CHANGE KILLERS

Change ~~Killers~~

MANAGING
RESISTANCE SO
PEOPLE AND
ORGANIZATIONS
THRIVE

JAN KADERLY

HOUNDSTOOTH
PRESS

CHANGE KILLERS
Managing Resistance So People and Organizations Thrive

FIRST EDITION

ISBN   978-1-5445-4659-9 *Hardcover*
      978-1-5445-4658-2 *Paperback*
      978-1-5445-4660-5 *Ebook*

*To the brave souls who take a leap of faith and give
a piece of themselves to an organization.*

Contents

INTRODUCTION 9

PART 1: RESISTANCE AND THE CAPACITY FOR CHANGE
RETHINKING CHANGE AND RESISTANCE 17
SEVEN BASIC NEEDS UNDERLIE RESISTANCE
AND SUPPORT FOR CHANGE 25
MANAGING NEEDS ON THREE
ORGANIZATIONAL LEVELS 41

PART 2: CHANGE KILLERS
HABIT AND ROUTINE.............................. 55
COMMITMENT 77
ORGANIZATIONAL IDENTITY 101
THE STATUS QUO EFFECT 127
BEST PRACTICES 153
GROUPTHINK 177
THREAT RIGIDITY 205
CHANGE CYNICISM 233

REFLECTIONS 253
ACKNOWLEDGMENTS 259
ABOUT THE AUTHOR 263
BIBLIOGRAPHY 265

Introduction

You—the change leader—thought you had it all worked out. You developed a plan that showed why change needed to happen, the good that would come from it, and how it would all come together. You kept everyone in the loop. Yet none of this mattered. The people who once nodded along didn't lift a finger. The moment of collective urgency faded into indifference and then solidified into doubt. What you thought was camaraderie evaporated into isolation. You alone gave voice to the need to do things differently. They weren't going to have any of it. They decided that change wasn't the solution, it was the problem.

You feel bewildered.

You feel like you failed.

You feel betrayed.

Like a riptide, resistance seemingly comes from out of nowhere—invisible, yet powerful enough to pull you and your change effort under. Resistance seems irrational, and no amount of logic you throw at it makes a difference. In the face of resistance, nothing makes sense.

There is another story that is the flip side of this one. It is the story of the change recipient, the person who is supposed to go along and support the change. Their experience can be equally bewildering, if not more so. For them, transformative change can come from out of the blue. For years they have managed—and made work—the processes or systems that are now being transformed. All this time, no one offered them much support to improve it or expressed much curiosity about how it worked.

For them, getting the job done takes all the time they have, and now one more thing—a big thing—has been added to the plate. Only platitudes are offered to reassure them that they will be given enough time, training, and leeway to make this work. Moreover, the people leading the change don't seem to know much about the details and are wondering:

Why did no one ask us about this?

What role will we play in this project that impacts everything we do?

Do any of our skills apply?

Why this, and why now?

THIS IS A BOOK ABOUT WHY WE RESIST CHANGE

This book is about resistance to organizational change, what causes it, and how change leaders can manage it. The book is a comprehensive analysis of resistance that examines eight phenomena of resistance in organizations—the change killers. By looking across many forms of resistance, themes emerged and a deeper logic could be seen. The deeper truth of resistance is that it is born of basic needs that are common to us all.

Even though the research started with various types of resistance—the change killers—the book begins with the seven basic needs that underlie resistance. By starting with the basic needs and the logic of resistance, you will have a richer understanding of the change killers and see this logic for yourself. You will also be immediately equipped to manage these needs in your daily life.

The flow of the book is as follows:

Part 1: Resistance and the Capacity for Change seeks to unfreeze your current conceptions of resistance and change, introduce you to the seven needs that underlie resistance or support for change, and advise you on how to manage these needs in complex organizations.

Part 2: The Change Killers details eight common forms of resistance within organizations. The change killers are phenomena that emerged from the crucible of real-world experiences that are also well-established in scholarly research on organizations. Each chapter goes into depth on a change killer and identifies its cause, consequences and, what you can do about them. In effect, the change killers are a diagnosis of common experiences within organizations, which are not well understood outside of scholarship.

The book ends with *Reflections*, my personal thoughts on how two years of researching and writing about resistance has changed my thinking in fundamental ways. To be more pointed and personal, it notes where I think I had things wrong and wish life offered a do-over.

Change Killers is a field guide—a practical tool—that a leader can use to anticipate, diagnose, and manage resistance to change. My goal is to bridge the practical needs of busy leaders with the penetrating insights of thinkers in the fields of psychology, social psychology, economics, management, and sociology.

While this book is the result of reading hundreds of peer-reviewed articles, it is not an academic book. I have synthesized the most authoritative thinkers and useful research. This book is intended to be an easy-to-use reference. Different types of change efforts will trigger different forms of resistance. The reference guide below will help you identify the types of resistance you might encounter.

Change Type	Habit & Routine	Commit-ment	Identity	Status Quo Effect	Best Practices	Group-think	Threat Rigidity	Change Cynicism
New Technology	✓	✓		✓	✓	✓	✓	✓
New Process	✓	✓		✓	✓	✓	✓	✓
New Strategy	✓	✓	✓	✓	✓	✓	✓	✓
New Product		✓	✓	✓		✓	✓	✓
New Brand		✓	✓			✓	✓	✓
New Leadership	✓	✓	✓	✓		✓	✓	✓
Reorganization	✓	✓	✓	✓		✓	✓	✓
Budget Cuts		✓	✓	✓		✓	✓	✓
Culture Change		✓	✓		✓	✓	✓	✓
Merger/ Acquisition	✓	✓	✓	✓	✓	✓	✓	✓

HOW THIS BOOK CAN HELP YOU BE MORE SUCCESSFUL

If we better understand resistance to disruptive organizational change, we can manage it and increase support and adoption of change.

Organizations are increasingly challenged to keep pace with high-velocity changes in technology and customer preferences. Increasingly, change is managed at a disruptive scale—more interconnected systems, processes, and teams are involved. The risk and financial investments are higher; thus change is often initiated from the top down. All of this creates change that can feel beyond our control, which is a breeding ground for resistance.

Change Killers will help leaders—CEOs, department heads,

project managers, and consultants—manage resistance and create support for change. This book will help you:

1. Make sense of resistance and understand it on a fundamental level
2. Build support for and adoption of major change
3. Be prepared to manage and navigate disruptive change efforts
4. Be a more empathetic and effective leader who can engage people on a deeper level
5. Manage disruptive change at different levels of the organization
6. Identify and harness the value of resistance in the information and engagement it provides

By understanding resistance on a deeper level and appreciating it as a common phenomenon, you can be a wiser leader who can bring people along to support rather than resist change. You can lead with ambition and empathy. You can champion change and the people it impacts. You can provide a vision of the future and allow people to shape it.

YOUR JOURNEY

I will take you on a journey where we loosen the grip of conventional notions of resistance so that a richer understanding can take root.

I will help *depersonalize* your own potentially painful experience in facing the resistance of others and help you see that it's not about you per se. At the same time, I will *personalize* the perspective of people resisting change within organizations.

As you read about the common forms of resistance in our workplaces—the change killers—I will empower you with a new understanding. I will help you see resistance as a natural expression of human needs, including your own. In all of the science and case studies detailed in this book, you will see a quite basic human struggle that cannot and should not be reduced to stereotypes.

My goal is to make your reading experience both professionally useful and personally enriching. And although this book is focused on resistance to organizational change, it is also meant to apply to life in general. Whether we are in our workplace, community, or home, we are always struggling to hold on, let go, and reach for something new.

As you read this book, you will see that, if managed well, resistance can provide value in your personal life and organization. In understanding resistance more deeply, you will understand yourself.

Resistance and the Capacity for Change

"If you want to truly understand something, try to change it."

—KURT LEWIN

The goal of Part 1 is to anchor you in a new understanding of—dare I say appreciation for—resistance. We are bombarded with the message "change or die," and we are trained to believe that, for the most part, change is synonymous with progress and resistance is synonymous with stagnation. While progress is impossible without change, not all change is progress. And, while resistance is by nature an oppositional force, resistance is not necessarily detrimental.

The first chapter, "Rethinking Change and Resistance," begins by reimagining change as a disruptive force undoing many things that provide stability and meaning in our workplace—impacting our lives in profound ways. This chapter ends with a head-on correction of our tendency to stereotype people as resistors.

The second chapter, "To Avoid Resistance We Must Address Seven Basic Needs," provides you with a blueprint to proactively manage resistance. This chapter introduces you to needs that underlie both resistance and support for change. Change triggers needs that are common to us all, and we—as change leaders—can either manage these needs to foster support for change or mismanage them and encounter resistance. This chapter is your tactical plan for using seven basic needs to manage change.

It is not enough to address an individual's needs in isolation. We are embedded in social groups and departmental structures, which can have a powerful influence on our attitudes and motivations.

The third chapter, "Managing Needs on Three Levels," gives you a detailed map of the organizational territory that must be aligned to create the conditions for successful change adoption. This chapter establishes a framework and tactics for managing the dynamics of individuals, groups, and the organization.

Rethinking Change
and Resistance

"People who are outspoken about their objections to a change proposal are often people who genuinely care about getting things right, and who are close enough to the inner workings of an organization to see the pitfalls in a plan."

—JEFFERY AND LAURIE FORD, 2010

This book provides an understanding of resistance to major and disruptive change—the type of change that displaces or modifies significant pieces of what came before. Disruptive change is different than constant change that happens every day as people improve what they do. Many people are agents of this type of bottom-up, localized change. Disruptive change often cuts across the organization, and it is often planned and led from the top down.[1] For most people in an organization, this type of change is initiated and, to some extent, defined by someone else.

---

[1]   Karl E. Weick and Robert E. Quinn, "Organizational Change and Development," *Annual Review of Psychology* 50 (February 1999), https://doi.org/10.1146/annurev.psych.50.1.361.

CHANGE IMPACTS PEOPLE'S LIVES

Disruptive change has major consequences for an organization and daily life within it. It can determine:

- **Who has the power to decide what is done and how it is done.** Major change can redistribute power within an organization. For instance, a CFO's influence will increase during major budget cuts.
- **Which skills are most and least valuable.** Major changes in strategy, technology, or process can necessitate learning new skills or bringing in new talent. As new skills are valued, old ones may be devalued.
- **The role that process plays in the course of business.** An operation that might have once been guided by an individual's discretion might become standardized.
- **The entire business model.** As organizations adjust to market demands or technologies, they may fundamentally change how they make money and operate. For instance, Kodak shifted its revenue sources from film to hardware sales with the advent of digital cameras.
- **A new understanding of the organization itself.** Disruptive change begets deeper soul-searching: *Is this what I signed up for?*

In other words, it alters something fundamental: how we work, how much say we have, how we relate to processes and technologies, how the organization values us, and how much we value it.

CHANGE IS AN UNDOING

Major change feels incredibly hard. It feels like there are forces keeping things in place—keeping *us* in place.

The fact is that we are held in place by real forces and dynamics within organizations. An organization's structure and processes create stable operations that reliably produce products and services. Organizations balance paradoxical demands that function as checks and balances (e.g., innovation and risk management), and inevitable departmental tensions can keep things from moving forward.

Moreover, we hold ourselves in place when we:

- Commit ourselves to our practice
- Train ourselves to be good at what we do
- Make our daily tasks second nature
- Form bonds with others who rely on us and we on them
- Make the organization's goals our own
- Actively perpetuate what was set in motion long ago

Like a tree, we put down roots that anchor us, create meaning, and form community—all of which help us thrive.

When we personally experience major change, we undo a part of ourselves. We may have to relinquish mindless ease as we expend significant effort to enact new processes. We may need to forever set aside skills that we worked hard to develop. We may have to let go of enriching relationships and colleagues. We may need to reconsider why we work for the organization at all.

When an organization initiates change, it undoes a part of itself. This may include dismantling a process or reconfiguring long-established teams, both of which worked well for years. It may result in taking a once reliable function and making it fragile or dismantling a legacy of proud accomplishment in one area and starting over fresh in another. Or perhaps a loyalty that was formed around one mission will be undone and built anew around another.

When we undertake major and disruptive change, we are undoing something that was important to us, something that satisfied a need, or something that made the system work. When these needs are not addressed or managed well, they will result in resistance to change.

In the face of major disruption, resistance is an attempt to restore a state of normalcy. Though counter-intuitive, resistance can be seen as a form of resilience.[2] It is our attempt to bounce back from shocks to the system on the organizational and individual levels.

RESISTANCE IS NOT THE *RESISTOR*

You will likely encounter resistance all along your journey as you sell your issue up the chain of command and across your organization. As time goes on and you overcome one issue after another, always building and strengthening your case of support, your commitment to your cause is growing. As your commitment grows, you become increasingly invested and wed to your idea.

Upon entering implementation—or any phase where you are working with newcomers to your process—you are engaging with people who have little background information on the project or understanding of why this change is needed now. Their commitment to your cause is naturally low. Conversely, your commitment is at its peak. You spent months or even years building support for change.

---

2   Karl E. Weick and Kathleen M. Sutcliffe, *Managing the Unexpected: Sustained Performance in a Complex World*, 3rd ed (Hoboken, NJ: John Wiley & Sons, 2015), 98.

THE COMMITMENT GAP

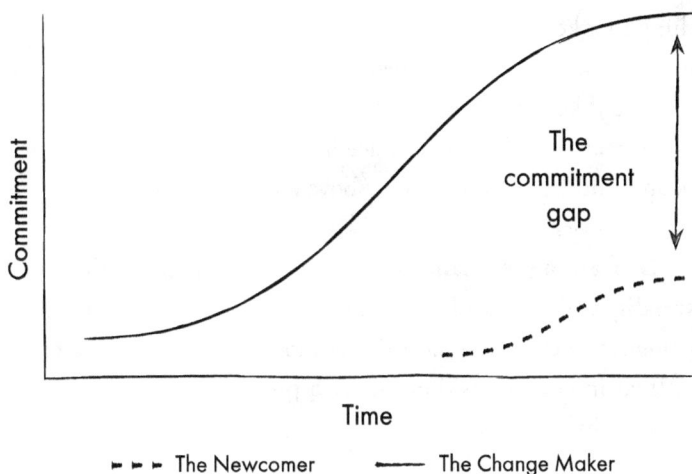

This gap between your commitment and that of newcomers is ripe for resistance. People may not agree with you, and you interpret them negatively. You will be most sensitive to the presence of roadblocks during early encounters with questioning newcomers. After all, it's your career and reputation at stake.

The newcomer's questions, concerns, and doubts will be at their highest level at a time when your tolerance might be at its lowest since you have come a long way and need things to move forward. In this situation, it is easy to interpret newcomers' questioning, doubts, and disagreements as the belligerence of resistors.

In fact, resistance is just a concept "managers use to label the behaviors and communications…they feel will increase the amount of work they must do to ensure a successful change." Moreover, resistors don't see themselves as obstacles; in their mind "their behaviors are consistent with and supportive of organizational objectives and values."[3]

But, these probing critical questions are valuable: "In the early stages of a change, any talk, even negative talk might be the only thing that keeps a change proposal alive."[4] Discussions that you may consider resistant deepen the understanding of the change effort and keep it in circulation. Rather than see early pushback as a threat, you should embrace it as an opportunity to engage people and learn from them. Above all, be careful not to stereotype resistors.

By framing resistance as a resistor, you focus on their personality traits instead of what they are saying. By focusing on *resistors*, you can interpret their questions and concerns as a result of their innate disposition, not as a problem in your plan. You might think of resistors as a threat—if you don't convert them, they could spell failure.

It's a lot easier for us to think of resistance as *resistors*, "over there, in them."[5] Resistors are people who stand in your way; they are human roadblocks on your path to success. When you think of resistance as *resistors*, the problem lies in them, not in you or your change effort. By focusing on resistors, change agents "shift responsibility from things under their control…to the characteristics and attributes of recipients."[6]

Unfortunately, by focusing on *resistors*, you can dismiss critical and critically valuable feedback that would improve your change

---

3   Jeffrey D. Ford and Laurie W. Ford, "Stop Blaming Resistance to Change and Start Using It," *Organizational Dynamics* 39, no. 1 (January–March 2010): 25, https://doi.org/10.1016/j.orgdyn.2009.10.002.

4   Ford and Ford, "Stop Blaming Resistance to Change," 27.

5   Jeffrey D. Ford, Laurie W. Ford, and Angelo D'Amelio, "Resistance to Change: The Rest of the Story," *Academy of Management Review* 33, no. 2 (April 2008): 362, https://doi.org/10.5465/amr.2008.31193235.

6   Ford, Ford, and D'Amelio, "Resistance to Change," 365.

efforts or prevent you from suffering the humiliating failure of a fundamentally flawed plan.

No good comes from thinking about *resistors*.

This is an attribution problem we should nip in the bud.

RESISTANCE IS A DIFFERENCE IN PERSPECTIVE

Resistance is a natural byproduct of people from different parts of an organization trying to make sense of the change, how it should work, and whether it will. Resistance happens when we exchange perspectives.

Once we resolve our attribution problem and stop thinking about resistors, we can focus on *what is said* instead of *who is saying it*.

We can then start to listen for signs that something is off:

- Is something technically wrong that we need to correct?
- Have we created the conditions for this effort to succeed?
- Have we addressed the needs of the people who will be required to adopt the change?

If we open ourselves to listening to another's perspective, we can learn from their resistance. We can strengthen our change effort by making work for the people who will be impacted by it.

CHAPTER SUMMARY

- Disruptive change is initiated by someone else and has a major impact on how we work (the role of process and technology), how much say we have in what we do (the redistribution of power), and how much the organization values our skills.
- An organization's ongoing processes, routines, structures, and

relationships produce reliable results. Disruptive change dismantles—undoes—some part of this stable operation.

- Change-makers can be too committed to their initiative as a result of the focus and perseverance needed to secure organizational support for major change.
- As a result of their high commitment to their initiative, the changemaker can be dismissive of criticism.
- "Resistor" is a label leaders use to make negative feedback a problem with a person, not their plan. Resistance is just a difference in perspective.
- Resistance has value. Critical dialogue about an initiative can keep the idea alive and provide important feedback that will make the plan better.

Seven Basic Needs Underlie Resistance and Support for Change

"The very senselessness of many jobs requires that people make sense of them."

—GERALD SALANCIK, 1977

Resistance occurs when basic needs are not satisfied.

This book dives deep into eight common forms of resistance within organizations and identifies the root causes of each one. Research shows that our resistance to change stems from fundamental needs. Resistance is triggered when our needs are not satisfied.

7 BASIC NEEDS THAT UNDERLIE SUPPORT OR RESISTANCE TO CHANGE

Ease

Integrity

Purpose

7
Basic
Needs

Control

Stability

Belonging

Competence

Below is the list of common types of resistance triggered by seven basic needs, with the corresponding change killer in parentheses. (To learn more about each one, see Part 2.)

- We resist changing habits because of our need for cognitive **ease**. (Habit and Routine)
- We resist something that feels threatening because of our need for **control**. (Threat Rigidity)
- We resist anything that our group is against because of our need to **belong**. (Groupthink)

- We resist trusting leaders who fail our sense of fairness because of our need for **integrity**. (Change Cynicism)
- We resist letting go of long-held practices because of our need to feel **competent**. (Best Practices)
- We resist major departures from the past because of our need for **stability**. (Status Quo Effect)
- We resist abandoning our commitments because of our need for **purpose**. (Identity and Commitment)

The seven basic needs cause some types of resistance and contribute to others. Our need to belong not only causes groupthink, it also contributes to the adherence to out-of-date best practices that are embraced by our peers and professional communities. Likewise, our need for control triggers threat rigidity and contributes to the status quo effect as we feel in control and can predict the status quo.

In short, these basic needs are the source of our resistance to change.

MANAGING SEVEN BASIC NEEDS IS THE DIFFERENCE BETWEEN SUPPORT AND RESISTANCE

Change activates basic needs that are common to us all. When our needs are threatened, they can trigger resistance. When they are supported, they can facilitate change.

Though they are achingly intuitive, it is important to understand these basic needs and how disruptive change can trigger them.

Below is a description of our seven basic needs.

EASE

We live in a tumultuous world and work in complex organizations that constantly pull at our attention. Our conscious (actively thinking) mind is a scarce resource (as little as 5 percent of our mental activity is deliberate). To navigate the demands of daily life, we heavily rely on unconscious and automatic thinking—we are on autopilot. We create mental shortcuts—automatic habits, routines, and easy decision-making hacks—that do not require thinking. As we function on autopilot, our deliberate conscious mind is freed to focus on complex problem-solving and creative thinking. Because of our need for ease, we will readily develop habits and routines that allow us not to think about what we do.[7]

Change can require us to deliberately perform tasks that were once second nature. This can result in mental fatigue and overwhelm.

PURPOSE

We need to find purpose in our work and meaning in our lives. We have a remarkable capacity to find and create purpose; we can even find meaning in banal jobs. As we create purpose, we identify with our work and become more committed to it. We will go above and beyond for a cause that we care about.[8]

Change can strip away our sense of purpose and make us feel alienated when we are reassigned to something we are not committed to.

---

7   Roy F. Baumeister et al., "Ego Depletion: Is the Active Self a Limited Resource?," *Journal of Personality and Social Psychology* 74, no. 5 (May 1998), https://doi.org/10.1037//0022-3514.74.5.1252; John A. Bargh and Tanya L. Chartrand, "The Unbearable Automaticity of Being," *American Psychologist* 54, no. 7 (1999), https://doi.org/10.1037/0003-066X.54.7.462; Wendy Wood and Dennis Rünger, "Psychology of Habit," *Annual Review of Psychology* 67 (January 2016), https://doi.org/10.1146/annurev-psych-122414-033417; John A. Bargh, "The Cognitive Unconscious in Everyday Life," in *The Cognitive Unconscious: The First Half Century*, edited by Arthur S. Reber and Rhianon Allen (New York: Oxford University Press, 2022).

8   Frank Martela and Anne B. Pessi, "Significant Work Is about Self-Realization and Broader Purpose: Defining the Key Dimensions of Meaningful Work," *Frontiers in Psychology* 9 (March 2018), https://doi.org/10.3389/fpsyg.2018.00363; Roy F. Baumeister et al., "Some Key Differences between a Happy Life and a Meaningful Life," *Journal of Positive Psychology* 8, no. 6 (August 2013), https://doi.org/10.1080/17439760.2013.830764; Patrick E. McKnight and Todd B. Kashdan, "Purpose in Life as a System that Creates and Sustains Health and Well-Being: An Integrative, Testable Theory," *Review of General Psychology* 13, no. 3 (September 2009), https://doi.org/10.1037/a0017152; Roy F. Baumeister and Kathleen D. Vohs, "The Pursuit of Meaningfulness in Life," in *Handbook of Positive Psychology*, edited by C. R. Snyder and Shane J. Lopez (New York: Oxford University Press, 2002).

STABILITY

The structures and processes of an organization are designed to create dependable behaviors that allow employees to operate independently and simultaneously with one another. This reliability of behaviors and processes allows organizations to function as a coordinated system. It also makes our lives within organizations steady. Stability enables organizations to produce the same results day after day. By nature, we need a sense of permanence—the feeling we will be the same tomorrow as we were today and yesterday.[9]

Change, especially major structural or process changes, can threaten the reliability of key functions and the stability of an organization. It can make us feel insecure and unstable.

COMPETENCE

Competence means that we have the skills and ability to perform our jobs. Competence comes with time—training, experience, and a history of performing functions well. Competence creates ease in the ability to do complex things effortlessly. Competence gives us the confidence to manage challenges. Because of our need for competence, we will try to be good at whatever we do.[10]

Change can damage or destroy our sense of competence and make us feel inept if our organization no longer values or needs our skills and abilities.

---

9 Stuart Albert and David A. Whetton, "Organizational Identity," in *Research in Organizational Behavior* Vol. 7, edited by Barry M. Staw and Larry L. Cummings (Greenwich, CT: JAI Press, 1985); Michael T. Hannan and John Freeman, "Structural Inertia and Organizational Change," *American Sociological Review* 49, no. 2 (April 1984), https://doi.org/10.2307/2095567.

10 Richard M. Ryan and Edward L. Deci, "Self-Determination Theory and the Facilitation of Intrinsic Motivation, Social Development, and Well-Being," *American Psychologist* 55, no. 1 (January 2000), https://doi.org/10.1037/0003-066X.55.1.68; James E. Maddux, "Self-Efficacy," in *Interpersonal and Intrapersonal Expectancies*, edited by Sławomir Trusz and Przemysław Babel (New York: Routledge, 2016); Abert Bandura, "Self-Efficacy Mechanism in Human Agency," *American Psychologist* 37, no. 2 (1982), https://doi.org/10.1037/0003-066X.37.2.122; Robert W. White, "Motivation Reconsidered: The Concept of Competence," *Psychological Review* 66, no. 5 (September 1959), https://doi.org/10.1037/h0040934.

BELONGING

Our need to bond with others is one of the most fundamental of human needs. We easily form bonds with strangers, ingratiate ourselves, and mimic to form a connection. Belonging to a group provides us with security, support, and the ability to cooperate and coordinate actions with others. The need to belong allows us to identify with groups, internalize the qualities of others, and conform.[11]

Change has the potential to break meaningful connections in our lives and cast doubt on the organization we thought we belonged to. When we feel like we do not belong or our bonds are broken, we feel alienated and profoundly lonely.

CONTROL

We need to believe that we are in control of our lives and feel like we have choices and the freedom to choose. When we have information, we can predict what will happen and feel in control. We need access to resources and the ability to influence a situation. The sense of control provides us with the assurance that we can navigate challenges. The sense of freedom and control is a precondition for making commitments. Because of our need for control, we will assume responsibility and command over things in our purview.[12]

---

11   Ryan and Deci, "Self-Determination Theory"; Tanya L. Chartrand and John A. Bargh, "The Chameleon Effect: The Perception-Behavior Link and Social Interaction," *Journal of Personality and Social Psychology* 76, no. 6 (June 1999), https://doi.org/10.1037/0022-3514.76.6.893; Roy F. Baumeister and Mark R. Leary, "The Need to Belong: Desire for Interpersonal Attachments as a Fundamental Human Motivation," *Psychological Bulletin* 117, no. 3 (1995), https://doi.org/10.1037/0033-2909.117.3.497; Robert B. Cialdini and Noah J. Goldstein, "Social Influence: Compliance and Conformity," *Annual Review of Psychology* 55, no. 1 (February 2004), https://doi.org/10.1146/annurev.psych.55.090902.142015.

12   Ryan and Deci, "Self-Determination Theory"; Susan E. Jackson and Jane E. Dutton, "Discerning Threats and Opportunities," *Administrative Science Quarterly* 33, no. 3 (September 1988), https://doi.org/10.2307/2392714; Barry M. Staw, Lance E. Sandelands, and Jane E. Dutton, "Threat Rigidity Effects in Organizational Behavior: A Multilevel Analysis," *Administrative Science Quarterly* 26, no. 4 (December 1981), https://doi.org/10.2307/2392337; Suzanne C. Thompson, "Will It Hurt Less If I Can Control It? A Complex Answer to a Simple Question," *Psychological Bulletin* 90, no. 1 (1981), https://doi.org/10.1037/0033-2909.90.1.89.

Change can make us feel out of control and disempowered especially if we are blindsided or excluded from decisions that affect our lives.

INTEGRITY

Integrity is the expectation that we will be treated fairly, honestly, and with respect. We form trusting relationships with people of integrity. That trust allows us to expend extra effort and go above and beyond on behalf of our team or organization. We believe that if we look out for the organization, it will look out for us. Because of our need for integrity, we will take a leap of faith and trust that the organization will live up to its end of the bargain.[13]

Change can damage integrity and erode trust if we believe that promises were not kept or people were treated unfairly.

Our basic needs are not only key to managing change and averting resistance, they may be the very forces that make organizations thrive. It may be that our need to belong and find purpose enables us to find a common cause, cooperate with others, and do the same thing day in and day out. These basic needs drive behavior that results in huge collective accomplishments, made possible by organizations.

These needs make disruptive change deeply challenging.

13   Roger C. Mayer, James H. Davis, and F. David Schoorman, "An Integrative Model of Organizational Trust," *Academy of Management Review* 20, no. 3 (July 1995), https://doi.org/10.2307/258792; Denise M. Rousseau, "Psychological and Implied Contracts in Organizations," *Employee Responsibilities and Rights Journal* 2, no. 2 (1989), https://doi.org/10.1007/BF01384942; James M. Kouzes and Barry Z. Posner, "The Credibility Factor: What Followers Expect from Their Leaders," *Management Review* 79, no. 1 (January 1990).

NEEDS AT A GLANCE

Need	Looks like...	Results in...	Without it, we feel...
Ease	Tasks are effortless Act on second nature Thinking is automatic	Efficiency	Overwhelmed
Purpose	Commitment to organization A sense of meaning in what we do	Dedication	Alienated
Stability	Sense of permanence Dependable actions Steady processes	Reliability	Unstable
Competence	Acquisition of skills Command over complexity Confidence to manage challenges	Capacity	Inept
Belonging	Forming bonds with others Seeking acceptance of groups Conforming to group norms	Cooperation	Isolated
Control	Predictability of what's to come Access to needed resources Influence over events	Accountability	Disempowered
Integrity	Expectation of reciprocity Expectation of fairness and respect	Trust	Cynicism

THE LOGIC OF RESISTANCE

The management of our basic needs is the difference between support for or resistance to change. When we look deeply at the cause of resistance within organizations, we can see an underlying and simple logic. Disruptive change can threaten our basic needs. If well-managed, this leads to support; if mismanaged, it leads to resistance. See illustration below.

BASIC NEEDS CAN SUPPORT OR RESIST CHANGE

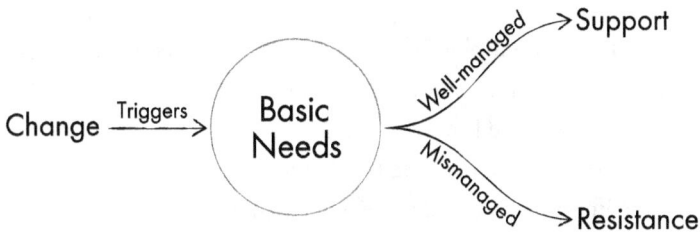

This framework explains why some change efforts work and others fail.

During the Great Depression, Joseph Scanlon was able to bring factory workers in management together in a successful effort to save a local steel mill. His approach is now considered a model because he successfully fostered the workers' needs for (1) **competence** in knowing how the company could realize greater efficiencies and cut costs; (2) **control** to determine how change could be implemented on the front line of the factory floor; (3) **purpose** in saving their company and local economy during extremely challenging times; (4) **belonging** by creating a unified team, the combined workers with management, and a common cause; and (5) **integrity** by creating a novel profit sharing program that rewarded workers and management equally.

The framework helps us make sense of failure.

A once dominant 50,000-person technology company needed to improve its declining cash flow. Its plan for major restructuring went from early support to outright mutiny among its employees when (1) the **integrity** of the company's new management eroded after they failed to live up to their promise of cutting work before jobs; (2) the **stability** of the organization was compromised by the deep and unsustainable budget cuts; (3) the employees' sense of **purpose** was eroded as the company sacrificed customer service, which most employees considered its core mission; (4) the **competence** of employees eroded as staffing cuts pushed them beyond their ability to deliver quality to their customers; and (5) daily **ease** turned to overwhelm as understaffed departments forced workers into extreme hours and relocations.

The implication is clear; the management or mismanagement of our basic needs can be the difference between support for or resistance to your change effort.

HOW TO MANAGE BASIC NEEDS

There are many practical things you can do that address people's basic needs and build their support for change. For each change killer, I provide solutions to manage and prevent resistance. The table below outlines several ideas for managing each need. I have provided a menu of options from which you can choose based on your organization and your situation.

HOW YOU CAN MANAGE BASIC NEEDS TO SUPPORT CHANGE

Our basic need for...	Can lead to *support* if you...
Ease	Chunk the project into small parts
	Sequence the training into manageable stepping stones
	Build habits and routines, bit by bit, with consistency
	Change the physical context (location) to break old habits/routines
Purpose	Authentically explain the need for change
	Connect change to something staff care about
	Publicly ask staff why and how they can support change
	Personally remind staff they are individually critical to the effort
Stability	Do not undertake other major changes at the same time
	Reassure staff that you are invested in their success
	Assure staff their job is not in jeopardy
	Decrease pressure to exceed goals during transition
Competence	Go for small wins (versus major transformations)
	Encourage practice and experimentation
	Invest time and money in training
	Communicate progress, however small
Belonging	Form a team to lead or support the change effort
	Leverage social influencers
	Connect the change effort to the organization's identity
	Remind staff that others rely on them
Control	Include staff early on in implementation planning
	Give staff discretion in how to enact the change
	Encourage adaptation in the adoption of new processes
	Over-communicate and avoid blind-siding
Integrity	Treat people with respect in communicating and listening
	Demonstrate that you treated people fairly in downsizing
	Keep your word—if you can't, then explain why
	Choose credible and trusted project leads and spokespeople

Just as you can manage and care for people's needs in support of change, you can easily and mindlessly mismanage them.

HOW YOU CAN MISMANAGE BASIC NEEDS TO TRIGGER RESISTANCE

The need for...	Can lead to *resistance* if you...
Ease	Change everything all at once
Purpose	Change the identity of the organization in a way that alienates core stakeholders
Stability	Make deep cuts in key parts of the organization and expect staff to exceed goals
Competence	Rush the project and cut time and resources for training
Belonging	Unfairly or overly criticize a tight-knit team's past work or decisions
Control	Do not consult staff about decisions that affect them
Integrity	Downsize lower-level staff but maintain executive perks

It is helpful to paint this picture even if it describes your behavior a little bit. It is worth a quiet reflection on how we might unintentionally trigger resistance by mismanaging the seven basic needs.

In short, our basic needs can be managed and mismanaged. How you manage these needs can be the difference between support and resistance to change.

BASIC NEEDS CAN COMPENSATE FOR EACH OTHER

Resistance to change is triggered when our basic needs are not cared for. There are practical things we can do to manage these basic needs and build support for change. But, if you are managing a disruptive change, you will not be able to satisfy all of the basic needs fully. Something will have to give.

In these cases, we can:

1. Identify how some needs will be negatively impacted or compromised
2. Shore up the needs that are depleted
3. Lean into other needs to compensate

In short, you can manage the needs holistically and use one to compensate for another. By managing them as a whole, you can restore a sense of balance.

As an example, let's take a deep budget cut that includes layoffs of longtime and well-liked employees, as well as a reorganization of their teams. In this situation, there will be pain, no matter what you do. Letting go of employees will break important social bonds and the reorganization will dismantle old teams, which will erode *belonging*. New workflows and processes will disrupt the *stability* and *ease* that some people rely upon.

CHANGE CAN TRIGGER OUR BASIC NEEDS
Example: Reorganization and Layoffs

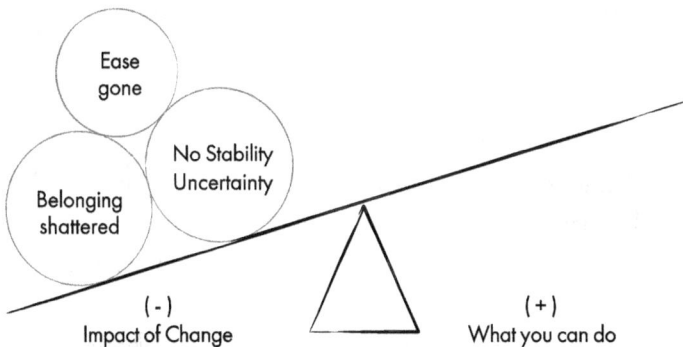

Ease gone

No Stability
Uncertainty

Belonging
shattered

(-)
Impact of Change

(+)
What you can do

In this case, where the need for *belonging* and *stability* are inevitably compromised, you can lean into *integrity* and *purpose*. To leverage *integrity*, you must, without equivocation, demonstrate the decision was made objectively and that laid-off employees were treated fairly. You must lean into *purpose* in order to connect this difficult decision to the needs and mission of your organization. Here you must communicate in an authentic and emotionally compelling way.

RESTORE BALANCE BY MANAGING THESE NEEDS
Example: Reorganization and Layoffs

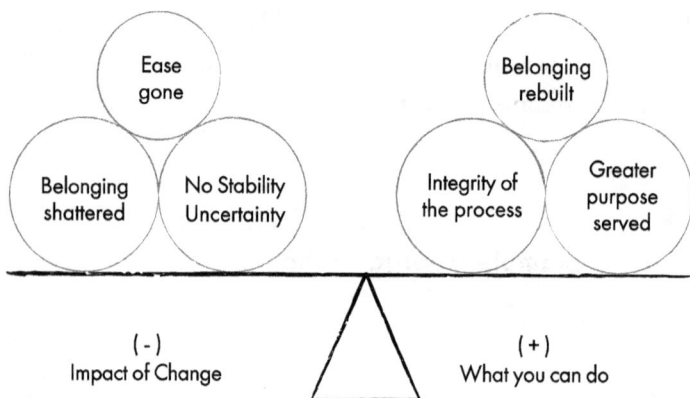

Your task as a changemaker is to:

1. Identify the needs that will be most negatively impacted by the change
2. Shore up the needs that will be most affected. Do what you can to mitigate negative impacts
3. Identify how you can satisfy other needs to make the person whole

The following worksheet shows the details of how you can map out a strategy for a specific change like this one.

CHANGE SCENARIO: DEEP BUDGET CUTS WITH LAY-OFFS AND A REORGANIZATION

Basic need	Impact of change (–)	What you can do (+)
Ease	Old routines that were second nature will change. New processes and workflows will require extra effort over weeks if not months.	Sequence the rollout of new processes. Don't demand all new operations, all at once.
Purpose	Staff may believe budget cuts compromise organization's ability to fulfill on its mission.	**Major impact.** **Clearly explain how this decision is in the best interest of the organization.** **Detail how the decision will help the organization meet its current and future challenges.**
Stability	Well-established functions will be disrupted as new teams and processes are formed.	Identify and communicate what remains the same.
Competence	NA	NA
Belonging	**Major impact.** **Several longtime & well-liked employees will be let go. Professional and social bonds will be broken. A tight-knit department will be disbanded and assumed in multiple areas.**	Extra effort should be made to welcome staff into their new departments. Create social opportunities, both 1:1 and group.
Control	**Major impact.** **Staff may feel a profound lack of control. Almost every part of their daily work like will be impacted.**	**Major impact.** **Communicate consistently and well in advance of changes. Avoid blindsides.**
Integrity	Some employees may not trust the process.	**Major impact.** **Clearly communicate decision-making processes.** **Explain alternatives that were considered, why this decision was made, and how the decision was objective.** **Demonstrate that laid-off employees were treated with utmost respect.**

CHAPTER SUMMARY

- Change activates seven basic needs that are common to us all. Resistance is triggered when these needs are not satisfied.
- Our seven basic needs are:
  - **Ease.** Habits and routines become second-nature and allow us to function on autopilot which frees up our active problem-solving mind.
  - **Purpose.** We need purpose in our work to have meaning in our lives and a reason to commit to hard and ambitious jobs.
  - **Stability.** We rely on consistent operations to reliably produce results and provide us with a consistency in our daily lives.
  - **Competence.** We need proficiency, skills, and abilities to perform tasks with ease and feel confident in managing challenges.
  - **Belonging.** We bond with others and form groups to help us cope, find security, and get things done.
  - **Control.** We need to have information, resources, and influence over how we work to be confident and satisfied.
  - **Integrity.** We need to trust that our organization will treat us fairly, honestly, and respectfully in order to go above and beyond.
- Disruptive change can trigger and threaten these basic needs. If you manage them well, they can support change. If you mismanage or ignore them, resistance can result.
- For a specific change initiative, you can proactively identify which needs will be negatively impacted. You can then determine how you can bolster these needs and lean into others to restore a sense of balance.
- In short, when some needs are negatively impacted you can compensate with others.

Managing Needs on Three Organizational Levels

"To become contextually conscious, contextually expert and contextually intelligent is to become far better positioned to lead wisely and well."

—BARBARA KELLERMAN, 2018

Organizations are complex as is life within them. We are nested within three levels of organization—individuals nested within groups or teams that are further nested within the organization and its structures. The job of the changemaker is to create conditions at the individual, group, and organizational levels that address our fundamental needs so that people can be effective agents of change.

Below is an illustration of the three levels.

CREATING CONDITIONS TO LEAD CHANGE ON 3 LEVELS

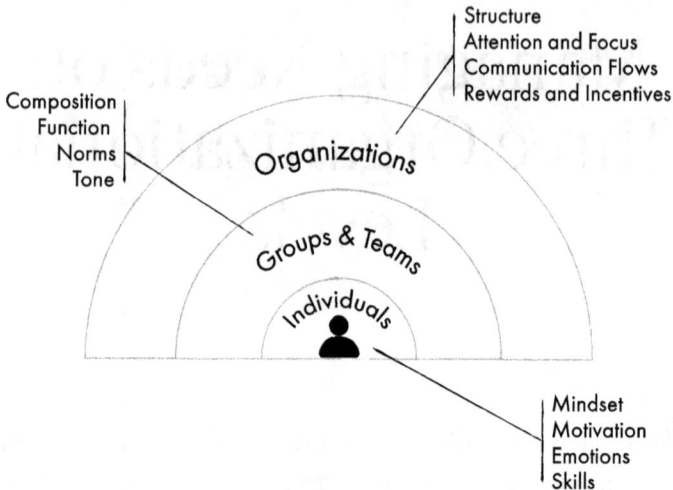

Structure
Attention and Focus
Communication Flows
Rewards and Incentives

Composition
Function
Norms
Tone

Organizations

Groups & Teams

Individuals

Mindset
Motivation
Emotions
Skills

You can manage the basic needs by creating conditions on each of these levels and calibrating them in concert.

Below is a brief description of each level and how we can influence them to create an environment that prevents resistance and facilitates change.

THE INDIVIDUAL

At the individual level, we can influence the mindset, motivations, and skills of individuals so that they see change as an opportunity, engage in the change effort, and build their competencies to support the future direction.

- **Mindset** describes a person's overall attitude or stance toward the change. Your job is to position change as an opportunity for people to grow personally and professionally. You can help people understand why change is necessary and how it will help the organization achieve its mission. You can explain why the current path will not work, which will help people loosen their attachments to the past to create the space for something new.
- **Motivation** describes the energy and engagement people bring to the change. Your job is to connect the change to something specific that people care about and clearly demonstrate how the change will improve it. This may be a goal or program that is important to them (e.g., customer satisfaction or membership), their occupation and the opportunity to deepen their expertise, or their connection to the organization itself (if it inspires loyalty). You can also foster direct engagement and create opportunities for people to inform the change effort.
- **Emotion** describes the feelings and intensity people experience at the prospect of change and through the process. Change may inspire relief and enthusiasm if it is a long-awaited solution to frustrating problems. Change might inspire anxiety and fear if people feel out of control. You can influence emotional responses to change by framing the change as an opportunity that inspires hope instead of a threat that ignites anxiety. You can also create an optimistic atmosphere through your own emotional tenor.
- **Skill** describes the ability of people to participate in the change effort and transition to the future state. You can provide training and support to build new skills. You can carve out the time for people to develop new competencies and explore what the change can be. During a change process, you can generally support people's personal and professional growth.

GROUPS AND TEAMS

Groups exercise significant influence on individuals. They sway our opinions, affect our moods, and influence our perceptions. The dynamics of a group can make or break a change effort. They can inspire comradery and a can-do spirit or sink an idea before it can see the light of day. Groups are multipliers; they affect all of the individuals within them.

Whether the group is a new or existing one, you can foster group dynamics that support your change effort by addressing four foundational issues of groups:

- **Group function**—engaging groups around the specific needs of your project. Teams can be helpful throughout a project's life cycle, including developing a concept, planning the initiative, providing high-level guidance, preparing for implementation, hands-on support during implementation, and evaluation of the results. You can even form a team to identify and address major obstacles. Throughout the process, make sure you have groups that can functionally support the needs of your initiative.

- **Group composition**—having the right people involved to support the effort. By engaging groups of people directly in the process you can leverage the perspective and support of others and increase their commitment to change. Be sure to include people whose support will be essential throughout the process and find a way to engage them. Be sure to include front-line staff and end users early on to help them understand, prepare, and plan for the change. You can also enlist positive people with social influence.

- **Norms**—the behaviors that are socially accepted and expected within a group (i.e., rules of the road). You can explicitly create norms within a group by identifying what the change might demand of a group and how they can support it through their behaviors. For instance, if your change requires innovation, the group may need to be more open and listen to new ideas, and provide feedback in a constructive way that strengthens a proposal instead of stopping it.

- **Tone**—the emotional resonance and mood within a group. The tenor of a group gathering can subtly or obviously affect the perceptions and judgments of individuals within it. A negative tone in a meeting can lead to negative judgments about a change effort. One person's negative attitude can be contagious. Likewise, a positive and optimistic tone can lead to greater support for change by creating the perception of an opportunity rather than a threat.

THE ORGANIZATION

At the organizational level, we can influence an organization's structure, attention and focus, communication, decision-making, and rewards and incentives to positively influence an individual's support for change.

- **Structure**—the formal reporting relationships and the determination of priorities within a group—is an important tool in aligning people with an organization's priorities. The formal structure can facilitate change when an entire team or department is focused on the change effort, its goal, and the overall approach. If the change effort is not a priority for a department or team, it may not get sufficient time, money, or staff. It is important to be wide-eyed about misalignments and tensions between departments that do not share the same priorities. This could be an important limitation to your change effort or require high-level interventions or coalition building.
- **Attention and focus**—the issues that get management's attention become the organization's priorities. You can find and

create opportunities to sell your issue as being key to the organization's strategy or important to its constituents. The process of getting and keeping attention and focusing on the importance of your change effort is vital to securing resources and support necessary for your success. This process is also unending.

- **Decision-making**—organizations have different approaches that are more or less inclusive and happen early or late in a project's life cycle. Decisions range from go-no-go decisions (should we do this?) to implementation decisions (how should we do this?). There are potentially many opportunities for decision-making that provide people with a sense of control and build commitment. We can ensure that people are brought into decision-making processes and have genuine opportunities to provide input. We can use decision-making forums to empower people who are critical to success and build their commitment.

- **Communication**—the formal and informal flow of communications determines who knows what and when. Whether information passes through gatekeepers or is broadcast to everyone all at once, you must tell the story of why change is needed at this point in time. Depending on the normal flow of information within your organization, you may need to develop new flows and types of communications to reach the people who will be essential to your success. Communication is essential to helping others make sense of the change. Communication helps people predict what is going to happen, which makes them feel more in control.

- **Rewards and incentives**—these can be created for both departments and individuals. On the *departmental* level, you should ensure that departmental goals are aligned with the change effort and the future direction of the organization.

You can leverage incentives and compensation structures for departmental leaders and their staff. On the *individual* level, you should genuinely praise people who are making progress toward the change effort, and provide them with meaningful rewards. Note: rewards do not need to be financial or large to motivate people.

CREATE CONDITIONS FOR SUCCESS ON THREE LEVELS

Successful change requires calibration of all three levels: the individual, group, and organization. For instance, you may have a highly motivated team pursuing an innovative new line of business. If they report to a senior executive who prioritizes traditional business over new, the effort will struggle to get the resources and support it requires.

To successfully lead major disruptive change efforts, you will need to manage or at least influence all three levels. If your role or situation does not give you sufficient influence over organizational dynamics (structure, attention and focus, decision-making, communications, incentives, and rewards), focus efforts where you can and be mindful of how misalignment at the organizational level might become an issue for your change effort. This approach will at least help you better diagnose problems you may encounter and develop fallback strategies.

The book is chock full of practical advice on how to avoid and navigate resistance. Below is a table that illustrates how our basic needs can be managed at the individual, group, and organizational levels. This is a snapshot that should kick-start your thinking about what you can do in your situation.

HOW TO MANAGE BASIC NEEDS AT THREE LEVELS

Basic Need	Individual	Group	Organization
Ease	Provide training that builds new skills slowly. Create new habits with care (clear cues, repetition, reward, feedback). Time and sequence the project to facilitate learning and new habit formation. Minimize unnecessary disruption to other habits/routines.	Minimize unnecessary disruptions to team function and composition. Create new routines between staff with care (clear cues, repetition, rewards, feedback).	Minimize unnecessary demands or disruptions in other areas of the organization. Ensure management provides time and support to impacted staff.
Purpose	Create public opportunities for individuals to express their support. Explain how the individual is critical to the change effort and others rely on them.	Explain how the group is critical to the change effort.	Develop a compelling story that explains the necessity of change. Ensure that the change is integrated into goals. Ensure that executives and departments are incentivized to support change.
Stability	Keep other areas of the job status quo during transitions. Reassure them with job security.	Maintain existing department and team structures during transition.	Minimize unnecessary demands or disruptions in other areas of the organization. Keep reporting structures the same during implementation.
Competence	Time to practice in system. Real-world experience in system. Communicate individual accomplishments. Remind a person of their past accomplishments.	Create a selective peer support group to acquire high-level training or work through complicated tasks. Communicate group accomplishments. Remind teams of their past accomplishments.	Reward individuals and teams who receive training. Include training and adoption in performance evaluations.

Basic Need	Individual	Group	Organization
Belonging	Connect an individual's identification to the organization with the change effort.	Create social opportunities around the change effort (parties, lunch and learn). Leverage team spirit and form teams to address key issues throughout the change effort.	Create an emotional connection between change effort and the mission.
Control	Communicate plans multiple times and well in advance: make the process predictable. Give people a say in how change is implemented. Bring people into the process early on. Solicit advice from key stakeholders.	Use team meetings to communicate plans and progress. Create advisory or working groups to provide input. Solicit advice from key teams.	Ensure that project and executive leadership are aligned on priorities. Ensure that people responsible for the change have the authority to make it happen. Revise job descriptions as necessary to reflect new roles or new leadership.
Integrity	Listen to individual concerns w/ genuine interest. Speak to people as peers, not lower-level staff. Be transparent and authentic in communicating the need for change.	Exercise caution in addressing lack of trust in group settings (better done 1:1). In group meetings, provide clear explanations of the need for change. Actively engage the group to provide feedback: "What are we missing?" Genuinely listen. Communicate how leadership is "walking the walk."	Leadership must do what they say. If this is not feasible, explain why. Choose credible project leaders. Directly address failed change efforts of the past.

MANAGE YOUR RESISTANCE FIRST

If you have the honor of leading a change effort, whether you're the CEO or a project manager, you have several advantages compared to other participants. You know more about the change that's coming. You believe in its possibilities, and you have some control over how it unfolds.

That said, change comes for us all. Large-scale complex and disruptive initiatives are beyond the control of any one person.

They hit bumps in the road and their success is called into question. They evolve into something different that you may not have anticipated or signed up for. They may require a skill that you don't have. Change takes on a life of its own.

You may begin your journey by initiating change, but at some point in the process, you react to it. At this point, you are a mere mortal encountering your own reluctance and resistance. To serve those who depend on you for guidance and to create conditions for their success in the organization, you will need to look out for your own basic needs.

CHAPTER SUMMARY

- Successful implementation of major change requires alignment between individuals, groups, and the organization and its structures. The changemaker must create conditions that foster support for change on all three levels.
- At the **individual level**, we influence the mindset, motivations, and skills of individuals so that they see change as an opportunity, engage in the effort, and build their competencies.
- At the **group level**, you can foster dynamics that support your change effort by forming groups to functionally address the specific needs of your project, involving critical people, developing norms that support the change, and ensuring the tone of group meetings is positive.
- At the **organizational level**, you can influence an organization's structure, attention and focus, communication, decision-making, and rewards and incentives to positively influence an individual's support for change.
- Misalignment between these levels can result in a lack of incentive and motivation to support change. Even if you can't

directly control these factors, it's important to understand and troubleshoot potential.

- You can manage the basic needs of people at every level of the organization.

- In leading disruptive change, you should expect to encounter your own resistance as the initiative becomes real and takes on a life of its own.

PART 2

Change Killers

**EIGHT REAL-WORLD PHENOMENON
OF RESISTANCE IN ORGANIZATIONS**

*"Things that could be named had lost their secret power over man, the
horror of the unknown. To know the name of a force, a being or an
object was (to primitive man) identical to mastery over it."*

—ANAGARIKA GOVINDA, 1937

EIGHT COMMON FORMS OF RESISTANCE:
THE CHANGE KILLERS

Switching things up, starting, and stopping demands a lot because
change threatens what we have worked hard to build and maintain. Thus, you should not be surprised when you encounter
resistance. Rather, you should be prepared.

You can prevent and manage resistance by understanding eight common forms of resistance within organizations: the change killers. Below is a brief description of the change killers detailed in Part 2.

- **Habits and Routines.** The change is running counter to the daily practices and routines that are now second nature to us.
- **Commitment.** The change is substantially different from something that we are committed to.
- **Identity.** We truly believed and internalized the organization's needs and we don't identify with the new direction.
- **Status quo effect.** The organization can't change sufficiently or quickly enough to meet the demands of its environment.
- **Best practices.** We adhere to popular practices when they may not be best for us.
- **Groupthink.** We collectively circle our wagons in mutual support and cling to past decisions.
- **Threat rigidity.** We feel threatened by the change and lean into what we know best and learned first.
- **Change cynicism.** We can't trust the organization or believe that this time will be any better than past change attempts.

Each change killer is a complex phenomenon that will tell its own story of resistance in Part 2. That said, the change killers also tell us a bigger story and a simpler one; they tell us how and why resistance occurs in the first place.

Habit and Routine

THE TWIN GODS OF DAILY LIFE

"The lack of conscious control can turn even the smallest habits into the uncontested masters of our lives."

—NYANAPONIKA THERA, 1968

Despite our deep investments and best intentions to try something new, habits and routines can be hard to make and break. Every day, all day, habits and routines quietly guide our behavior. Here are a couple of scenarios where habits undermined change.

- For many years, staff maintained their own customer and sales data on their own spreadsheets. They complained about how onerous the process was. Executives had trouble understanding the full revenue picture with such fragmented information. Finally, the company decided to spend more than $2M on a technology solution. The project launched, and yet the company could not get some of the staff to input information into the system. For more than two years, a handful of hold-outs continued to rely on the Excel spreadsheets they used and begrudged for years. They could not change their daily practice.

- A retail company needed to decrease the time spent resolving its customer service issues. Requests for refunds over a modest amount had to go to a manager for approval, which resulted in significant delays. The company hired a consultant who proposed a new workflow that would empower frontline staff to resolve almost all refund requests on the spot. Yet, some of the staff felt insecure about making these decisions and continued to rely on supervisors to give the go-ahead on refund decisions. Despite a change in the formal process, the informal communication routines remained intact.

Habits and routines play dual roles in making change. On the one hand, they can anchor us to the past, on the other hand, they can create reliable behaviors for the future.

THE NATURE OF HABIT AND ROUTINE

Habits and routines are patterns of behavior that develop through repetition until they become easy, if not mindless. Both habits and routines can become automatic as a result of our mind's need for ease.

HABITS AUTOMATICALLY PURSUE REWARDS

Habits are repeated actions that we do in pursuit of a reward that becomes associated with a cue in our environment. As we repeat the action in the same context over and over again, we begin to pursue the reward automatically. Over time, the context (the time of day, or a location) becomes the cue that triggers habitual behavior. For instance, we may start a morning exercise routine with great effort; however, as we repeat the process and enjoy the invigoration it offers, we begin to associate mornings with exercise. Over time, mornings become the cue for exercise, and we automatically do it. The same logic applies to evening cocktails.

Our workplaces teem with habits and thrive on them. We may automatically respond to emails when we hear the bell announcing a new message so that we feel on top of our communications. Or we create to-do lists at the beginning of the day so that we feel in control.

Habits can be hard to break because our memory of the cue, and the rewards associated with it, are lasting even when we forget why we started the habit in the first place. Essentially, a habit forms and "turns the world around you—your context—into a trigger to act"[14]

ROUTINES ARE COLLECTIVE HABITS

Like habits, routines are also repeated patterns of behavior. Organizational routines are distinctively collective and require multiple people to carry them out. *An organizational routine is "a repetitive recognizable pattern of interdependent actions involving multiple actors.*"[15] For instance, a hiring practice is a routine that happens frequently and follows a standard sequence of actions that involve multiple people, including the hiring manager, the job applicant, and the HR department.

Below are some key features of routines.

- **Routines must be performed frequently to become regular.** Something that happens once is not a routine.

- **Routines are collective interactions of people.** Routines can

---

14 Wendy Wood, *Good Habits, Bad Habits: The Science of Making Positive Changes That Stick* (New York: Farrar, Straus and Giroux, 2019), 44.

15 Martha S. Feldman and Brian T. Pentland, "Reconceptualizing Organizational Routines as a Source of Flexibility and Change," *Administrative Science Quarterly* 48, no. 1 (March 2003), https://doi.org/10.2307/3556620.

span departments and hierarchies. Unlike habits, routines are always social.[16]

- **Routines are triggered.** They can be triggered as part of a sequence of events (e.g., a customer inquiry triggers the creation of a case) or by a performance threshold (e.g., subpar performance triggers an improvement plan).[17]
- **Routines work in specific conditions.** Though they are standardized, routines work in distinct organizations, teams, or moments in time. Routines that work well in one context may not work well in another.[18]

Routines arose at some point to perform a function, solve a problem, or do something more efficiently and reliably. As they are followed and improved upon over time, they become an ingrained practice passed on to generations of new employees. **Routines represent the learning of all the people who performed them before.**[19]

THE CAUSE OF HABITS AND ROUTINES

William James described it well: "Consciousness drops out of every process where it is no longer needed."[20]

---

16   Markus C. Becker, "Organizational Routines: A Review of the Literature," *Industrial and Corporate Change* 13, no. 4 (August 2004): 646, https://doi.org/10.1093/icc/dth026.

17   Becker, "Organizational Routines," 653.

18   Becker, "Organizational Routines," 652.

19   Linda Argote and Jerry M. Guo, "Routines and Transactive Memory Systems: Creating, Coordinating, Retaining, and Transferring Knowledge in Organizations," *Research in Organizational Behavior* 36 (2016): 68, https://doi.org/10.1016/j.riob.2016.10.002.

20   Quoted in Bargh, "The Cognitive Unconscious in Everyday Life," 89.

OUR NEED FOR EASE CREATES AUTOMATIC BEHAVIORS AND JUDGMENTS

Our ability to actively and consciously deliberate about something is a surprisingly limited resource that our mind reserves for its highest and best use. Psychologists believe that the conscious mind guides our behavior as little as 5 percent of the time.[21] For the rest of the time, our subconscious mind performs several vital functions effortlessly—we function on autopilot. It scans our environment and makes split-second unconscious judgments of people and situations as accurately as those we spend five minutes mulling over.[22] It constantly queues up behaviors in response to what it sees. It mimics the body language, tone, and mannerisms of others to create camaraderie with others. It even activates goals when we enter certain situations (e.g., our goal to be accepted is triggered in a room full of strangers) to help us take advantage of opportunities without even trying. We could not do all of this work deliberately.

These subconscious functions are known as automaticity—our mind's ability to unknowingly respond to something in our environment. Automaticity supports many daily functions so that our active conscious thinking is freed to focus on other things— new experiences that require deliberate attention. Our ability to operate on autopilot provides us with cognitive ease, an essential human need.

Automaticity explains the prevalence of habits and routines in our daily lives. Almost 45 percent of our day is spent performing habits mindlessly. We develop habits so that we don't have to think

---

21   Bargh and Chartrand, "The Unbearable Automaticity of Being," 464.

22   Bargh and Chartrand, "The Unbearable Automaticity of Being," 475.

about what we are doing; "once we surrender to our habits, our minds are free to perform higher tasks."[23]

Likewise, organizational routines make things easier and speed things up. They remove the need to figure out how something is done or make decisions. Routines "economize on limited information processing and decision-making capacity."[24] They free up the mind of an organization to actively deliberate about other more important things that require deliberation.

THE VALUE OF HABITS AND ROUTINES

Habits and routines make life easier. They give us a sense of ease in the form of continuity—today will be like yesterday and tomorrow will be like today. They give us a sense of familiarity, predictability, fluency, efficiency, and even safety.[25]

HABITS AND ROUTINES PROVIDE COGNITIVE EASE AND SHORTCUTS IN DAILY LIFE

They allow us to perform actions without having to determine how to do so over and over again. They require less thinking which allows our active mind to focus on non-routine events that demand our active evaluation and response. When a long and interconnected sequence of activities is summarized as a routine— say a "hiring process" that involves lots of steps between multiple actors and departments—we have an easy way to reference and know what we mean. We have a working knowledge of the "hiring process" routine without spelling out what is involved. In this way,

---

23   Wood, *Good Habits, Bad Habits*, 47.

24   Becker, "Organizational Routines," 657.

25   Wood, *Good Habits, Bad Habits*, 205–207.

routines are easy-to-understand labels that help us make sense of a "sea of activity that would otherwise be overwhelming."[26]

HABITS AND ROUTINES CREATE A SENSE OF STABILITY

When our world feels uncertain, we lean on habits and routines to provide stability and comfort. During unpredictable times, routines help us simplify complex situations; they "fix certain parameters...[and] increase predictability and at the same time free limited cognitive resources."[27]

ROUTINES CREATE SIMULTANEITY AND PREDICTABILITY ACROSS AN ORGANIZATION

When an organization has well-established routines across its departments, people in one area know what others are doing in another. Generally speaking, they rarely surprise each other. Consider an airplane taking off. The captain examines the flight path while the first officer inspects the plane, while ground operations refuel and load food, all while air traffic controllers review weather and flight-plan information. Every actor in this interconnected system of routines relies on the other to do their job simultaneously.

Routines also create predictability between staff and management. An effective routine can carry out the directives of management and avoid the need for micromanagement every step of the way. In turn, staff enacting the routine exercise their discretion.[28] In between this top-down direction and its execution

---

26   Feldman and Pentland, "Reconceptualizing Organizational Routines," 107.

27   Becker, "Organizational Routines," 658.

28   Becker, "Organizational Routines," 656.

is a gray area known as the "zone of indifference" that allows for wiggle room in how things get done.

ROUTINES ARE AN ORGANIZATION'S MEMORY AND APPLIED KNOWLEDGE

Initially, routines "represent successful solutions to particular problems."[29] As they are constantly repeated, routines are adapted as people learn and improve a practice. Routines capture the contributions of the people who execute them. In this way, routines are a repository of knowledge within an organization and serve "an organization's memory and play a central role in transferring organizational memory through time."[30]

ROUTINES ARE A SOURCE OF CONSTANT CHANGE

We modify routines as we enact them. We are constantly using our own judgment to make the routine work in specific situations. In this way, routines are a source of constant flexibility and continuous change.[31]

In sum, it is natural to take routines for granted; they are mindless by nature. Their familiarity should not belie their importance in our personal or organizational lives. Without them, we would be exhausted and adrift.

---

29   Becker, "Organizational Routines," 660.

30   Argote and Guo, "Routines and Transactive Memory Systems," 69.

31   Feldman and Pentland, "Reconceptualizing Organizational Routines."

THE DANGERS OF HABITS AND ROUTINES

There is a flip side to every benefit that we enjoy from habits and routines. With the ease of not thinking comes a mindlessness in situations that demand our attention. With repetition and predictability comes rigidity. Habits and routines anchor us to the past in ways that we may not even be aware of.

Let's unpack the downsides of both individual habits and organizational routines.

HABITS AND ROUTINES ARE HARD TO BREAK

Though they may have begun with a deliberate choice, habits and routines become mindless patterns of actions automatically cued by our environment. Like deep grooves of the mind, habitual and routinized behaviors can be intractable.

HABITS AND ROUTINES DULL OUR AWARENESS

Habits and routines perpetuate the past even when the need and conditions no longer hold. Their repetition dulls our senses as we come to expect things to be the same and don't expect things to deviate from the norm. Routines can function like social scripts that prescribe roles that make us feel inauthentic.[32] Habits and routines can have a "deadening, stultifying, and narrowing influence" on our behaviors.[33]

Research shows that "people with strong habits hold expectations about the environment that reduces their capacity to detect

---

32   Blake E. Ashforth and Yitzhak Fried, "The Mindlessness of Organizational Behaviors." *Human Relations* 41, no. 4 (April 1988): 316–317, https://doi.org/10.1177/001872678804100403.

33   Nyanaponika Thera, *The Power of Mindfulness* (The Buddhist Society, 1968), 48.

when it changes"[34] This explains why we may overlook or normalize potential warning signals and system malfunctions—the system has never failed, must be something wrong with the alarm (e.g., Three Mile Island).[35] Habitual patterns of behavior are "conservative forces that reduce openness to new information and that perpetuate well-practiced behaviors despite people's intentions to do otherwise."[36]

HABITS AND ROUTINES REPLICATE THE PAST

Habitual patterns of behavior, once anchored to the past, become second nature, which we mindlessly abide through repetition and reward. Changes made to routines are often incremental, and the fate of routine is largely determined by its origin.[37] Routines and habits are conservative forces.

ROUTINES CREATE DEPENDENCY ON A CERTAIN WAY OF DOING THINGS

As we routinize operations, we get stuck on a path. We build competency and chart a path with a potentially sub-par process or system. "Path dependency," also known as "competency traps," occurs when you get used to doing something a certain way—you do not look for something better even if it exists.[38]

---

34 Bas Verplanken and Wendy Wood, "Interventions to Break and Create Consumer Habits," *Journal of Public Policy & Marketing* 25, no. 1 (April 2006): 92, https://doi.org/10.1509/jppm.25.1.90.

35 Ashforth and Fried, "The Mindlessness of Organizational Behaviors," 316.

36 Verplanken and Wood, "Interventions to Break and Create Consumer Habits," 95.

37 Becker, "Organizational Routines," 653.

38 Becker, "Organizational Routines," 653.

ROUTINES CAN LEAD TO INERTIA

The inherent stability of routines can become a "pathology."[39] We largely stick with our routines. We do not challenge them or seek better alternatives. We ignore the feedback that they may not serve us well. We stay on our path—suboptimal as it may be—because we feel comfortable and competent. The problem is that, more often than not, uncertainty calls for new thinking to understand the world around us and develop a course of action that meets the moment. Our reliance on routines can steer us away from creativity and innovation.

WHAT YOU CAN DO

It is easy to interpret resistance as the result of personal intention when in fact it is born of habit and routine. Our need for cognitive ease is fundamental, and this need drives mindless patterns of behavior that are as human as the opposable thumb.

That said, you can help people create new habits that become reliable behaviors and break those habits that do not serve you well.

INTERRUPT THE AUTOPILOT WITH ACTIVE THINKING

At their worst, habits and routines lead to mindless actions that are anchored to the past and hold us back when our situation demands something new. Their repetition dulls our senses and understanding as we expect things to be as they were. Our goal is to understand "what actually happens to us and in us."[40] We need to see and understand things as they are—not as we think

---

39   Becker, "Organizational Routines," 659.

40   Thera, *The Power of Mindfulness*, vii.

they should be. While habits and routines simplify and mold the world around us to conform to our expectations, we must pay attention to the nuances, discrepancies, and unique particulars of how the world really is.[41]

There are several strategies to interrupt automaticity with active, mindful thinking.

- **Notice what's different about your situation and look for discrepancies and novelties.** Discrepancies can be a sign that your expectations are out of sync with reality. Discrepancies could be unexpected failures such as bad performance reviews or strategies that no longer work. Discrepancies are opportunities to reevaluate habitual thinking. New and novel situations call for a new approach to how you understand and navigate them. If you're starting a new job, you should not bring the old assumptions that accumulated over the years with your previous employer.

- **Create opportunities for active thinking.** You can create mindful attention.[42] We can proactively engage in active thinking through activities such as performance discussions, strategic planning sessions, and market or environmental assessments. The SWOT analysis—strengths, weaknesses, opportunities, and threats—is a good primer to talk about the need for change or at least a re-evaluation of how things are done.

- **Talk about your habits and routines and name them.** Talking about habits and routines can facilitate change. When we give a name to something that we experience, like a pattern of behavior, we begin to control it. To name is to tame it.

---

41 Karl E. Weick and Kathleen M. Sutcliffe, "Mindfulness and the Quality of Organizational Attention," *Organization Science* 17, no. 4 (August 2006): 518, https://doi.org/10.1287/orsc.1060.0196.

42 Meryl Reis Louis and Robert I. Sutton, "Switching Cognitive Gears: From Habits of Mind to Active Thinking," *Human Relations* 44, no. 1 (January 1991): 60, 65, https://doi.org/10.1177/001872679104400104.

Talking and reflecting can help a group look at the situation from different perspectives, identify what is working and not working, name the problem, and imagine alternative solutions.[43]

BREAK HABITS AND ROUTINES THAT HOLD YOU BACK

We learn some habits and routines consciously through training and others unconsciously through repetitive action. Just as we learn them, we can forget them. The process of forgetting involves letting go of knowledge and breaking patterns of behavior.

You can replace old ways of doing things with new ones by introducing doubt about the established practice and then exposing your team to alternative practices and experimentation. People will let go of the old ways as they appreciate and eventually adopt the new.

Let's go through each step of this process.

Introduce and Surface Doubt with the Old Way of Doing Things

We justify what we do and discard that which threatens our status, reputation, and sense of competence. In order to break through this instinctual defense, you must explicitly demonstrate that the established practice is no longer sufficient or reliable. As long as "current beliefs and methods seem to produce reasonable results, people do not discard their current beliefs and methods."[44]

---

43   Katharina Dittrich, Stéphane Guérard, and David Seidl, "Talking about Routines: The Role of Reflective Talk in Routine Change," *Organizational Science* 27, no. 3 (January 2016): 679, https://doi.org/10.1287/orsc.2015.1024.

44   William H. Starbuck, "Unlearning Ineffective or Obsolete Technologies," IOMS: Information Systems Working Papers, NYU Working Paper no. 2451/14188 (New York University, New York, 1996), 725–728, https://papers.ssrn.com/sol3/papers.cfm?abstract_id=1284804.

It is important to proceed with empathy and avoid criticizing past decisions. Doing so could trigger defensiveness, which only increases a person's commitment to the status quo.

One approach is to make it clear that it was right for the organization to adopt the current practice at the time—it was the best available option. Next, explain how changing conditions require a new approach. Have your team explore their dissatisfaction with the current system and reiterate their reasons why you must change.

Begin Training and Experimentation with New Systems and Processes

By quickly engaging your team, you build confidence, competence, and eventually ease in a new practice. This also prevents inertia and doubt from setting in. Old patterns of behavior will be discarded as the new ones take hold. New knowledge will displace the old.[45] Successful experimentation creates motivation to continue and communication with others about success encourages later adopters to follow suit.

Change the Physical and Social Context That Triggers Habits and Routines

Habits and routines take hold in specific contexts and environments. Habits are triggered by a specific context including times of day, locations, or people. Similarly, organizational routines are embedded in team relations which are supported by their physical proximity to one another.

---

45 Marlena Fiol and Edward O'Connor, "Unlearning Established Organizational Routines – Part I," *The Learning Organization* 24, no. 1 (January 2017): 25, https://doi.org/10.1108/TLO-09-2016-0056.

Changing the physical location and environment is another strategy for disrupting established patterns and facilitating new perspectives and experiences. Just as moving to a new house can help break bad habits triggered by the old one, changing one's work setting can do the same.[46]

Another strategy is to restructure staff and absorb them into other parts of the organization. This can dismantle the web of relationships, processes, and knowledge that can be an obstacle to change.

CREATE NEW HABITS AND ROUTINES

Whether you are a young startup or an established organization launching a new initiative, you may need to create new habits and routines. The process of habit formation provides a template for establishing reliable patterns of behavior.

The basic steps of deliberately creating a habit or routine are:

1. **Map out the behaviors.** Make the steps as simple as possible. Your routines need not be overly prescriptive; they can leave room for interpretation.

2. **Create a consistent context for the new behavior.** Clearly identify the trigger or cue that prompts the routine (e.g., new customer data is entered into the CRM system as soon as someone is identified as a prospect). Habits and routines rely on a stable context and triggers for action.

3. **Repeat the behavior.** In the beginning, this will be a concerted and deliberate process. Be sure to give people time to adequately train or adjust to the new way of doing things. You will need to remind people to perform the routine through

---

46   Verplanken and Wood, "Interventions to Break and Create Consumer Habits," 96.

multiple channels: posters, Post-It notes, meetings, emails, etc.—think of this as a communication campaign.

4. **Reward the behavior and provide positive feedback.** Positive feedback can create a sense of competence and confidence. This also means removing stress from the process and avoiding negative experiences.

5. **Reflect upon how the routine is going.** Engage everyone involved in the process of improving the routine. Getting input from multiple perspectives can ensure the process works. Do not over-hype the new process as this can lead to disappointment.

Outside of creating new habits from scratch, you can effectively create new habits by transitioning people from the old to the new. Below are strategies for this more gradual process.

- **Create new routines by adapting existing ones.** Learning something new and changing behavior can be challenging. You can create new routines by modifying current ones to achieve your goals. People are more likely to learn new things when they can "relate it to their areas of expertise. When they can't, they might...resist adopting it."[47]

- **Transition from the current state to the new through experimentation.** Experimentation with a new approach can ease the change from a long-established routine to a new one. Experimentation is less threatening than a hard stop. It also allows learning about the new system to take place gradually. As people experiment with the new system and have positive and motivating experiences, they will slowly phase out the old.

47 Pablo Martin de Holan, Nelson Phillips, and Thomas B. Lawrence, "Managing Organizational Forgetting," *MIT Sloan Management Review* 45, no. 2 (Winter 2004): 45, https://sloanreview.mit.edu/article/managing-organizational-forgetting.

Whether you are creating new routines or adapting old ones, it is important to capture and share positive experiences and new learnings. Innovations can die on the vine from a "failure to capture" what people learned and what works. This lack of documentation can result in an organization forgetting about what it learned. Personal learning and positive experiences should be "made institutional...[and] new knowledge must be made explicit...then the information must be communicated to other parts of the organization."[48] When experimenters document and share their positive experiences with others, they create both knowledge and momentum for the organization.

AVOID BAD HABITS AND ROUTINES

It would be so helpful to know if the mindless patterns of behavior and thought that guide almost half of our waking day were serving us well or poorly. Unfortunately, it is hard to know if our habits and routines are helpful or what exactly causes success or failure.

Amidst this uncertainty, there are a few strategies to help avoid bad habits and routines.

- **Don't over-learn success or failure.** If you identify the wrong cause of a failure, you may become too conservative and not attempt a venture that could, under different circumstances, lead to success. Conversely, if you miscalculate the cause of success, you may be overly optimistic and not exercise enough caution or restraint in the future.[49]

- **Treat work (and life) like one big experiment.** Treating our work like an experiment opens up our minds to new insights and creates opportunities for surprises. By nature, experi-

---

48   Marin de Holan, Phillips, and Lawrence, "Managing Organizational Forgetting," 48.

49   Marin de Holan, Phillips, and Lawrence, "Managing Organizational Forgetting," 50–51.

mentation is less committing because we haven't staked our reputations on the outcomes. When we experiment, we are willing to deviate from normal or optimal practices in order to test our assumptions.[50] Moreover, when we experiment, we seek our feedback and pay close attention.

CHAPTER SUMMARY

- Habits and routines are automatic, mindless behaviors that can be an obstacle to change as they replicate and tie us to the past. They can enable change if they are adapted and developed to support new ways of doing things.
- Habits and routines are behaviors that develop through repetition until they become easy, if not mindless, patterns.
- Routines are collective habits that involve many people across an organization, represent a sequence of events, and are improved upon over time.
- Our mind automates habits and routines so that we don't need to think about them. This frees up our mind to actively deliberate about problems and more important issues.
- Habits and routines provide us with mental shortcuts, ease, and predictability in daily life. Organizational routines are developed and adapted over time and contain solutions that people devised to problems.
- Habits and routines can be hard to break; they continue when conditions no longer call for them and create a predictability that dulls our awareness. They can lead to inertia when we do not seek better alternatives.
- To overcome habitual thinking and behaviors, you can stimulate active and mindful thinking by noticing the subtle things

---

50   Starbuck, "Unlearning Ineffective or Obsolete Technologies," 727–730.

in your environment, creating opportunities for deliberate thinking, and talking about habits.

- You can break habits and routines by introducing doubt about the old ways of doing things, beginning training and experimentation with new systems and processes, and changing the physical and social context.
- You can create new habits and routines by identifying the desired behaviors, creating consistent cues (triggers) for the behavior, repeating rewards, and reflecting on them. It is important to capture and share positive experiences and new learnings.
- To avoid the onset of habits and routines that may not serve you well, it is helpful to take life in stride. Don't overlearn success or failure (you likely won't know what exactly caused either), and treat life like a big experiment (don't overly commit, and be open to learning).

CASE IN POINT: RESISTANCE OF BEHAVIOR CHANGE

NUDGING HANDWASHING IN HOSPITALS

Since the eighteenth century, handwashing has been considered an essential practice in medicine. By the early nineteenth century, handwashing was adopted globally, and currently it is understood to be a critical practice to reduce infectious disease spread.[51] Yet only 40 percent of doctors and nurses comply with hospital hand hygiene guidelines.[52]

Over the past decade, many hospitals have adopted a "nudge" strategy to essentially create handwashing habits. Nudge strategies typically include placing sanitizer dispensers and visual reminders at key locations, such as doorways, and by a patient's bedside—where doctors and nurses spend much of their working time. Thus every time a doctor or nurse enters the room or stands by a patient's bed, they are reminded to wash their hands. And with every bedside visit, handwashing is repeated and becomes automatically associated with standing by the bed.

Some studies have found that nudging results in a 60 percent increase in handwashing among doctors and nurses.[53] A review of forty-two nudge trials shows that 80 percent of nudge strategies had a positive effect when combined with traditional education and training.[54]

---

51 Ramezan Ali Ataee et al., "Bacteriological Aspects of Hand Washing: A Key for Health Promotion and Infections Control," *International Journal of Preventative Medicine* 8 (March 2017): 16, https://doi.org/10.4103/2008-7802.201923.

52 Vicki Erasmus et al., "Systematic Review of Studies on Compliance with Hand Hygiene Guidelines in Hospital Care," *Infection Control and Hospital Epidemiology* 31, no. 3 (March 2010): 283–294, https://doi.org/10.1086/650451.

53 Fabrizio Elia et al., "A Nudge Intervention to Improve Hand Hygiene Compliance in the Hospital," *Internal and Emergency Medicine* 17, no. 7 (October 2022): 1899–1905, https://doi.org/10.1007/s11739-022-03024-7.

54 Erasmus et al., "Systematic Review of Studies on Compliance with Hand Hygiene Guidelines in Hospital Care"; Sze Lin Yoong et al., "Nudge Strategies to Improve Healthcare Providers' Implementation of Evidence-Based Guidelines, Policies and Practices: A Systematic Review of Trials Included within Cochrane Systematic Review," *Implementation Science* 15, no. 1 (July 2020): 50, https://doi.org/10.1186/s13012-020-01011-0.

CASE IN POINT: RESISTANCE TO DELIBERATE THINKING

SELF-CONTROL IS IN FACT EXHAUSTING

Psychologist Roy Baumeister and his colleagues set out to determine whether our ability to actively choose to do something is a limited resource. They conducted four experiments that tested whether our performance of one volitional task that required active deliberation decreases our ability to perform another. They tested four types of active choice and their impact on our stamina to perform another task that requires our active mind.

All four experiments showed that our ability to regulate ourselves, resist temptation, make active choices, stifle emotions, and persist in the face of challenge all draw from the same limited resource. When we do these things once, we have less strength to do them a second time.[55] These tests demonstrate our need to delegate tasks to our subconscious and make decisions automatically. If we had to make every decision deliberately, we would be absolutely exhausted.

- **Experiment 1: Resisting chocolate.** Participants who resisted chocolate and instead ate radishes spent eight minutes solving a puzzle. Participants who ate chocolate spent nineteen minutes solving a puzzle. Resisting temptation cut stamina in half!

- **Experiment 2: Making a single choice.** Participants who chose which pre-written speech to make spent less than fourteen minutes solving a puzzle. Participants who were assigned their speech spent twenty-three minutes solving the puzzle. The act of making a deliberate choice diminished stamina by almost 50 percent.

- **Experiment 3: Suppressing emotions.** Participants who suppressed their emotions during a funny or sad video clip performed significantly worse in solving puzzles than those who did not stifle their feelings. Regulating emotions decreased problem-solving abilities.

---

55   Baumeister et al., "Ego Depletion."

- **Experiment 4: Performing complex tasks.** Participants who performed mentally demanding tasks were given the opportunity to stop watching a boring video of a blank wall. This experiment shows that a prior exertion of self-regulation negatively impact our ability to make active decisions (opting out of watching a blank wall). In other words, depleted people did what was easiest and made passive choices.

In sum, each active decision depletes our ability to make another. Baumeister's research shows how important it is that we are able to automate decisions and behaviors in daily life.

Commitment

AN ANCHOR TO THE PAST (AND FUTURE)

"The secret of happiness and virtue is liking what you've got to do. All conditioning aims at that: making people like their inescapable social destiny."

—ALDOUS HUXLEY, *BRAVE NEW WORLD*

Commitment to our work gives us purpose and meaning, it motivates and sustains us. The danger is that when we commit to the current version of the organization (its processes, priorities, or values), our commitments can become outdated as the organization changes.

Commitment takes on many forms, some helpful and others harmful. Here are a few scenarios of how commitment can play out:

- Staff on a membership team were committed to high-touch personal member engagement. They did not agree with using technology to service more members with less effort. They truly believed that relationships would suffer without a more personal approach. They showed little interest in learning the new technology. As the organization moved on, they could not let go of their previous commitments. In time, some were let go.

- A CEO was deeply committed to expanding the geography of their entertainment venues. After years of planning and fundraising, construction began. Costs and timelines ballooned. Initial assumptions of the business plan became untenable. Rather than pull the plug, the CEO aggressively increased revenue projections to offset increased costs and added years to the timeline. As objective indicators suggested that the project should stop, the CEO's commitment escalated. Eventually, the project's backers pulled out. The CEO resigned.

- A team of product designers is deeply committed to the process of testing and experimentation. Failing fast and learning is a core value system to them. They thoroughly evaluate the performance of every product they develop, no matter how rudimentary. They willfully and transparently publish all results, even abysmal ones. Their commitment to experimentation means they willfully adopt a rigorous system of corporate control: performance monitoring, and reporting.

- The Amway corporation inspires its sales team to achieve higher and higher goals by asking each salesperson to commit their individual goals to writing: "Whatever the goal, the important thing is that you set it, so you've got something for which to aim—and that you write it down. There is something magical in writing things down."[56] Amway knows that we want to be consistent with our commitments.

---

56 Robert B. Cialdini, *Influence, New and Expanded: The Psychology of Persuasion* (New York: Harper Collins, 2021), 319.

THE NATURE OF COMMITMENT

You may think that commitment begins with a belief that something is worthwhile and this belief eventually drives actions. *A large body of research shows that commitment begins with behavior.*

COMMITMENT BEGINS WITH ACTION

Let's start with a clear definition. *Commitment is a force that binds us to a course of action.*[57]

Commitment begins with an action that is then justified by the mind: "To act is to commit oneself."[58] When we commit to something, we commit to behavior, because, "behavior is a visible indicator of *what we are*, and what *we intend to do*."[59] When we say that we will do something by next Monday, we have determined and constrained our future behaviors, at least through Monday. *Committing behaviors both bind and constrain us.*

VOLITIONAL, VISIBLE, AND IRREVERSIBLE ACTIONS COMMIT US

For an action to create a commitment, it needs to be volitional, visible, and irreversible. Let's unpack each of these:

- **Volition.** Volition is an essential ingredient of commitment. Volition "is the cement that binds the action to the person and that motivates him/her to accept the implications of his/her

57 John P. Meyer and Lynne Herscovitch, "Commitment in the Workplace: Toward a General Model," *Human Resource Management Review* 11, no. 3 (Autumn 2001): 308, https://doi.org/10.1016/S1053-4822(00)00053-X.

58 Barry M. Staw and Gerald R. Salancik, eds., *New Directions in Organizational Behavior* (Chicago: St. Clair Press, 1977), 4.

59 Gerald R. Salancik, "Commitment Is Too Easy!," *Organizational Dynamics* 6, no. 1 (Summer 1977): 63, https://doi.org/10.1016/0090-2616(77)90035-3.

acts."[60] Generally speaking, we accept the consequences of our actions out of a sense of personal responsibility. Getting someone to do something without their volition is entrapment.[61]

- **Visible.** Visible acts can be observed by others. Their visibility creates public expectations for our future behaviors. For instance, asking for volunteers in a public meeting creates commitment because others bear witness. Conversely, anonymous actions allow us to deny our intentions and change our minds.[62]

- **Irreversibility.** Acts that cannot practically be undone create constraints on our future options. Quitting a job or firing someone is practically irreversible as pride and embarrassment make it inconceivable to reverse course.

THE CAUSES OF COMMITMENT

We commit to tasks, jobs, organizations and causes for many reasons. We need to be consistent with our previous actions and find purpose in what we do. We will commit to something in order to belong.

OUR NEED TO BE CONSISTENT MEANS THAT WE FOLLOW THROUGH

Our personal integrity and need to be trusted leads us to be consistent with our commitments.[63] Our commitment is automatic and sometimes ill-considered.

---

60   Salancik, "Commitment Is Too Easy!," 69.

61   Salancik, "Commitment Is Too Easy!," 67.

62   Salancik, "Commitment Is Too Easy!," 64.

63   Mayer, Davis, and Schoorman, "An Integrative Model of Organizational Trust," 716, 719.

Once an active commitment is made, then self-image is squeezed from both sides by consistency pressures. From the inside there is press to bring self-image in line with action. From the outside there is a sneakier pressure—a tendency to adjust this image according to the way others see us.[64]

This consistency effect causes us to make good on previous statements, and to act in concert with the past. The famed "foot in the door" sales technique preys upon the consistency effect. By agreeing to a small request, such as a petition signature, we are more likely to agree with a larger one, like a donation.[65]

Consistency is seen as a virtue and sign of strong leadership, personal strength, and integrity in the business and political world. Conversely, being phony or inconsistent is ranked as the worst thing a person could be.[66]

OUR NEED FOR PURPOSE CREATES COMMITMENT

Our work and career is an important source of meaning and purpose in modern life.[67] When we are committed, we *identify* with the organization, desire to be part of it, and *internalize* the organization's values as our own.[68]

Purpose can take the form of:

64 Cialdini, *Influence, New and Expanded*, 294.

65 Jonathan L. Freedman and Scott C. Fraser, "Compliance without Pressure: The Foot-in-the-Door Technique," *Journal of Personality and Social Psychology* 4, no. 2 (1966), https://doi.org/10.1037/h0023552, 195.

66 John A. Bargh, "It Was Social Consistency that Mattered All Along," *Psychological Inquiry* 29, no. 2 (October 2018): 61, https://doi.org/10.1080/1047840X.2018.1480586.

67 Baumeister and Vohs, "The Pursuit of Meaningfulness in Life," 611.

68 Charles O'Reilly and Jennifer A. Chatman, "Culture as Social Control: Corporations, Cults, and Commitment," in *Research in Organizational Behavior* Vol. 18, edited by Barry M. Staw and Larry L. Cummings, 170, (Greenwich, CT: JAI Press, 1996).

- **An objective goal** that we are trying to achieve, such as improving our knowledge or skills[69]
- **A subjective fulfillment** such as greater satisfaction or work/life balance[70]
- **A value system** that "provides a compass for right and wrong" that guides our perceptions and behaviors and creates a sense of "purposeful action"[71]
- **The positive impact we have on others** and the motivation we have to help[72]

By finding purpose, we are connecting the present to the future; "the future events lend direction to the present so that the present is seen as leading towards an eventual purpose."[73] A sense of purpose and meaning provides us with a sense of stability amidst change and helps us cope with the challenges and feel in control.

OUR NEED TO BELONG AND CONFORM CREATES COMMITMENT

The norms and culture of an organization shape our behavior and determine our commitments. The norms of an organization are rules of thumb, everyday "expectations about what are appropriate

---

69 Baumeister and Vohs, "The Pursuit of Meaningfulness in Life," 610.

70 Baumeister and Vohs, "The Pursuit of Meaningfulness in Life," 610.

71 Brent D. Rosso, Kathryn H. Dekas, and Amy Wrzesniewski, "On the Meaning of Work: A Theoretical Integration and Review," *Research in Organizational Behavior* 30 (January 2010): 111, https://doi.org/10.1016/j.riob.2010.09.001.

72 Adam M. Grant, "Relational Job Design and the Motivation to Make a Prosocial Difference," *Academy of Management Review* 32, no. 2 (April 2007): 404, https://doi.org/10.5465/amr.2007.24351328.

73 Baumeister and Vohs, "The Pursuit of Meaningfulness in Life," 610.

and inappropriate attitudes and behaviors."[74] When we care about those with whom we work, we want to be accepted and live up to their expectations. **When we believe we are *being noticed* by someone who matters, our behaviors conform to the group's norms and our attitudes and beliefs soon follow.** We will adjust our beliefs and commitments to be consistent with our actions. Note: our ability to rationalize our behavior is so great that it can even overcome doubts and result in a changed belief.[75] If we break a norm, we risk being professionally shunned by our friends and colleagues.

THE VALUES OF COMMITMENT

Commitment brings many benefits to people working within organizations. It infuses banal activities with purpose. It creates employees who are willing to give it their all without asking for additional pay. With its ability to lift spirits and performance, commitment is essential to ambitious and risky change efforts.

COMMITMENT BRINGS PURPOSE AND MEANING TO WORK AND LIFE

We are "hardwired to seek meaning," pursue important goals, and support a broader purpose.[76] We experience commitment as a positive emotional attachment to something that has intrinsic value to us. **The sense of purpose helps us navigate challenges and be more resilient and rebound from setbacks.** Purpose can

---

74   Charles O'Reilly, "Corporations, Culture, and Commitment: Motivation and Social Control in Organizations," *California Management Review* 31, no. 4 (Summer 1989): 12, https://doi. org/10.2307/41166580.

75   O'Reilly and Chatman, "Culture as Social Control," 167.

76   Baumeister and Vohs, "The Pursuit of Meaningfulness in Life," 613.

help manage stress that results from unpredictable and uncontrollable situations. For instance, caregivers who connect their hard work to the important goal of helping loved ones with degenerative diseases experience better health outcomes than guilt-induced caregivers. Purpose can lead to more efficient individual and team efforts as we focus on actions that fulfill our purpose.[77]

COMMITMENT IMPROVES PERFORMANCE

Committed employees go the extra mile. They dedicate personal time to their job and take on additional responsibilities. Committed employees have less intention to leave the organization, and are absent less than others. Organizations that adopt management practices that build commitment (e.g., training, comprehensive rewards, employee security, self-managed teams, decentralized decision-making, information sharing, and reduced status differential) demonstrate superior outcomes in learning, skill development, innovation, customer service, productivity, cost reduction, and flexibility.[78] Commitment can be a source of competitive advantage.

COMMITMENT SUSTAINS ACTION IN DIFFICULT SITUATIONS

Commitment instills people with a stronger desire and willingness to work harder because they believe in what they are doing. This is especially helpful when the chips are down. Commitment sustains "action in the face of difficulties… Without commit-

---

77   McKnight and Kashdan, "Purpose in Life as a System that Creates and Sustains Health and Well-Being," 246.

78   Richard T. Mowday, "Reflections on the Study and Relevance of Organizational Commitment," *Human Resource Management Review* 8, no. 6 (Winter 1998): 394, https://doi.org/10.1016/S1053-4822(99)00006-6.

ment individuals would be less likely to pursue goals for which the outcomes are uncertain."[79] Commitment compels people to "push headlong on a course of action when the outcomes of the action are themselves not known. For an organization that faces an uncertain environment, the selective use of a commitment can allow it to take actions that pay off or not."[80]

COMMITTED EMPLOYEES REQUIRE LESS OVERSIGHT

Committed employees internalize the organization's goals and act instinctively on its behalf.[81] We experience our commitment as a result of our own "personal determination" rather than a command by someone else.[82] But, the reality is that we commit to organizational goals and norms because we conform to our peers. In this way, commitment is a form of social control that engenders "positive feelings of solidarity, and a greater sense of autonomy."[83] Because committed employees pursue the organization's objectives innately, they require less active oversight and can be trusted with more autonomy. Flexible work systems, independent teams, and decentralized decision-making can function effectively with committed employees.

79   Salancik, "Commitment Is Too Easy!," 63.

80   Staw and Salancik, eds., *New Directions in Organizational Behavior*, 44.

81   Charles A. O'Reilly and Jennifer A. Chatman, "Organizational Commitment and Psychological Attachment: The Effects of Compliance, Identification, and Internalization on Prosocial Behavior," *Journal of Applied Psychology* 71, no. 3 (1986): 493, https://doi.org/10.1037/0021-9010.71.3.492.

82   O'Reilly and Chatman, "Culture as Social Control," 163.

83   O'Reilly and Chatman, "Culture as Social Control," 165.

THE DANGERS OF COMMITMENT

While commitment has many emotional and functional benefits for employees and organizations, it can restrict the voices we listen to and the options we consider. It can create a rigid adherence to the past and can easily escalate beyond reason.

COMMITMENT CAN RESTRICT CRITICAL PERSPECTIVES

A group that is committed to common goals and norms can be homogenous in its thinking. As the group upholds its commitments, it can potentially silence critical yet well-intentioned voices. The solidarity of a tight-knit team bound by strong commitments can restrict diverse perspectives that could improve the organization.[84]

COMMITMENT CAN LEAD TO RIGIDITY

As we infuse our actions with purpose, we become wedded to them, and potentially stuck in our ways. Commitment can come mindlessly, "having done a thing once in the past, alone justifies doing it that way again."[85] The repetition of behaviors can lead to commitment that reinforces the behavior. We cling to our patterns, become tied to a course of action, and do not seek or entertain alternatives. We become rigid.

---

84   O'Reilly and Chatman, "Culture as Social Control," 167, 170.

85   Staw and Salancik, eds., *New Directions in Organizational Behavior*, 41.

COMMITMENT CAN ESCALATE A
FAILING COURSE OF ACTION

Leaders are expected to be decisive and stick to their guns. Generally speaking, indecision is not tolerated. Most organizations do not look kindly on failure. When faced with negative consequences of their decisions, leaders might justify their past actions by escalating their commitment, rather than pulling back. The need to demonstrate competence and rectify past losses with future gains is incredibly strong.[86] Commitment to a faltering course of action easily escalates even as the objective evidence suggests that it is time to stop.

WHAT YOU CAN DO

Building commitment is critical to the success of your change effort. Commitment motivates and sustains people in challenging and ambiguous situations. It may also be necessary to manage commitments to the past and loose their grip. Lastly, commitment can escalate even in the face of failure.

I will provide you with strategies for (1) building commitment; (2) loosening outdated commitments; and (3) deescalating commitments.

CHOOSE THE OBJECT OF COMMITMENT

Building commitment is an intentional process that begins with the question, *Building commitment to what?* Your job as a change leader is to identify the commitment that makes sense and will tap into the deeper motivations of your team.

---

86 Barry M. Staw, "The Escalation of Commitment to a Course of Action," *Academy of Management Review* 6, no. 4 (October 1981): 583, https://doi.org/10.2307/257636.

You can build commitment to an organization, occupation, goal, policy, or course of action. The object of commitment should reinforce the behaviors needed to support your change effort. Below are a few examples.

- If you are implementing a CRM, focus commitment on *improving the customer's experience.*
- If you are developing new products, build commitment to the *process of innovation and experimentation.*
- If you are implementing a new workflow between teams, focus commitment on the *value of being dependable to others.*

Commitment focused on the organization itself can inspire broader behaviors such as lower turnover and absenteeism, improved performance, and contributions beyond the job description.[87]

When you build commitment to the right thing, employees will want to see an initiative succeed. They will go above and beyond what is required and do what is needed.[88]

FOCUS ATTENTION ON WHAT IS IMPORTANT

With many change initiatives, the transition from the old way to the new can be rife with uncertainty and ambiguity. Uncertainty about the future creates a disquieting void that you can fill with new commitments. You must consistently signal what your team should focus on and why it is important.

Major changes can be long and complex and hit bumps in the road. You will need to create focus and maintain motivation by:

---

87   Meyer and Herscovitch, "Commitment in the Workplace," 310.

88   Meyer and Herscovitch, "Commitment in the Workplace," 311.

1. **Setting incremental and achievable goals.** People can see their progress in small and short-term wins.
2. **Publicly noticing the significant efforts** people are making and behaviors that you are hoping to see. The simple act of noticing, and letting people know that you notice can be a powerful reinforcement of the behaviors that support change.[89]

INSPIRE BELIEF THAT THINGS ARE WORKING

Transformational change can take years to realize returns, and it is often unclear whether things are working. Moreover, major change can be achieved through the steady accumulation of minor tweaks. **You can leverage small happenings in a way that reinforces your mission and motivates your team.** The attainment of milestones, anecdotal results, or just trying something new can be opportunities to reflect and celebrate the change afoot.

As a leader, you are crafting the story of change. It is your job to explain and justify why the change effort is important and valuable. It is your job to motivate people in the face of senselessness and uncertainty. Put another way, "Evidence that something is working is probably less important than the belief that it is working. For it is belief that sustains the activity, not the evidence."[90]

CREATE SYSTEMS OF PARTICIPATION

Substantial research demonstrates the power of participation to create commitment. Yet we've all had experiences where people roll their eyes about such efforts. You, however, can create meaningful

---

89 O'Reilly and Chatman, "Culture as Social Control," 172.

90 Salancik, "Commitment Is Too Easy!," 72.

participation that actually works with the right stakeholders, at different times in a project's lifecycle and with the right approach.

Who should participate? In short, anyone who is essential to the success of your project or could block your progress. An empirical study of eighty-two change efforts showed that *successful change efforts involved stakeholders at the upper and peer levels of the organization far more than unsuccessful ones.* The same study also showed that *successful change efforts involved stakeholders at lower levels* three times more than unsuccessful attempts.[91]

Participants can include:

- Senior executives with budget authority
- Staff from other departments who will be impacted by the change
- Front-line staff who will be responsible for implementing or adopting a change
- Outside experts can bolster a business case or provide technical expertise
- Critics and supporters who can provide valuable problem-solving information

Opportunities for participation can take place through the course of a project and in various forms. You can *formally* engage your stakeholders through:

- **A planning team** formed early in the process that develops the scope and approach
- **A steering committee** that can provide executive support and advice
- **A working team** that helps you manage the project, engage

---

91   Jane E. Dutton et al., "Moves that Matter: Issue Selling and Organizational Change," *Academy of Management Journal* 44, no. 4 (August 2001): 724.

and communicate with stakeholders, and identify and resolve key issues

- **An implementation team** that translates the broad directive into specific plans for their area and identifies and works through problems
- **Ad-hoc groups** that work on specific issues that pop up during the project

Teams such as these require significant management time and ability to keep them focused and aligned. That said, they may be worth the effort for complex and risky efforts that impact multiple areas.

Effective participatory systems can help you manage the complexity, share in the risk, and secure resources. Ineffective ones can derail.

Below are the building blocks for successfully building commitment through participation.

- **Participants must agree to join the effort and be active.** Participating in the process is a choice, not an assignment. This is key to building commitment.
- **Establish the norm that the team's role is to make the initiative workable.** As they identify problems, they can identify the path for solutions and track progress.
- **The group must be able to exercise discretion and make real choices.** Research shows that participatory management programs are more likely to fail when groups lack the technical skills and decision-making authority to implement their recommendations.[92]
- **Their contributions and choices should be public.** Avoid

---

92   Edward E. Lawler and Susan A. Mohrman, "Quality Circles After the Fad," *Harvard Business Review* 63, no. 1 (January 1985), https://hbr.org/1985/01/quality-circles-after-the-fad.

anonymous mechanisms, such as polling or voting, that provide anonymity.

- **There must be trust in the process.** If staff feel that their participation is for appearances only, they will become cynical of the process and you might lose support.

In sum, our "active participation in the design of a plan of action implies both willingness and ability to accomplish it… the power of participation and directing future behavior comes from the person being held responsible for a decision with salient implications."[93]

REWARD PEOPLE

Positive feedback, recognition, and small rewards can increase and reinforce commitment to a change effort. Conversely, research suggests that large monetary rewards can negatively impact our motivation as we focus on cash, rather than achieving something important.[94]

PROTECT TRUST IN THE PROCESS

Be genuine in your participation methods. Participation needs to reinforce the participant's value in the eyes of the organization. You need to demonstrate that you will genuinely consider suggestions. Disingenuous efforts of participation will very likely fail.[95] When it comes to trust, quality matters.

---

93 Staw and Salancik, eds., *New Directions in Organizational Behavior*, 35.

94 O'Reilly and Chatman, "Culture as Social Control," 173.

95 Anuradha Chawla and E. Kevin Kelloway, "Predicting Openness and Commitment to Change," *Leadership & Organizational Development Journal* 25, no. 6 (September 2004): 494, https://doi.org/10.1108/01437730410556734.

You will need to demonstrate that the change process is fair; this is especially true for changes that involve layoffs. The process should be objectively evaluated, represent the good of the organization, and be sensitive to the needs of employees, especially those who are negatively impacted. You must communicate the fairness of the process, especially to your most committed employees. **The perception of unfairness and injustice can destroy commitment.**[96]

AVOID DEFENSIVENESS BY JUSTIFYING PAST COMMITMENTS

Criticizing someone's past actions will only inspire justifications of them, which will only reinforce previous commitments. You can help someone let go of their previous commitments by acknowledging why their decisions made sense at the time. When we feel justified about our past actions, we become less defensive and more willing to change.[97]

ENGAGE WITH CRITICAL PERSPECTIVES

Opposition to change can happen when leaders fail to explain the realities and constraints facing the organization to staff. By including staff, and even critics, in the decision-making process, you invite them "to accept the premises of the situation—and thus to plan within the same constraints that they may have previously opposed."[98]

---

96   Joel Brockner, Tom R. Tyler, and Rochelle Cooper-Schneider, "The Influence of Prior Commitment to an Institution on Reactions to Perceived Unfairness: The Higher They Are, The Harder They Fall," in "Process and Outcome: Perspectives on the Distribution of Rewards in Organizations," special issue, *Administrative Science Quarterly* 37, no. 2 (June 1992), https://doi.org/10.2307/2393223.

97   Salancik, "Commitment Is Too Easy!," 79.

98   Salancik, "Commitment Is Too Easy!," 75.

You will need a plan for managing objections that (1) harnesses the value of critical feedback, and (2) avoids the potential of someone's criticism becoming a commitment to the project's failure. By voicing concerns or criticisms in front of others, people can commit themselves to a program's failure. Even unwittingly they may feel the need to prove themselves right and your program wrong.

To engage with critical perspectives:

- **Adopt a mindset that you do not have all the answers and the plan is not perfect.** Your humility takes pressure off of you and invites people to help solve problems. You can demonstrate your openness to critical feedback by consistently asking:
  - What am I not seeing?
  - What is the weakness of this plan?
- **Track problems and their resolution.** By tracking issues throughout the process, you can channel objections into a problem-solving system. Create a document that tracks all concerns, solutions, and methods used to solve them. You may need to prioritize this list into low, medium, and high importance.

This strategy has another obvious, if not challenging, benefit. The critic may have a perspective in which your constraints can be overcome or bypassed altogether. For this to work they must be willing to listen to you, and you must be willing to listen to them.

DE-ESCALATE COMMITMENTS TO FAILURE

Projects can require months if not years of our commitment to selling, planning, and getting the work off the ground. It's very easy to get wrapped up, revved up, and blinded by our commitments.

Our desire to demonstrate our competence is strong. When we

are personally responsible for a negative consequence, we may be motivated to rectify our past losses and increase investments to a failing course of action.[99] **We can easily convince ourselves that all we need is a little more time and money to be proven right.**[100]

We should be on guard for the tendency to justify ourselves, cherry-pick our indicators of success, and keep projects going that need to stop. We need to be ready to change or reverse course.

Below are several strategies to de-escalate commitments to failure.

COMMIT TO THE PROBLEM, NOT THE PROGRAM

Commitment to a specific course of action is likely only one way to solve a problem. By distinguishing the underlying problem from the specific program that you are currently pursuing, you can give yourself the flexibility of finding another solution should the initial one fail.[101]

REDUCE THE FEAR OF FAILURE AND SOCIALIZE ITS POSSIBILITY

High stakes and the fear of failure increase the pressure to make good on bad ideas.[102] Though it is important that people be

99   Barry M. Staw, "Knee-Deep in the Big Muddy: A Study of Escalating Commitment to a Chosen Course of Action," *Organizational Behavior and Human Performance* 16, no. 1 (June 1976): 41, https://doi.org/10.1016/0030-5073(76)90005-2.

100   Staw, "The Escalation of Commitment to a Course of Action," 578.

101   Jerry Ross and Barry M. Staw, "Organizational Escalation and Exit: Lessons from the Shoreham Nuclear Power Plant," *Academy of Management Journal* 36, no. 4 (August 1993): 728, https://www.jstor.org/stable/256756.

102   Itamar Simonson and Barry M. Staw, "Deescalation Strategies: A Comparison of Techniques for Reducing Commitment to Losing Courses of Action," *Journal of Applied Psychology* 77, no. 4 (1992): 425, https://doi.org/10.1037/0021-9010.77.4.419.

accountable, the penalties for failure can be minimized and temporary. Under most circumstances, we should avoid the threat of losing one's job or future promotions. You can also include the possibility of failure in the plan itself. This will make withdrawal from the project legitimate and normal.

ESTABLISH MINIMUM TARGET LEVELS FOR SUCCESS BEFORE LAUNCH

It is quite easy to interpret data through rose-colored glasses. Having clear objectives set in advance will make it harder to be overly optimistic when in fact the results are negative.

EMPHASIZE THE PROCESS VS. OUTCOMES OF DECISIONS

You can evaluate a decision regardless of the outcomes it achieves, the idea being that "a good decision cannot guarantee a good outcome. All real decisions are made under uncertainty. A decision is therefore a bet, and evaluating it as good must depend on the stakes in the odds, not on the outcome."[103]

CONSIDER THE ADVICE OF OUTSIDERS

Engage and listen to people who have no reputational investment in the original decision. They can leave their ego aside and bring a sense of objectivity.

---

103 Simonson and Staw, "Deescalation Strategies," 425.

CHAPTER SUMMARY

- Commitment can be an obstacle to change when our commitments become outdated as the organization changes. Conversely, we can commit to change when we are given the choice to support and see purpose and meaning in the new direction.

- Commitment is formed through volitional, visible, and irreversible actions. When we freely make public commitments, we indicate what we intend to do.

- We have a powerful drive to be consistent and follow through with our commitments not only to maintain our own sense of ourselves but to make good on how others perceive us.

- We commit to organizations and causes that provide us with a deeper and longer-term sense of purpose. We also commit to the norms or beliefs of an important group in order to belong.

- Commitment provides us and organizations with enormous value; it provides purpose and meaning to life, improves job performance, helps us persevere, and enables greater autonomy.

- Commitment is problematic when it restricts people from sharing critical perspectives, leads to rigidity and mindless repetition, and escalates failing courses of action without safeguards to haul it.

- You can build new commitments and loosen old ones by carefully choosing the object of commitment, focusing attention on what's important, inspiring belief that things are working, and creating ways for people to participate in decisions that affect them and rewarding their participation. Building commitment means engaging with people who may be critical of your plan.

- You should avoid creating a situation in which people feel the need to defend their previous commitments; this will cause them to dig in.

- You can de-escalate commitments to failure by committing to the problem and not a specific solution, reducing the fear of failure, establishing kill switches, emphasizing the importance of the decision-making process (versus outcomes, which people may continue to pursue), and soliciting advice from outsiders.

CASE IN POINT: RESISTANCE AVERTED

THE SCANLON PLAN AND THE TRIUMPH OF COLLECTIVE MANAGEMENT

In the early 1930s, a steel company was about to go out of business like many others during the Great Depression. The president of the local union, Joseph Scanlon, a one-time boxer, accountant, and millworker, did not want his workers to join the ranks of so many unemployed Americans. He knew productivity improvements could boost profits and reduce costs.[104]

He deeply believed in drawing upon the experience of all members of an organization to solve problems, and he knew that most organizations did not realize the full potential of their staff. He also believed that employees could solve an organization's problems if they were provided the maximum amount of information and data about the company's constraints and issues.[105]

Scanlon devised a plan to engage management and employees to save the steel plant.

Essentially his plan invites employees to consider the organization from the man-

---

104 Salancik, "Commitment Is Too Easy!," 75.

105 Fred G. Lesier and Elbridge S. Puckett, "The Scanlon Plan Has Proved Itself," *Harvard Business Review* 47, no. 5 (1969): 110.

agement perspective and, in turn, management is invited to hear how employees would solve their problems.

Key features of the original Scanlon plan and others adopted since:

Direct Employee Participation

Employees participate through departmental committees, composed of members of management and employees elected within their department. The committee discusses and screens suggestions for operational improvements, which are approved by departmental managers. A higher-level advisory group allocates resources to approved suggestions. All suggestions are transparently tracked, and decisions and results are shared with their originators.

For this committee structure to work, genuine participation is required by employees, who are expected to submit ideas, and executives, who are expected to listen and follow through on good ideas.

The Plan Has a Clear Performance Measurement and Target

Many organizations use productive efficiency to measure their Scanlon Plans. Others have called for environmental performance to be a measure.[106] Customer satisfaction could be another. The key feature is that the performance measure applies to the organization as a whole.

A Monthly Bonus Is Awarded to All Employees Based on the Achievement of the Target

The incentive structure of the Scanlon plan is collective, not individualistic. Scanlon believed that "individual's incentives put the direct worker in business for himself, pitted him against the broader interest of the company, and produced

---

106 Jacob A. Massoud, Bonnie F. Daily, and James W. Bishop, "Reward for Environmental Performance: Using the Scanlon Plan as Catalyst to Green Organisations," *International Journal of Environment, Workplace and Employment* 4, no. 1 (January 2008), https://doi.org/10.1504/IJEWE.2008.022255.

in equities and the wage structure that in turn led to poor employee morale."[107] Scanlon believed that rewards should be based on the success of the organization overall, and should be shared collectively by management and employees.

Through direct employee participation, cooperation between employees and management, and collective reward systems, the Scanlon plan yields many improvements within an organization.

- **Direct participation in solving the problems of the organization improves employee satisfaction and commitment.** Scanlon did not believe that work was inevitably unpleasant or that satisfaction could only be derived outside of it. His plan was designed to make work more meaningful through learning, problem-solving, and cooperation.
- **The organization learns through monthly deliberations between employees and management around the challenges facing the organization.** The organization becomes more flexible as it is constantly evaluating and implementing improvements and solutions to its economic and competitive problems.
- **Employees do not consider change to be a threat.** Management shares plans and concerns well in advance of any major changes. Moreover, employees are engaged in the design of solutions. They become active and creative agents in the change effort.[108]

Lastly, as employees, management, and experts across the organization work together to suggest, evaluate, implement, and track solutions, the overall functioning of the organization improves. What could be fractures within an organization become true interdependencies as each party listens, trusts, and understands the others' perspectives. They are working together to achieve a collective goal, which is collectively rewarded.

---

107 Lesieur and Pucket, "The Scanlon Plan Has Proved Itself," 110.

108 Gilbert K. Krulee, "The Scanlon Plan: Co-Operation Through Participation," *The Journal of Business* 28, no. 2 (April 1955): 111, https://www.jstor.org/stable/2350903.

Organizational Identity

THAT'S NOT US

"Too often what organizations claim to be when nothing is on the line is not how they act when everything is on the line."

—ALBERT AND WHETTEN, 2006

There are moments in the life of an organization that cut deep—reputational crisis, deep budget cuts, loss of a founder, or arrival of a new CEO—that bring forth a question that most of the time lies dormant: "Who are we?" The answer to this question can lead to resistance or support for change.

Below are a few examples of how organizational identity can impact change.

- Kodak had an early opportunity to pioneer digital cameras. When an enterprising engineer presented one of the first-ever digital cameras, the management team responded, "That's cute, but don't tell anyone about it." Kodak's management team held tight to its conception of the company as a pure filmmaker. It could not fathom filmless photography.[109]

- A new CEO joined a national sports organization with long-established traditions and a highly exclusive reputation. The CEO's highest priority was to make the sport more racially, sexually, and economically inclusive. A fierce grassroots backlash ensued claiming the sport had lost its way. This cultural divide would ensnare the CEO for years to come.

- After years of aggressive growth, a leading software company well known for its strong employee-centered culture faced economic headwinds that led to lay-offs and a strong focus on sales targets. Employees who took pride in the organization's focus on equity and fairness found the roll-back of benefits and emphasis on quotas over wellness to be a betrayal of the organization's defining commitments. Some took to social media, others started looking for new jobs. The organization's reputation as a strong culture builder changed from the inside out. It was now all about sales.

These defining moments arouse deep introspection, confusion, and anxiety; they wake the sleeping giant of organizational identity. Deliberate management of identity can inspire support and commitment. Careless treatment can lead to a deteriorating cycle of forcing change that only begets resistance.

We will unpack the nature of organizational identity and our deep need for it.

---

109 Ryan Raffaelli, Mary Ann Glynn, and Michael Tushman, "Frame Flexibility: The Role of Cognitive and Emotional Framing in Innovation Adoption by Incumbent Firms," *Strategic Management Journal* 40, no. 7 (February 2019), https://doi.org/10.1002/smj.3011.

THE NATURE OF ORGANIZATIONAL IDENTITY

Identity can be a complex topic. In this section, we will unpack what it is and how it defines and distinguish an organization over time. Identity is more than just a claim, it is an understanding that is shared. We will also explore the stuff—an organization's values, process, history, or products—that can made an identity.

ORGANIZATIONAL IDENTITY IS CENTRAL, ENDURING, AND DISTINCTIVE

Let's start with a working definition. *An organization's identity consists of features that in the eyes of its members are central to its character, make it distinctive from other similar organizations, and are seen as having continuity over time.*[110]

Next, let's unpack each of these dimensions.

- **Central.** Central features are those that define an organization's "soul" or its "essence." Central features are the organization's "deepest commitment[s]—what they would repeatedly commit to be through time and across circumstance."[111] Central features can be an organization's values, products, services, or practices that are essential to "who we are."[112] These core features define the organization's identity. Without them, there's really no identity to speak of.[113]

- **Distinctive.** Organizations and people have a deep need to distinguish themselves from others. Without distinction, an organization's central features would not be identifying. Dis-

---

110 Albert and Whetten, "Organizational Identity," 265.

111 David A. Whetten, "Albert and Whetten Revisited: Strengthening the Concept of Organizational Identity," *Journal of Management Inquiry* 15, no. 3 (September 2006): 224, https://doi.org/10.1177/1056492606291200.

112 Dennis A. Gioia et al., "Organizational Identity Formation and Change," *Academy of Management Annals* 7, no. 1 (June 2013): 125, https://doi.org/10.5465/19416520.2013.762225.

113 Gioia et al., "Organizational Identity Formation and Change," 167.

tinguishing characteristics define the boundary of a group and determine who is in and who is out. They provide group members with a personal uniqueness from those outside and similarity with each other. Similarly, organizations seek to be like others in their category and be recognizable as a "type of organization." At the same time, they seek to be different from any specific competitor.[114]

- **Enduring.** An organization's central features endure over time. The sameness of the core features provides much-needed stability within an organization. The loss of continuity can inspire grief and anxiety. *Note that it is more important that people believe that the identity is enduring than that it actually stays the same.* Beneath the surface of an enduring identity, change is often afoot—a dynamic we shall explore later.

We identify with the organization when we define ourselves by the same attribute that we see in the organization and "the level of organizational identification indicates the degree to which people come to see the organization as part of themselves."[115] **When organizational identification is strong, we incorporate a large part of what is distinctive, central, and enduring about the organization into what we see as distinctive, central, and enduring about ourselves.**

When we identify with the organization, our well-being and behaviors are impacted by what others think. When people think highly of our organization, we feel proud, and we bask in the "reflected glory."[116] When others have low regard for our employer,

---

114 Whetten, "Albert and Whetten Revisited," 222.

115 Jane E. Dutton, Janet M. Dukerich, and Celia V. Harquail, "Organizational Images and Member Identification," *Administrative Science Quarterly* 39, no. 2 (June 1994): 242, https://doi.org/10.2307/2393235.

116 Dutton, Dukerich, and Harquail, "Organizational Images and Member Identification," 240.

we feel stress and possibly shame. Our sense of self rides on the waves of our organization's reputation.

IDENTITY MORE THAN A CLAIM

An organization's identity—the central, enduring, and distinctive features that define "who we are"—is manifest through the *claims* it makes about itself and the *meanings* that others ascribe to these claims.

Visionary *claims* an organization makes about itself include the language, labels, and images that the organization uses to define itself. Organizational claims often come from the top down, from senior management. But, *claims and labels alone are not enough.*

An organization's identity must be felt and understood by its members. Identity is negotiated. An organization's identity is a shared understanding that is negotiated by people with different perspectives. It is also negotiated with the external world that either validates or invalidates its worth.

The *meanings* associated with an organization's claims about its identity may vary. Different people understand the organization in different ways. Thus, an organization's claims can have multiple meanings. For instance, when the president of a university claims it is a "Top 10 School," staff interpret this in very different ways. This claim is inspiring because of its breadth. It allows staff to interpret it for themselves and see themselves in it—whether they work in the Chemistry or Admissions department.

Identity is formed through actions. Identity is honed through trial and error. We have to try it on and see how it works in guiding our actions. Action can be a powerful way of discovering what identity should be. An organization that defines itself as an "innovation company" will continually reinforce this claim through its innovation practices.

FOUR WAYS PEOPLE IDENTIFY WITH ORGANIZATIONS

We can identify with different aspects of an organization. An organization's products, processes, values, or history can offer us stuff to work and align with.

Product-Based Identity: "Who We Are" Is What We Offer

Many companies base their identity on the core products that they offer. Another photography company, Polaroid, saw itself narrowly through the lens of the type of film it made. In contrast, Netflix transitioned from a DVD rental company to a digital subscription service. When "who we are" is tightly bound to a specific product, an organization might struggle to evolve its product line.

Process-Based Identity: "Who We Are" Is How We Work

Process can be a source of identity for organizations that credit processes with their distinction and success. Professional practices are often a source of identity: "We are a science-based organization," "We are an innovation company," or "We are a data-driven creative agency." Identity could be formed from a distinctive decision-making process: "We are member driven."

Values-Based Identity: "Who We Are" Is What We Care About

One can see the role values play in organizational identity during times of crisis—when the organization's actions betray the values of its members and their sense of "who we are." BP faced a lethal crisis after the DeepWater Horizon disaster. Public outcry prompted an organizational introspection and resulted in the new identity. "Beyond Petroleum" represented BP's new commitment to exploring "new ways to live without oil." Years later, BP was one of the top ten green brands positioned above Greenpeace.[117]

Heritage-Based Identity: "Who We Are" Is Our Traditions

Organizations with a long and storied legacy may base their identity on their history, founding, milestone achievements, and corporate folklore. These organizations might display myth-making artifacts, oil portraits of early leaders, and timelines of their history (often featured on their websites). New employee orientation includes the organization's history and the stories that everyone tells, which can be a constraint to innovation if it is seen as a deviation from the shared cultural heritage.

THE CAUSES OF ORGANIZATIONAL IDENTITY

The need for a central, enduring, and distinctive self is planted deep within us as individuals and organizations. Our need to belong causes us to identify ourselves as similar to some and yet different from others. Our need for stability causes us to create and adhere to an sense of "sameness over time" in ourselves and our organization.

WE NEED TO BE DIFFERENT FROM SOME AND THE SAME AS OTHERS

We distinguish ourselves from some people by likening ourselves to others. Our identity reflects two fundamental human needs: our need for assimilation (how we are similar to others) and a need

117 Jennifer Natsu, "BP Tops Greenpeace in Green Brands Survey," Environment + Energy Leader, March 26, 2008, https://www.environmentalleader.com/2008/03/bp-tops-greenpeace-in-green-brands-survey.

for uniqueness (how we are different from others).[118] **Personal identity is developed socially through our belonging to different groups that define us as being similar to those within our group and different from those outside of it.** Group identities "allow us to be the same and different at the same time."[119] This is the nature of belonging.

WE NEED TO FEEL CONSISTENT OVER TIME

A sense of identity allows people to "satisfy their inherent needs to be the same yesterday, today, and tomorrow."[120] Psychologist Eric Erickson observed how World War II veterans returning home suffered from the loss of continuity with their previous selves. He believed that the need for a continuous self is fundamental and developed his notion of ego identity as "a sense of sameness over time." **Our deep need for sameness and continuity can make change hard and painful. This is why we might experience change as a loss.**[121]

THE VALUE OF ORGANIZATIONAL IDENTITY

Both individuals and organizations benefit from when people see themselves in their organization. The workplace can become an arena of personal expression. A strong sense of purpose can clarify and motivate. Identity can be a competitive advantage.

---

118 David A. Whetten and Alison Mackey, "A Social Actor Conception of Organizational Identity and Its Implications for the Study of Organizational Reputation," *Business & Society* 41, no. 4 (December 2002): 397, https://doi.org/10.1177/0007650302238775.

119 Marilynn B. Brewer, "The Social Self: On Being the Same and Different at the Same Time," *Personality and Social Psychology Bulletin* 17, no. 5 (October 1991): 477, https://doi.org/10.1177/0146167291175001.

120 Whetten and Mackey, "A Social Actor Conception of Organizational Identity," 396.

121 Albert and Whetten, "Organizational Identity," 272.

PEOPLE CAN BE THEMSELVES AND BELONG

Our deep need for personal identity can be satisfied by identifying with our organizations. Organizational identity allows individuals to more fully realize themselves in their workplaces. Specifically, the benefits of identifying with one's organization are:

- **Self-expression.** When our self-conception is aligned with our organization's identity, we can truly express ourselves and exhibit a full range of "who we are" and what we value.[122] We don't have to hide our true selves.
- **Ease.** This alignment of personal and organizational helps us fit in. We can easily navigate an environment that represents our values and reflects who we are.[123]
- **Personal growth.** As the organization grows and evolves its identity, staff can imagine "possible selves" and realize new versions of who they can become.[124]
- **Self-esteem.** When that organization with which we identify is respected by others, it can make us feel good about ourselves and enhance our self-esteem.[125]
- **Belonging.** When we identify with an organization, we belong to a group of similar others.
- **Security.** Identity provides a sense of continuity over time. Identity makes the organization feel stable.

---

122 Dutton, Dukerich, and Harquail, "Organizational Images and Member Identification," 244.

123 Dutton, Dukerich, and Harquail, "Organizational Images and Member Identification," 244.

124 Dutton, Dukerich, and Harquail, "Organizational Images and Member Identification," 257.

125 Dutton, Dukerich, and Harquail, "Organizational Images and Member Identification," 240.

ORGANIZATIONS HAVE CLARITY AND A MOTIVATED STAFF

For organizations, identity can provide clarity and motivate staff. It can be a powerful catalyst and obstacle to major change.

Specifically, the organization benefits of fostering strong identity include:

- **Clarity of purpose.** Identity provides an organization with a sense of its deepest and enduring commitments.[126] This deep purpose does not need to be continually re-discovered.

- **Clarity in decision-making.** Fork-in-the-road decisions—budget cuts, major new products, acquisitions, etc.—boil down to the question of "Who are we?" When quantifiable solutions and facts fail to answer the deepest questions, identity is the "court of last resort."[127]

- **Legitimacy.** Stakeholders and staff alike value stability and predictability. An enduring identity creates consistent organizational behavior over time, which is rewarded with legitimacy.[128]

- **Corporate citizenship.** When we identify with our organization, we are much more likely to go the extra mile as "exertion on behalf of the organization is also exertion on behalf of the self."[129]

- **Impetus for change.** Identity can be a springboard for change when an organization's actions do not align with its sense of self. The organization's understanding of "who we are" can pull the organization's practice into alignment with its core commitments and values.

---

126 Whetten, "Albert and Whetten Revisited," 224.

127 Whetten and Mackey, "A Social Actor Conception of Organizational Identity," 397.

128 Gioia et al., "Organizational Identity Formation and Change," 161.

129 Dutton, Dukerich, and Harquail, "Organizational Images and Member Identification," 256.

THE DANGERS OF ORGANIZATIONAL IDENTITY

During times of change, an organization's identity can hold people back and keep them from learning and adopting new practices. When the identity itself changes, this can be experienced as a personal loss. We will unpack the downsides to individuals and the organization.

PEOPLE CAN FEEL ANXIETY, LOSS, AND THREATENED

We experience the downsides of organizational identity when the organization's identity changes. These negative experiences include:

- **Pain and anxiety.** Just as identity provides a sense of stability, identity change can be experienced as a real loss and break with who we were. Identity change can cause "psychic pain, discomfort, anxiety, conflict, and overall loss of self-esteem."[130]
- **Perceptions of threats.** Changes in organizational identity can be experienced as a threat to our sense of self, or belonging in the organization. Our future status and value are called into question.
- **Defensive reactions.** When we perceive change as a threat, we defend ourselves by denying there's a problem or idealizing the past that is never coming back.[131]

ORGANIZATIONS CAN BECOME RIGID AND ENTRENCHED

An organization's identity can hold it back when it needs to evolve. For an organization, the downsides of a strong identity include:

---

130   Gioia et al., "Organizational Identity Formation and Change," 133.

131   Andrew D. Brown and Ken Starkey, "Organizational Identity and Learning: A Psychodynamic Perspective," *The Academy of Management Review* 25, no. 1 (January 2000): 105–106, https://doi.org/10.2307/259265.

- **Cognitive conservatism.** Identity endures because its members and stakeholders perpetuate it and expect identity to remain the same. Narrow definitions of "who we are" halt innovation and limit new product development. Blockbuster could not conceive of itself beyond a brick-and-mortar store and succumbed to a death by streaming.[132] Many traditional newspapers failed to develop compelling digital offerings until it was too late.
- **Entrenched practices.** Identity can be embedded in how we work—our defining practices, routines, and abilities. When change in strategy threatens established practice, resistance may result. People will seek to preserve the practices that define them, especially if it threatens their sense of competency and status.
- **We do not learn.** Change can upend fundamental notions of what makes us special and threaten our individual and collective identities. Change causes anxiety that we instinctively retreat from. And in this retreat, we do not learn. And when we do not learn, we do not grow.[133]

On the individual and organizational level, major change can threaten strong and stable identities. These negative experiences can be obstacles to your change initiative. There is a great deal you can do to embed your change in the identity of an organization and evolve the organization's understanding of "who we are."

---

132 Raffaelli, Glynn, and Tushman, "Frame Flexibility," 1021.

133 Brown and Starkey, "Organizational Identity and Learning," 109.

WHAT YOU CAN DO

There are several strategies for leveraging the power of organiza-tion identity to support major change efforts. Several of these recommendations involve loosening the hold of the incumbent identity to make room for an expanded and refined definition of "who we are."

MAKE SENSE AND GIVE SENSE TO OTHERS

Major change can challenge our conceptions of "who we are." Threats to commonly held notions of an organization's identity can trigger resistance if not rejection as employees reassert their understanding of what the organization stands for.[134] Against the backdrop of this possibility, the changemaker must help the organization make sense of its situation and give sense to others.

Sensemaking is the process by which we interpret a situation and create meaning out of ambiguity. As the term implies, it is the proj-ect of making sense out of our world. Leaders do this all the time. When they develop strategy, they scan their environment looking to discern opportunities and threats. With this understanding, they define the organization's capability. They have defined the context in which they can organize actions and align the organi-zation. Leaders then read the tea leaves of ambiguous data and attempt to figure out whether the organization is succeeding or failing. Again, more sensemaking.

In sensemaking, we develop an understanding for ourselves. *Sensegiving is the process by which we help others understand the world.* In sensegiving, leaders help others see a clear narrative in

---

134 Rajiv Nag, Kevin G. Corley, and Dennis A. Gioia, "The Intersection of Organizational Identity, Knowledge, and Practice: Attempting Strategic Change Via Knowledge Grafting," *Academy of Management Journal* 50, no. 4 (August 2007), https://doi.org/10.5465/amj.2007.26279173.

an inherently messy world. In sensegiving, leaders paint a picture in clear and evocative terms that help others make sense of what the organization is doing, guide their actions, and affirm the direction that it is heading.[135]

In many, if not all, of the recommendations below, the change-maker will go between *making sense* and *giving sense* to the change afoot and what it means to the organization and its conception of itself.

Below is a practical list of things you can do to mitigate the potential resistance identity inspires and harness the power of identity to support your change effort.

DETACH "WHO WE ARE" FROM "WHAT WE DO"

As we have learned, "who we are" can be defined in a lot of ways. An organization's central, enduring, and distinctive features may be strongly tied to its core products and services. Over time a product-based identity can be very limiting as the organization needs to evolve and adapt to its changing environment and customer needs.

"Who you are" can and should represent the deeper values and identity that persist over time. "What we do" changes as the organization adapts, responds, and stays relevant; it should be defined elastically. **By decoupling "who we are" from "what we do," people can stay loyal to a deeper and enduring notion of an organization while it changes.**

Even though Amazon started off as an online bookseller, it very flexibly framed its mission to be the "world's most customer-centric company." This flexible framing has allowed it to sell and

---

135 Dennis A. Gioia and Kumar Chittipeddi, "Sensemaking and Sensegiving in Strategic Change Initiation," *Strategic Management Journal* 12, no. 6 (September 1991): 446, https://www.jstor.org/stable/2486479.

do just about everything under its sprawling corporate umbrella. Conversely, Polaroid tightly coupled "who we are" to the type of film it produced until the bitter end.[136]

EXPAND YOUR CATEGORY

By going up a level of abstraction, you can expand the boundaries of what can legitimately be explored and done by your organization. If an organization too narrowly defines "what we do," it unwittingly constrains the possibilities for innovation. For instance, Fuji shifted its internal frame of reference from "film" to a higher-level category of "imaging and information." Ball Corporation expanded its frame of reference from a bucket company to a "world-class container company" that includes glass, aluminum, and plastic containers of all varieties.[137] Likewise, if you consider a "zoo" as an attraction, you unlock the possibility of many innovative experiences that do not involve animals. These small pivots can have big implications.

CREATE EMOTIONAL ATTACHMENTS TO "WHO WE ARE"

Disruptive change and innovation can be a threatening and alienating experience. You can mitigate this by creating emotionally resonant stories about "who we are" that tap into the values, beliefs, or cultural heritage of the organization.

By reminding people of why they care and what they love about their organization, you can create a continuity to the past while you engineer change for the future. Anchor this emotional attachment to a deeper level within the organization—

---

136 Raffaelli, Glynn, and Tushman, "Frame Flexibility," 1021.

137 Raffaelli, Glynn, and Tushman, "Frame Flexibility," 1026.

deeper than specific products, services, or processes—something that the organization has always stood for. Ball Corporation created a slogan, "We can!" to capture its history of innovation and can-do spirit.

EMBED THE FUTURE IN THE PAST

As changemakers chart a bold new vision for the organization, they risk losing the support of those who feel a deep connection with the organization's history. Situate your vision of the future within the history of the organization. You can frame a future vision of the organization as a reflection of its past:

> As old cultural practices…are infused with new meaning, new claims [of identity] can be convincingly presented as a rediscovery of shared values, the awareness of which had gradually faded over time. Furthermore, embedding new claims in the cultural heritage of the organization emphasizes the connection with "who we have been" rather than "who we want to become."[138]

Essentially, the organization is becoming what it always has been, even if details change. This strategy can provide comfort and reassurance in an organization with a strong cultural heritage. This is how Danish speaker manufacturer Bang and Olufsen corrected a failing brand drift to "luxury" during the 1980s. It "rediscovered" its Bauhaus traditions of "simplicity and essentiality" and framed its new strategy as a return to its heritage

---

138 Davide Ravasi and Majken Schultz, "Responding to Organizational Identity Threats: Exploring the Role of Organizational Culture," *Academy of Management Journal* 49, no. 5 (June 2006): 453, https://doi.org/10.5465/AMJ.2006.21794663.

of delivering excellence with modesty. Products made from gold were out, aluminum was back.[139]

PROJECT A NEW IMAGE AND WORK TOWARD IT

You may need to stake a claim on a future version and pull the organization toward it in situations where stakeholders are demanding change or the future state is compellingly clear.

One such situation involves a crisis in which the organization did not live up to its reputation or values. This was the case when Shell Oil faced public outcry over its initial plans to sink the oil tanker Brent Spar in the North Atlantic. The public response to their plan triggered a deep listening and introspection that resulted in a public commitment that the company would not only be "technically competent" but "socially responsible." In this case, Shell put forth a public image and commitment that then pulled the organization's actions into alignment with its new identity.[140]

This strategy can work proactively. Leaders can project a compelling image of the organization that signals how the organization needs change. A hearing aid manufacturer successfully transitioned its identity from a focus on production to service by adopting the slogan "Think the Unthinkable," and creating a metaphor for the organization ("The Spaghetti Organization") that signaled new ways of working (e.g., paper-free organization and flexible working environments). An aggressive press push achieved international headlines that shook loose the old identity

---

139 Ravasi and Schultz, "Responding to Organizational Identity Threats," 447–448.

140 Dennis A. Gioia, Majken Schultz, and Kevin G. Corley, "Organizational Identity, Image, and Adaptive Instability," *Academy of Management Review* 25, no. 1 (January 2000): 68, https://doi.org/10.2307/259263.

and provoked internal discussions and movement toward the CEO's new vision.[141]

You can project a new and compelling image that then inspires the behaviors of the organization you want to become. In short, you project what you want to become.

CREATE AMBIGUITY, THEN INTRODUCE THE VISION

Major change efforts, especially strategic ones, alter how we see the organization and ourselves within it. We are asked to set aside previously held assumptions and embrace new ones that will enable the organization to shift gears and adapt. This could include the most basic understanding of what the organization does. Shell went from an oil company to an energy explorer. Amazon went from an online bookseller to a low-cost online commerce platform.[142]

During periods of major strategic change, you can introduce ambiguity into commonly held assumptions about who the organization is and what it does. **Ambiguity can dislodge old meanings, shake up complacency, and create a fruitful, if not disquieting, void.** There are a couple of ways to do this:

- Announce the change effort as a big deal; this alone can shake things up. Send a clear signal of the need for and mandate to change.
- Use hypothetical examples to casually introduce and field test potentially challenging ideas.

Proclamations of change and provocative scenarios will loosen the grip of the status quo and create an atmosphere of ambigui-

---

141 Gioia, Schultz, and Corley, "Organizational Identity, Image, and Adaptive Instability," 77.

142 Raffaelli, Glynn, and Tushman, "Frame Flexibility," 1024.

ty.[143] **Then ambiguity creates the conceptual space for a new vision.** Your job is to help others make sense of the new vision and see themselves within it. This vision should be compelling but broad enough to give people leeway to see how it applies to them. For example, Hewlett-Packard's vision was to become "the partner of choice for our customers" and Home Depot's was to be "the employer, retailer, investment, and neighbor of choice in the home improvement industry."[144]

Ambiguity creates the void for a broad vision that is then filled in by a workable understanding of the staff. The broad vision allows for diverse stakeholders to interpret and enact the meaning in different ways, as they each see themselves as pursuing the larger goal.[145]

EXPLORE ALTERNATIVE FUTURES TO REIMAGINE THE ORGANIZATION

We know that organizations have to adapt, yet we deeply crave stability. Scenario planning is a less emotional way to challenge an organization's identity. By imagining radically different notions of the future, we question fundamental premises of our current organization.

Scenario planning allows us to play in very different worlds and "experiment and role-play for different futures," which helps us cope with the anxiety of change.[146] In scenario planning, we can move from stability to exploration. Like a game, scenario

143 Gioia and Chittipeddi, "Sensemaking and Sensegiving in Strategic Change Initiation," 439.

144 Dennis A. Gioia, Rajiv Nag, and Kevin G. Corley, "Visionary Ambiguity and Strategic Change: The Virtue of Vagueness in Launching Major Organizational Change," *Journal of Management Inquiry* 21, no. 4 (May 2012): 367, https://doi.org/10.1177/105649261244722.

145 Gioia, Nag, and Corley, "Visionary Ambiguity and Strategic Change," 368.

146 Brown and Starkey, "Organizational Identity and Learning," 112.

planning invites us to think of the unthinkable and create space to reimagine ourselves.

DOUBT THE PAST, EXPERIMENT, AND BOND WITH THE NEW

Like ambiguity, doubt is another way to create conceptual space to re-imagine the organization's identity. Doubt can loosen attachments to the past and allow for experimentation with new ways of doing things. As doubt reduces the value of the old organization, experimentation and compelling vision increase the value of the new identity.

You can introduce doubt by explicitly stating what is no longer working in the current system. This can be done by stating what the company is *not* doing well. Point out products that are in decline or customer bases that are shrinking. Be clear on changes in your environment that you are *not* prepared for. The overall goal is to rupture people's beliefs and weaken their ties to the "old" organization.[147]

Note, in this anxiety-provoking phase, you should make employees feel personally valued even if their old organizational roles are not.

Doubt creates opportunities for experimentation. Experimentation motivates staff and begins to build ties to the new organization. Experiments "make it safe for people to adopt and enact roles that lead to a new understanding of the self, especially when the new is very different from the old."[148] By experimenting, people can safely imagine their "possible selves."

As people begin to engage with new ways of working and

---

147 C. Marlene Fiol, "Capitalizing on Paradox: The Role of Language in Transforming Organizational Identities," *Organizational Science* 13, no. 6 (December 2002): 659, https://doi.org/10.1287/orsc.13.6.653.502.

148 Fiol, "Capitalizing on Paradox," 660.

trying out the new identity for themselves, they can begin to see themselves and the new organization. You can build consensus around the goals and values of the new organization that point in a direction and yet have the leeway to include a variety of perspectives and encompass change over time.

CHAPTER SUMMARY

- An organization's identity becomes important during times of fundamental change—reputational crisis, deep budget cuts, loss of a founder, or arrival of a new CEO. How members of the organization answer the question of "Who are we?" can facilitate change or lead to resistance.

- An organization's identity consists of the features that are perceived to be *central* to its character, make it *distinctive* from other similar organizations, and have *continuity* over time. We identify with the organization when we define ourselves by the attributes that we see in the organization.

- Organizational identity consists of the *claims* an organization makes about itself and the *meanings* others ascribe to it. Some identity claims are deliberately broad to allow staff to see themselves and their work within them.

- We can identify with different aspects of an organization, including the organization's products, processes, values, or history.

- Identifying with an organization allows us to belong to a distinctive group. It also allows us to experience a continuity over time.

- When we personally identify with an organization, we can more fully express and develop ourselves, and we easily fit in with our organization. We can have great self-esteem, a sense of belonging, and security.

- A clear sense of identity helps organizations understand their purpose, which facilitates decision-making. Identity can provide stability and legitimacy or be the catalyst for change. It fosters greater loyalty from its members.
- When an organization's identity changes, it can cause people to experience pain and anxiety, feel threatened, become defensive, and idealize the past.
- An organization's identity can also keep it from changing as organizations have trouble conceiving of themselves differently, become entrenched in their practices, and retreat from learning new things.
- You can use organizational identity to foster support for change by helping people make sense of the change, detaching "who we are" as an organization from "what we do," expanding your category (e.g., film becomes imaging), and creating emotional attachments that tap into why they care.
- When the future direction is significantly different from the past, you can embed the future in the past, go back to your roots, and become who you have always been.
- If the organization's identity is out of alignment with its actions (and reputational crisis is on the horizon), you can project a new image and work toward it.
- If the identity is too narrow for where the organization needs to go, you can use a more ambiguous identity to provide flexibility in action and allow people to interpret the claim for themselves. You can also use doubt about the viability of the existing identity or scenario planning to loosen attachments.

CASE IN POINT: RESISTANCE OF OUR SELF-CONCEPTION

THE REVOLT OF ENGINEERING PRACTICE
AGAINST IDENTITY CHANGE

A team of leading scholars detailed the tumultuous journey of an anonymous large American technology firm that attempted to transform itself from R&D innovator to a company driven by customer needs (i.e., from technology-push to market-pull).[149] The case documents the attempt to change organizational identity by grafting on new knowledge and skills to usher in a new identity.

The company began as an R&D division staffed by scientists and engineers who pushed cutting-edge technology out to markets and achieved considerable success as a leader in technology innovation. Innovation and research were considered a core distinctive factor of the organization and a driver of its preeminence.

When the parent company was acquired by a large conglomerate, the R&D division was spun off as a separate organization. It was now subject to market forces and would have to build its own customer base and revenue to sustain itself. To do this, it would have to build marketing and business development capacity.

This transition to an independent company was "a major jolt for the organization. All of a sudden the same scientists and engineers, whose main jobs for years have been to work on projects that excited their intellect, now had to be responsive to market demands...science for science sake was no longer a viable option."

It was not feasible to develop the new skill sets internally; they would need to hire from the outside. When the technology bubble burst in the 1990s and venture capital dried up, the pressures to develop markets increased. The new company

---

149 Nag, Corley, and Gioia, "The Intersection of Organizational Identity, Knowledge, and Practice," 825–826, 835–836, 840. All quotes in this case study come from this source.

did a radical re-organization to focus on markets and business development. The organization developed a Venture Management Group composed of senior marketing executives who reported directly to the CEO.

Several key shifts occurred:

- The organization's identity was shifting from a technology-push company (led by technology innovation) to a market-pull company driven by market and customer needs.
- The premium knowledge base shifted from science and research to marketing and business development. Consequently, power shifted from scientists and researchers to marketing professionals.
- Work practices changed. Scientists and researchers once set the agenda and process informally and interpersonally. Now standard operating procedures governed knowledge sharing and reporting. Decisions flowed through the Venture Market Group.

The attempts to graft on a new identity by hiring new skill sets and building new capabilities and processes did not work. The science and engineering staff resisted the change as they sought to preserve their existing identity.

The new operating procedures for developing and approving technology projects were too disruptive and unsettling to the scientists' preferred informal and creative processes.

More importantly, the "dramatic change in work practices undermined members' sense of their...identity ('It's just not who we are')... They saw the shift in emphasis towards venture and away from basic technology research as a threat to a deeply held and strongly valued collective identity."

The new practices of being a market-driven company were at odds and incompatible with the identity of being a world-class research and innovation company.

As the science and engineering staff resisted the new procedures, the Venture Management Group asserted its authority. As one member stated, "I have the power to force the issue here. I can force these scientists to follow SOPs, otherwise they won't get funding."

The Venture Management Group's assertion of authority resulted in an escalation of resistance that in turn escalated their imposition of authority. The escalatory cycle would prove to be the downfall of the transformation effort. Resistance was too strong.

The Venture Management Group was dissolved, business development staff quit, and the attempt at strategic transformation was suspended. The organization reverted to its founding strategy of pushing technology innovations to the market while it adapted some of the business development practices from the transformation period.

In retrospect, the reason for the transformation's failure is clear: "Once identity is threatened and attempts to preserve it are enacted, a strong deterrent to changes...is created. This cycle then escalates when change agents respond to deterrents with re-energized attempts to impose change, which again threaten power relations, thus continuing the cycle."

The Status Quo Effect

THE ALLURE OF DOING NOTHING NEW

"...it is in the nature of man's mind. A thing which you enjoyed and used as your own for a long time, whether property or opinion, takes root in your being and cannot be torn away without your resenting the act and trying to defend yourself, however you came by it."

—OLIVER WENDALL HOLMES, 1897

Organizations must respond to their customers' expectations, their competitor's offerings, and/or broader economic and social forces. For organizations of any size and age, there will be a lag between the intent and the realization of change. Moreover, the greater the change, the longer it might take as "transformation always involves overcoming large amounts of organizational inertia."[150] The question is, *How great is the lag between your pace of change and that of the world around you?*

You may have experienced this lag as you try to push something new forward and feel the organizational pull for things to

---

150 Richard P. Rumelt, "Precis of Inertia and Transformation," 2003, 10, https://www.studocu.com/row/document/national-university-of-sciences-and-technology/electrical-engneering/berkeley-precis/64596594.

stay in place. The pull of the status quo is real. Here are a couple of examples:

- Year after year, this well-established and large organization's budget stayed the same. One marketing executive discovered that securing funding for a new digital marketing initiative was a multiyear herculean task that was subjected to the highest scrutiny. In contrast, other print-based expenditures, allocated years before, were continually reallocated despite their waning performance.

- No one in this organization liked their technology system. Every year, more efficient, easier-to-use, and cheaper solutions were coming out. But after ten years of using the old system, almost every file was created with it and everyone knew how to use it, even if they didn't like it. The sheer scale and integration of the system made it hard to imagine switching.

This inability to change despite compelling reasons to do so is a function of our organizations, at least the stable ones. The tendency to stay in place is also a byproduct of our own preferences, behaviors, and decision-making processes. This is the status quo effect.

NATURE OF THE STATUS QUO EFFECT

Let's start with some working definitions.

Status quo effect is the psychological tendency to maintain the status quo or do nothing in the face of potentially superior alternatives.[151] *Clinging to the status quo results in inertia, which is*

---

151 William Samuelson and Richard Zeckhauser, "Status Quo Bias in Decision Making," *Journal of Risk and Uncertainty* 1, no. 1 (March 1988): 8, https://doi.org/10.1007/BF00055564.

persistence of existing behaviors.[152] In short, the status quo effect is our psychological bias to do nothing new, and inertia is actually doing nothing; the former is a preference, the latter a behavior.

WE ARE BIASED TOWARD INACTION

Our bias for inaction pervades our personal, social, and working lives. It explains why we choose the same brand of toothpaste and go to the same vacation spots year after year. It explains why incumbent politicians have huge advantages and re-elections and why any redistribution of public money and power is so fraught with resistance. It also explains why most organizations do not reallocate their resources to any significant degree.[153]

If things are running well, the status quo is fine, and "inertia is costless and arguably beneficial" as the ease of predictable operations is a virtue.[154] The problem comes when an organization's actions are not fast or effective. Inefficiency may be the symptom of inertia that you recognize. In other words, you may not notice inertia until you experience or notice a lag.

CAUSES OF STATUS QUO EFFECT

Significant change in strategy, structure, or process takes time, costs money, and holds risk, which is why "firms change only with great difficulty."[155]

---

152   Greta L. Polites and Elena Karahanna, "Shackled to the Status Quo: The Inhibiting Effects of Incumbent System Habit, Switching Costs, and Inertia on New System Acceptance," *MIS Quarterly* 36, no. 1 (March 2012): 22, https://doi.org/10.2307/41410404.

153   Stephen Hall, Dan Lovallo, and Reinier Musters, "How to Put Your Money Where Your Strategy Is," *McKinsey Quarterly*, March 1, 2012, https://www.mckinsey.com/capabilities/strategy-and-corporate-finance/our-insights/how-to-put-your-money-where-your-strategy-is.

154   Rumelt, "Precis of Inertia and Transformation," 2.

155   Rumelt, "Precis of Inertia and Transformation," 2.

There are many causes of the status quo effect and inertia. First and foremost, organizations are built to be reliable and stable. Significant change can involve too much risk at too great a cost and challenge our need for control and a sense of competency. Lastly, the status quo provides us with ease in daily life.

ORGANIZATIONS PROVIDE STABILITY AND RELIABILITY

Organizations are a costly way of solving problems. In fact, there may be a "strong tendency for organizations to become ends in themselves and to accumulate personnel and an elaborate structure far beyond the technical demands of work."[156] So why do they exists?

Modern organizations exist to provide "reliable performance" and "account rationally for their actions."[157] To achieve this, organizations standardize routines and create stable structures of roles, communications, and coordination. This "common knowledge" becomes a reliable precedent that guides and constrains successive generations of staff.[158] Thus, the persistence of existing behaviors—inertia—is the consequence of stable structures, routines, and shared understanding.

Major re-organizations that go deep into the organization's fundamentals can be highly unstable as working relationships are reshuffled, new routines are developed, old ones are revised, and communication flows are redesigned. The cost, risk, and time needed for previously simple tasks increase dramatically. Restructuring is a time of deep vulnerability and liability for an

---

156 Hannan and Freeman, "Structural Inertia and Organizational Change," 152.

157 Hannan and Freeman, "Structural Inertia and Organizational Change," 153.

158 Paul A. David, "Clio and the Economics of QWERTY," *The American Economic Review* 75, no. 2 (May 1985), https://www.jstor.org/stable/1805621.

organization.[159] This liability of structural change is a compelling reason to maintain the status quo.

OUR NEED FOR COMPETENCY AND CONTROL HOLDS THINGS IN PLACE

We stick with past decisions, even ones that will never pay off, to maintain our sense of competence and control. We are reluctant to "cut our losses" because of our need to justify past decisions and maintain our authority. Once a choice is made, we stay the course and even discard information that might suggest we were wrong. Major change may require leaders to "repudiate prior commitments" which might compromise their status and power. Unfortunately, by sticking with our status quo choices, we can maintain the illusion of control.[160] Leaders invested in the status quo may be a significant source of inertia.[161]

We may lack the competency to enact change. While some of us may be comfortable with "stretching" ourselves beyond our normal bounds, others may get discouraged, especially if the gap is too great.

EASE AND LAXITY PERPETUATE ILL-SUITED HABITS AND NORMS

We can't give up our habits. Organizations work well when the processes that link the work of one function to another require little thought. Routines are often habitually followed without understanding their origin, even if it is no longer relevant. The

---

159 Hannan and Freeman, "Structural Inertia and Organizational Change," 160.

160 Samuel and Zeckhauser, "Status Quo Bias in Decision Making," 40.

161 Rumelt, "Precis of Inertia and Transformation," 8–9.

pull of habitual behaviors can be stronger than the incentives to change them.

We tend to normalize problems. In well-established industries, a common reactive mindset is one that believes troubles are industry problems rather than organizational ones. This line of thinking quickly leads to shrugging shoulders as if there's nothing we can do.[162]

Our vision is insufficient and too narrow. Changes in the competitive landscape, technology, or customer taste may require a dramatic change. Some organizations fail to see the limitations of what they are doing or the full scope of the change required. (See the Polaroid case study at the end of the chapter.)

CHANGE INVOLVES TOO MUCH UNCERTAINTY AND RISK

The high cost of switching to something new yields an advantage to the current state.[163] Switching costs include everything from learning and training, to stress and anxiety, to productivity drops during implementation. With potentially high costs, major change must yield significant benefits.

Searching for new alternatives takes real effort. It is much easier to assume that our initial thinking was sound and still holds true compared to the mental effort of finding and analyzing new options.[164]

We are averse to loss and imagine change as making things worse. We have a "strong tendency to remain at the status quo because the disadvantages of leaving it loom larger than advantag-

---

162 Rumelt, "Precis of Inertia and Transformation," 6.

163 Polites and Karahanna, "Shackled to the Status Quo," 27.

164 Samuel and Zeckhauser, "Status Quo Bias in Decision Making," 35.

es."[165] In fact, the more options offered, the greater the advantage to the status quo. Even if we are made better off, if we lose anything in the process, we consider it unfair. This phenomenon is known as loss aversion.[166]

We regret doing something more than doing nothing. We often assign more responsibility to making a decision than ignoring the situation. Consequently, we suffer more regret resulting from a decision compared to inaction. We will go so far as to actively avoid making decisions to avoid regret—a phenomenon known as *regret avoidance*.[167]

ORGANIZATIONS CONTAIN DIVERSE INTERESTS AND PERSPECTIVES

People see situations differently. They may have irreconcilable perspectives regarding the nature of the problem, and thus the nature of the change required. If consensus is required, inertia may result.[168]

Competition can undermine collective action. Change may require cooperation across departments to act for the common good. Yet, incentives for departments to change may be at cross-purposes. If the organization's culture is competitive, departments may act out of self-interest and maintain their control. Inertia may result from such political deadlocks.[169]

No one wants to be the first mover. When a risky new ini-

---

165 Daniel Kahneman, Jack L. Knetsch, and Richard H. Thaler, "Anomalies: The Endowment Effect, Loss Aversion, and Status Quo Bias," *Journal of Economic Perspectives* 5, no. 1 (Winter 1991): 198–199, 203, https://doi.org/10.1257/jep.5.1.193.

166 Kahneman, Knetsch, and Thaler, "Anomalies," 203.

167 Samuel and Zeckhauser, "Status Quo Bias in Decision Making," 38.

168 Rumelt, "Precis of Inertia and Transformation," 7–8.

169 Rumelt, "Precis of Inertia and Transformation," 7.

tiative is launched that requires leadership, it can be easier for everyone to wait to see how things go for the first mover. If no one wants to be the brave first mover, collective action may be blocked.[170]

THE VALUES OF THE STATUS QUO EFFECT

The consequences of the status quo effect depend on the situation. If things are humming and the demands of your environment are within your ability to meet them, the status quo is efficient and effortless. It can yield important benefits to your organization.

ORGANIZATIONS WITH CONSISTENT ROUTINES AND TRACK RECORDS HAVE AN ADVANTAGE OVER NEWER ONES

Older organizations have demonstrated higher degrees of reliability and accountability. In contrast, new organizations "rely on the cooperation of strangers. Development of trust and smoothly working relationships takes time. It also takes time to work out routines."[171] It is easier for established organizations to continue existing routines than for new organizations to create new ones. Not surprisingly, organizational death rates dramatically decline with age.[172]

---

170 Rumelt, "Precis of Inertia and Transformation," 9.

171 Hannan and Freeman, "Structural Inertia and Organizational Change," 157.

172 Hannan and Freeman, "Structural Inertia and Organizational Change," 158.

THE STATUS QUO EFFECT PROVIDES PREDICTABILITY
AND EASE IN DAILY LIFE AND OPERATIONS

When our daily patterns and work routines are consistent, our work with others is smooth, as we know what to expect from each other. When we can count on today's routine being the same as yesterday's, our minds can focus on matters that demand our deliberate attention.[173]

In sum, inertia—the continuity of our behaviors—provides people and organizations with stability.

THE DANGERS OF THE STATUS QUO EFFECT

If your environment is turbulent and requires rapid change, the preference for doing nothing and the persistence of existing behaviors means that your organization's response will be inadequate.

THE STATUS QUO CAN BE A DEAD WEIGHT ON
AN ORGANIZATION'S ABILITY TO ADAPT

When an organization decides to respond to a situation, its dependable structure—its roles, communications, and routines—can have a dead-weight quality that causes lag in the response. The lag between the timing of someone's intention to change and the desired outcome can be too long for the attention span of decision-makers. They will move on to other issues before addressing difficult structural barriers.[174] In fact, changes that impact different parts of the organization may be too complicated and risky, which results in practices that are "locked in."[175]

---

173 Becker, "Organizational Routines," 657.

174 Hannan and Freeman, "Structural Inertia and Organizational Change," 155.

175 David, "Clio and the Economics of QWERTY."

WE DON'T EXPLORE OR ADOPT BETTER ALTERNATIVES

A bias toward the status quo can result in a decision-making process that *undervalues* the benefits of something new and *overvalues* the benefits of the current state.

When a situation demands change, we are more likely to stay in our comfort zone rather than deal with uncertainty. We are more likely to accept inefficiency and damaging stagnation over growth and impact. Our bias for the status quo potentially results in nothing better being undertaken.

INERTIA CAN STALL OUT CHANGE EFFORTS AND ERODE SUPPORT

When we delay a change effort and allow existing behaviors to persist, people can become more attached to the current state. Doubts deepen during project delays, even among supportive people. Doubts could be overcome and fears allayed if people get engaged in the change quickly and become familiar with it.

Inertia can also result in attempts to delay implementation and a lack of interest in gaining familiarity with a new system or process. It can lead to renewed support and enthusiasm for the old system and current state as a "known quantity." It can silence any intention to change and lead to a "lock-in" of existing behaviors.[176]

WHAT YOU CAN DO

The status quo effect might require intervention at the individual and organizational levels. It is, after all, a byproduct of our psychological bias and organizational structure.

---

176 Polites and Karahanna, "Shackled to the Status Quo," 29.

FOCUS ATTENTION ON WHAT NEEDS TO CHANGE

To alter the status quo, you must focus your organization and its leadership on the need for change. There is often a cacophony of issues being sold at any one time. Getting the attention of decision-makers—a process known as *issue selling*—is a critical early step in enacting change. Organizations act on issues that command the limited and selective attention of their decision-makers.[177]

Issue selling describes the behind-the-scenes work of change agents operating below the level of top management. Issues sellers are "mindful and proactive orchestrators of change who, with intent, try to bring streams of issues, solutions, and opportunities together in ways that focus attention and invite action on issues."[178] This type of bottom-up change is ongoing and always evolving.

Researchers studied eighty-plus attempts of middle managers advocating for change within a large, well-established, and risk-averse hospital system—a typically large and bureaucratic organization—that was facing competitive pressures to lower costs and improve quality.[179] This research details how middle managers navigated change. The following are insights from the successful attempts to sell issues that can be applied to a variety of inertia-prone organizations:

- **Package the initiative as fitting within the organization's strategy** rather than challenging it. Some were deliberately toned down to appear incremental and conform to the organization's priorities and goals.

- **Use the logic of a business plan** and detail the financial

---

177 William Ocasio, "Towards an Attention-Based View of the Firm," *Strategic Management Journal* 18, no. S1 (December 1998): 203, https://doi.org/10.1002/(SICI)1097-0266(199707)18:1+<187::AID-SMJ936>3.0.CO;2-K.

178 Dutton et al., "Moves that Matter," 732.

179 Dutton et al., "Moves that Matter," 718.

aspects of the proposal, the marketing, the strategy operations, and other business perspectives.

- **Persistence is key.** Continuously sell your proposal and raise the issue many times over an extended period; this is especially true if the change is substantial. You may need to sell your proposal in "bits and pieces."
- **Be opportunistic and look for fortuitous moments** that allow you to sell your issue. You can artfully tie your issue to something else that gets the organization's attention. Be entrepreneurial.
- **Be politically savvy in knowing who to enlist and how to motivate their support for your change.** Successful issue sellers were nuanced in finding the opportune time to present their cause and how to connect it to issues people cared about.
- **Consider forming a coalition of peers and leadership** to grow the scope, increase visibility, and build commitment for your change effort. Bringing in outside experts can lend legitimacy and authority to your proposal.[180]

In sum, successful issue selling means you actively and continuously engage the right people with your issues, at the right time and in the right way.

DO NOT LET THE INERTIA SET IN, KEEP PEOPLE MOVING

Even small steps can keep people focused and committed to the change. If a system implementation is delayed, engage people in training or bring in outside experts for talks. In short, keep taking action. Remember: action builds commitment and inertia erodes it.

---

180 Dutton et al., "Moves that Matter," 723.

DECREASE THE COSTS AND RISKS OF CHANGE

We are already inclined to overestimate the value of what we have and underestimate the value of something new. Any additional "costs" of change can make the process of building support that much harder. Here are three things you can do to level the playing field:

- **Familiarize people with change quickly to reduce uncertainty and stress.** Familiarity with the new way of doing business builds personal confidence and, eventually, ease. Familiarity can reduce uncertainty and stress.
- **Accommodate disruption during the transition.** Developing new ways of working and learning new skills takes time and may disrupt current operations. Create realistic goals during transitions to reduce stress.
- **Frame the change as a continuation or gain (never a loss).** We focus on losses more than gains, which blinds us to the benefits of change. Frame the change as a continuation of something people care about (e.g., "this new system will help us better serve our customers"). Be very explicit—not subtle—about what is gained.

DEVELOP METHODS TO REALLOCATE RESOURCES

Taking funds from one business unit and giving them to another can be fraught with conflict. Yet, if the organization needs to shift gears, reallocation is absolutely critical. McKinsey & Company identified several strategies that can help organizations overcome budgetary inertia[181]:

- **Create investment categories: "seed"** for new business, **"nurture"** for building up business, **"prune"** for taking resources

---

181   Hall, Lovallo, and Musters, "How to Put Your Money Where Your Strategy Is."

away, and **"harvest"** for divesting. By socializing different phases of investment, you create opportunities for new investment and normalize the fact that some investments should end.

- **Shift the burden of proof for resource allocation away from "we did it last year."** You can establish clear criteria upfront for reinvesting in an existing program (e.g., the new marketing initiative needs to outperform previous baselines).
- **Review investments on a granular versus high level.** McKinsey found that most companies review investment decisions at the divisional or business unit level. At this high level, there is not enough detailed information to evaluate a program's performance.

GO FOR SMALL WINS

The prospect of major change in a steadfast organization can be daunting. Social psychologist Karl Weick suggests that we can structure major issues into a series of *small wins*—controllable opportunities that produce visible results.[182]

Structuring big change as small wins has many benefits:

- **Once small wins are accomplished, they create momentum** for the next one, which brings allies and additional resources to your cause.[183]
- **Small wins are like miniature experiments** that facilitate learning and adaptation. It is easier to see cause and effect with a small win.[184]

---

182 Karl E. Weick, "Small Wins: Redefining the Scale of Social Problems," *American Psychologist* 39, no. 1 (1984): 43, https://doi.org/10.1037/0003-066X.39.1.40.

183 Weick, "Small Wins," 43.

184 Weick, "Small Wins," 44.

- **Small wins may be more stable and less risky than large ones.** If lots of things have to come together to produce a large win, lots of things can go wrong. Small wins "preserve gains" because the failure of one doesn't unravel the accomplishment of others. The worst thing that can happen with a small win is a small flop; the risk of large-scale failure is greatly reduced.
- **Small wins are more effective than large changes in producing commitment.** People have a closer relationship with small wins. On a human level, "small wins are not only easier to comprehend but more pleasurable to experience."[185]

Small wins create a sense of confidence that unlocks the very resources we need to manage the problem; "a small win reduces importance ('this is no big deal'), reduces demands ('that's all that needs to be done'), and raises perceived skill levels ('I can do at least that')."[186]

RESTRUCTURE FOR INNOVATION: CREATE AN AMBIDEXTROUS ORGANIZATION

A heavy reliance on existing customers, products, and services can be a significant source of inertia that stifles innovation. People fear that new products can cannibalize existing ones and potentially the jobs that go with them. New markets threaten to divert resources away from existing ones. Yet, you may need to innovate and develop new capabilities that go in a different direction while you manage the existing business. You will need an organizational structure that maintains the discipline and reliability of the exist-

---

185 Weick, "Small Wins," 45.

186 Weick, "Small Wins," 46.

ing business while you foster innovation with experimentation and flexibility.

Researchers conducted a longitudinal study across thirteen firms and twenty-two innovations from different industries including IBM, *USA Today*, Polaroid, HP, Firestone, and BF Goodrich among others.[187] Firms employed four different organizational designs to manage their innovation streams:

1. **Ambidextrous team.** An autonomous innovation unit reporting to a senior executive with targeted integration across the organization.
2. **Embedded team.** Innovation streams are embedded into existing functional units, and a senior team is responsible for existing business and innovation.
3. **Cross-functional team.** Headed by a project manager who is not a member of the senior team and receives limited leadership support.
4. **Spin-out team.** A highly autonomous unit is created with little integration across the organization.

The research conclusively demonstrates that an ambidextrous organizational design yields significantly better innovation outcomes while maintaining—if not growing—existing business.

An ambidextrous organization has several key features that define its structure and its culture:

- **A distinct unit is created that operates with relative autonomy** within the parent organization.
- **The innovation unit has targeted integration with members of the senior team** and other functional teams within the

---

187 Michael Tushman et al., "Organizational Designs and Innovation Streams," *Industrial and Corporate Change* 19, no. 5 (October 2010): 1331–1366, https://doi.org/10.1093/icc/dtq040.

parent organization to leverage resources within the organization and share learnings.

- **The innovation team reports to a senior member** of the executive team and is supported by the general manager or president.
- **The innovation manager has complete freedom** to define the work processes and culture of the innovation team.
- **The group is physically separated** from the teams that run existing business.
- **The president and the senior team operationalize dual strategies** that support the existing business as well as the new ventures.
- **Senior leadership is able to articulate an overarching aspiration** that could speak to and motivate the maintenance side of the business as well as the innovation side.
- **Senior executives and managers were incentivized by "common fate incentives"** that were rewarded only if the existing business and innovation team succeeded.
- **The motivations and culture of the core business and innovation team were distinct.**

Notably the other innovation designs (embedded, cross-functional, spin-out) suffered from problems that are predictable in hindsight:

- Cross-functional teams were led by a lower-level project manager who did not receive enough strategic or political support.[188]
- Highly autonomous spin-offs lacked integration with the organization's senior management and faced resistance.
- Embedded teams could not nurture innovation while managing existing business (four out of five shifted to ambidextrous designs).

---

188 Tushman et al., "Organizational Designs and Innovation Streams," 1347.

Ambidextrous organizational structures provide the ability to manage existing business while you explore radically new possibilities.[189] It allows an organization to maintain the status quo—its bread and butter business—while it explores potentially disruptive innovation.

CHAPTER SUMMARY

- There is a tendency for organizations—as well as a bias in our own thinking—to stay the same even when they need to change.
- Status quo effect is the psychological tendency to maintain the status quo or do nothing in the face of potentially superior alternatives. The result of clinging to the status quo is inertia—the persistence of existing behaviors.
- There are many causes for the status quo effect. Organizations need stability to reliably produce the same outcomes day after day. Diverse perspectives and competition within organizations can keep things from moving forward.
- On a personal level, we maintain the status quo and stick with previous decisions to feel more in control and competent. The status quo provides us with a sense of ease. Change involves uncertainty as the cost of searching for new alternatives and switching gears can be high.
- The status quo effect has a couple of irrational causes. When we fear we will lose something with a change, we will cling to what we have regardless of what we might gain. Last, we are more likely to regret taking action than doing nothing.

---

189 Michael L. Tushman and Charles A. O'Reilly, "Ambidextrous Organizations: Managing Evolutionary and Revolutionary Change," *California Management Review* 38, no. 3 (July 1996): 11, https://doi.org/10.2307/41165852.

- The status quo effect has value in providing organizations and people with stability and predictability.
- The status quo effect can damage organizations when the environment demands a faster change than the organization can muster. Organizations can be less likely to explore alternatives, and change efforts can stall.
- To alter the status quo, you must focus your organization and its leadership on the need for change. You may need to develop methods or reallocate resources so that change efforts can be funded.
- You can decrease the perceived costs of change so that people feel less risk in it. You should not let inertia set into your change effort. By focusing on small wins, you can create a viable path for change and sustain momentum.
- You may need to restructure the organization so that it maintains the discipline and reliability of the existing business while you foster innovation with experimentation and flexibility in a distinct unit.

CASE IN POINT: RESISTANCE OF THE EXECUTIVE MINDSET

POLAROID'S BUSINESS MODEL AND ITS BATTLE WITH THE INERTIA

When executives work together for many years, they share beliefs—a "dominant logic"—that shapes how they interpret the world, understand problems, and search for solutions. The mindset of executives can be a source of inertia that constrains an organization.

In the case of Polaroid, the culture and capabilities that once made the company an unparalleled pioneer in instant photography held the company back when it needed to transition from analog to digital photography.[190]

Polaroid was founded in 1937 by Edwin Land, one of the earliest inventors of instant photography. By 1948, Polaroid introduced the first instant camera (weighing in at five pounds). Land was an ambitious leader. His motto was, "Don't do anything that someone else can do. Don't undertake a project unless it is manifestly important and nearly impossible."[191] For decades, Polaroid introduced ground-breaking cameras with the quest to increase the quality and decrease the processing time of its instant photographs.

Polaroid's strategy was to invest in long-term research and development projects that pushed the envelope on the technology of film and film processing. Polaroid's technologies created demand rather than responding to the market.

---

190 Unless otherwise stated, all information about Polaroid, its products, and its executive strategies come from: Mary Tripsas and Giovanni Gavetti, "Capabilities, Cognition, and Inertia: Evidence from Digital Imaging," in "The Evolution of Firm Capabilities," special issue, *Strategic Management Journal* 21, no. 10/11 (October–November 2000): 1147–1161, https://www.jstor.org/stable/3094431.

191 "The Vindication of Edwin Land," *Forbes* 139 (May 4, 1987): 83.

In the 1980s, the decade preceding the introduction of digital photography, Polaroid pursued two paths: (1) create instant digital prints that would rival the quality of 35mm; (2) accelerate research and development in digital photography.

In 1981, it formed an Electronic Imaging Group and laboratory staffed by new hires. By 1989 more than 40 percent of its research and development dollars were devoted to digital imaging. As a result, the company made huge advances in digital technology. Polaroid sensors generated 1.9 million pixels, well beyond most of the competition, which generated only 480,000. Polaroid developed early algorithms that resulted in lossless compression. These were major breakthroughs at the time.

Despite its technological advances in digital, Polaroid was unable to shift its mindset around its business model and product development. Like many other camera companies before digital, Polaroid made money from film instead of camera hardware (a.k.a. the "razor blade" business model that produces profits from the blades instead of the razors). In order to compete profitably in the hardware arena, it needed to focus on low-cost hardware manufacturing and rapid product development and innovation. This would increase margins on hardware and bring innovative products to market much more quickly.

Polaroid executives could only understand digital imaging through the lens of a technology challenge, not a market opportunity. As a consequence, Polaroid did not invest in low-cost electronics manufacturing or evolve to develop products quickly or market them effectively.

Mounting internal tensions between company executives and the Electronic Imaging Group resulted in lengthy delays in the development and commercialization of the digital camera. Even though Polaroid developed a digital camera in 1992, the company sat on the product until 1996. By the time it was announced, forty other firms were selling digital cameras.

Despite the fact that Polaroid was able to dramatically shift its R&D capabilities from analog to digital, its business model was stuck in historical precedents and mired in inertia. The results were striking: sales decreased after thirty years of at least 20 percent annual growth. By 1994, Polaroid lost $180M in digital imaging. In 1995, losses climbed to $190M.

In 1996, a new CEO, Gary DiCamillo, was brought on board believing that the "value of large scale inventions had disappeared. Instead, Polaroid was focused on rapid incremental product development." He decreased the funding for technology and R&D.

Even though Polaroid commanded the ability to pivot its technology from digital to analog, it could not transition its business strategy from the "razor blade model." Senior managers "strongly discouraged search and development efforts that were not consistent with the traditional business model, despite ongoing efforts from newly hired members of the electronic imaging division to convince them otherwise."

In short, the Polaroid executive team "was able to develop new beliefs for digital imaging only as long as those beliefs were consistent with the instant photography business." Once the strategy challenged their fundamental assumptions, inertia set in.

CASE IN POINT: RESISTANCE OF HISTORY

WHEN ONE DAMN THING FOLLOWS ANOTHER RESULTING IN THE QWERTY KEYBOARD

Notice the keyboard of your computer or mobile phone and the arrangement of the keys on the top row: QWERTY. You are beholding what is known as the QWERTY keyboard created almost 150 years ago during the advent of the first typewriters. The QWERTY keyboard's persistence is the result of *path dependency*, a historical sequence of events that at first may be accidental or happenstance, but builds momentum over time, eventually constraining our options and locking us into specific practices.[192] Organizations and industries continue down a path in part due to the investments they make, the coordination and learning that build up around a practice, and the expectation that others will adopt the practice as well.[193] Path dependency is one dynamic that creates the stability of the status quo.

The QWERTY keyboard is the product of chance events, not systematic or rational choices. It is the story of how "one damn thing follows another."

The QWERTY keyboard was the invention of Christopher Latham Sholes, a Wisconsin printer and mechanical tinkerer. Many were developing typewriter models, and Sholes was but the fifty-second person to invent a typewriter. He, along with his manufacturing partner, Remington and Sons (the famed arms manufacturer), was able to solve the problem of keystroke clashing and jamming that bedeviled other models. In a stroke of marketing genius, he placed all of the letters needed for a salesman to rapidly spell the name of the product in one row: TYPEWRITER.

---

192 Unless otherwise stated, all information about the QWERTY keyboard comes from David, "Clio and the Economics of QWERTY," 332.

193 Marie-Laure Djelic and Sigrid Quack, "Overcoming Path Dependency: Path Generation in Open Systems," *Theory and Society* 36, no. 2 (March 2007): 164, https://doi.org/10.1007/s11186-007-9026-0.

In the early days, the QWERTY machine was not economically dominant—sales volumes were relatively small and the company almost went into bankruptcy. Nor was the QWERTY technically compelling. Many competitive keyboards were developed in the early days of typewriters. Thomas Edison developed an electric print wheel that became the basis of teletype machines. For more than forty years, August Dvorak tried to unseat the QWERTY keyboard with his DSK simplified keyboard that increased typing speed by 40 percent.

Yet, the QWERTY keyboard remains the industry standard even in the digital age. How could this be?

Early typists learned touch typing (versus hunt and peck typing) using the QWERTY keyboard. By the 1890s, employers began to hire and train QWERTY touch typists, which created even more momentum for other typists to learn QWERTY. This early labor pool of QWERTY typists and employers created economic incentives for manufacturers to produce QWERTY typewriters. It was also inexpensive for manufacturers to convert typewriter hardware to QWERTY.

In short, the QWERTY typewriter was the best economic choice for typewriter manufacturers in the 1890s because enough typists knew how to use it, which created sufficient demand from employers. This resulted in the typewriting industry prematurely standardizing the wrong system that remains with us today.

Economic historian, Paul David highlights three factors that contributed to our path dependency on QWERTY that has lasted for more than 130 years: (1) the interrelatedness and dependence of the QWERTY hardware on the skills of touch typists; (2) the standardization of hardware across manufacturers that resulted in the scaled adoption of QWERTY; and (3) the practical irreversibility of switching to an alternative that does not have a labor pool that could use it. Path dependency might be found in situations that have interdependence between hardware and software (human skill), scale of adoption, and irreversibility.

And so we see how an early "historical accident" of the early training of QWERTY touch typists, led to a convergence around the wrong standard that has "locked in" the industry for decades to come.

In untold aspects of our lives, we are surrounded by QWERTY keyboards; and even though we are "perfectly 'free to choose,' [our] behavior, nevertheless, is held fast in the grip of events, long forgotten, and shaped by circumstances in which neither [we] nor [our] interest figured."

Best Practices

A DEADENING MIMICRY

"The manager's situation is much like that of a lost, but experienced, spelunker groping her way to safety by reading the information contained in the walls, floor, and atmosphere of the cave."

—EUGENE BARDACH, 2004

Nothing seems to stir the hearts and minds of executives and practitioners alike as the concept of "best practices." Once born and adopted within the manufacturing sector, best practices have spread like a kudzu vine over the past forty years to envelop almost all industries and practices with the allure of a universal standard that surpasses all others.

Here are a few examples of widely-lauded practices that produce questionable results and yet persist.

- For decades compensation consultants promoted the idea that CEO pay (in the form of stocks and options) should be tied to shareholder value and include large lump sum parachute payments tied to no performance measure. Never mind the fact that CEOs alone cannot control stock price, CEO pay ratcheted upwards. As companies publicly reported compensation, no one wanted to be in the bottom 25 percent. The results have been widening pay inequities, increasing cynicism about leadership, and perverse incentives to cut corners (e.g., risky mortgage approvals or Enron's off-balance sheet transactions that hid poor performance).[194]

- The annual performance review—the appraisal of an employee's performance by their superior—is one of the most common and dreaded rituals of organizational life. Despite their ubiquity, the performance review is "almost always rated as failures by both employees and management."[195] And, there is little if any evidence that performance evaluation improves employee performance. Why would it? The underlying assumption is "that forcing supervisors and managers to act as judges, evaluating employee behavior, rewarding compliance, and sanctioning deviation from externally imposed plans" will increase motivation or improve performance is fundamentally flawed. Yet, it persists as an indispensable HR practice.[196]

Though it may begin as an innovation, a best practice can become a codified and bureaucratized practice, buttressed by the belief that it represents the optimal approach.

With the promise that we too can be the "best" if we adhere to its doctrines, "best practices" can be the obstacle to trying something unproven, innovative, and unique. The confidence of using the "best practices" can keep us from more critically evaluating the effectiveness of what we are doing or searching for something better.

---

194 Jay Lorsch and Rakesh Khurana, "The Pay Problem," *Harvard Magazine*, May–June 2010, https://www.harvardmagazine.com/2010/05/the-pay-problem.

195 Kevin R. Murphy, "Performance Evaluation Will Not Die, But It Should," *Human Resource Management Journal* 30, no. 1 (October 2019): 14, https://doi.org/10.1111/1748-8583.12259.

196 Murphy, "Performance Evaluation Will Not Die, But It Should," 26.

THE NATURE OF BEST PRACTICES

Best practices can be found in every sector—from higher education to hospitality—and in every organizational function—from human resources to supply chain management.[197] One can see best practices functioning in high-level maxims such as "customer centricity" or "authentic leadership" or in very detailed practices such as coding or executive compensation.[198] The basis for claiming a best practice can vary widely from the rigorous testing common in technical and scientific fields to the inspiring pronouncements made by charismatic leaders.

KNOWLEDGE THAT WORKS FOR EVERYONE

Let's define this ubiquitous term: *A best practice is a knowledge about what works that can be replicated by others.* Best practices develop when one group is engaged in an activity that produces good results that another group attempts to reproduce.[199] In essence, *best practices begin as local knowledge about what works in one place that is converted into universal knowledge about what generally works the best.*[200]

---

197 Higher Education: "Safer Schools and Campuses Best Practices Clearinghouse," U.S. Department of Education, accessed May 22, 2024, https://bestpracticesclearinghouse.ed.gov. Hospitality: Judy A. Siguaw and Cathy A. Enz, "Best Practices in Hotel Operations," *Cornell Hotel and Restaurant Quarterly* 40, no. 6 (December 1999), https://ecommons.cornell.edu/items/120d253e-0cd0-4428-b2ae-487176163ca6. Human Resources: "Best Practices for Employers and Human Resources/EEO Professionals," U.S. Equal Employment Opportunity Commission, accessed May 24, 2024, https://www.eeoc.gov/initiatives/e-race/best-practices-employers-and-human-resourceseeo-professionals. Supply Chain Management: David Blanchard, *Supply Chain Management Best Practices*, 2nd ed. (Hoboken, NJ: John Wiley & Sons, 2010).

198 Kirk Paul Lafler and Mary Rosenbloom, "Best Practice Programming Techniques for SAS Users," Paper 176-2017, presented at SAS Global Forum (SGF) 2017, https://support.sas.com/resources/papers/proceedings17/0175-2017.pdf; Frederick D. Lipman and Steven E. Hall, *Executive Compensation Best Practices* (New York: Wiley, 2008).

199 Gabriel Szulanski and Sidney Winter, "Getting It Right the Second Time," *Harvard Business Review* 80, no. 1 (January 2002): 64, https://hbr.org/2002/01/getting-it-right-the-second-time.

200 Michael Quinn Patton, "Evaluation, Knowledge Management, Best Practices, and High Quality Lessons Learned," *American Journal of Evaluation* 22, no. 3 (September 2001): 330, https://doi.org/10.1177/109821400102200307.

Note: **Best practices are different from lessons learned. Lessons learned are localized and more personal insights. To say something is a best practice is a much bolder claim.**[201]

Whether they have been tested and verified or just passed along as the buzz at the latest conference, best practices are talked about and shared. We seek them out and we pass them along.

The question becomes, How much stock can we put into this learning and how much confidence should we place in the practice? Do we really know what leads to success in the first place? How much of what we learn from another's experience is relevant to the particularities of our own?

We have much to learn from the experience of others, but bad ideas can spread just like good ones. All practices, even those considered best, should be subjected to a skeptical gaze on a regular basis. Most importantly, we should trust what we see more than what we want to believe (or those before us wanted to believe).

THE CAUSES OF BEST PRACTICES

Our need to find, follow, and share best practices is part and parcel of our desire to feel and appear competent, increase the ease of our own decision-making, and learn from the experience of others to reduce our risk.

WE WANT TO FEEL AND BE RECOGNIZED AS COMPETENT

We need to feel like we are good at what we do. Adopting a best practice that is approved by our community provides reassurance of our proficiency. Competence is a fundamental need—a key part of self-determination—that makes us feel more confident

---

201 Patton, "Evaluation, Knowledge Management, Best Practices, and High Quality Lessons Learned," 313.

and effective in what we do.[202] Our feelings of competence and control increase our vitality and motivation; this is especially true when we feel supported.

Sharing a best practice with others can enhance our status and "convey an impression of being 'with it.'"[203] In effect, we are "in the know" by aligning ourselves with another's success. We secure our own self-esteem by "basking in the reflected glory" of another.[204]

WE SPREAD IDEAS THAT SOLVE PROBLEMS

The need to learn from the experience of others is profound—fumbling through our situation with trial and error is time-consuming, costly, and potentially painful. We are especially prone to acquire information from others' decisions that are "risky, important, complex or riddled with uncertainty."[205] In talking to others about what has worked for them, we can "reduce risk, simplify, complexity, and increase [our] confidence [we] are doing the right thing."[206] In other words, when the situation "does not speak for itself, people turn to each other for cues."[207]

202 Ryan and Deci, "Self-Determination Theory and the Fascilitation of Intrinsic Motivation," 70.

203 Jonah Berger, "Word of Mouth and Interpersonal Communication: A Review and Directions for Future Research," *Journal of Consumer Psychology* 24, no. 4 (May 2014): 588–589, https://doi.org/10.1016/j.jcps.2014.05.002.

204 Robert B. Cialdini et al., "Basking in Reflected Glory: Three (Football) Field Studies," *Journal of Personality and Social Psychology* 34, no. 3 (1976): 374, https://doi.org/10.1037/0022-3514.34.3.366.

205 Berger, "Word of Mouth and Interpersonal Communication," 594.

206 Berger, "Word of Mouth and Interpersonal Communication," 594.

207 Ronald S. Burt, "Social Contagion and Innovation: Cohesion versus Structural Equivalence," *American Journal of Sociology* 92, no. 6 (May 1987): 1290, https://doi.org/10.1086/228667.

WE DECEIVE OURSELVES INTO BELIEVING
WHAT WE SAY AND HEAR

We have a psychological bias to remember our accomplishments and forget our failures. As a result "leaders create, and re-create their own reality so often that soon it becomes almost impossible for them to distinguish the actual truth from what they recall, as being true, even if they wanted to do so."[208] This can result in people confidently proclaiming half-truths or falsehoods to be best practices.

For listeners, it is tempting to selectively believe what they want to be true. This is especially the case for best practices that function more like philosophies or ideologies. These best practices are often combined with inspiring stories that "offer morals that fit what we want to believe, and many offer hope."[209] Claims that leaders should be genuine and vulnerable may speak more to what we want the world to be, rather than what it really is. Typically, we do astonishing little due diligence to assess the accuracy of what we hear.

BEST PRACTICES OFFER EASE AND
CONSENSUS IN DECISION-MAKING

More pressing than finding trustworthy information is "finding ways to ignore as much as possible of the otherwise overwhelming hoard of facts."[210] The social acceptance of a best practice provides a confidence in decision-making that would have otherwise relied on a time-consuming search and evaluation of alternatives.

"Best practices" also offer a shared understanding of "the best

---

208 Jeffrey Pfeffer, *Leadership BS: Fixing Workplaces and Careers One Truth at a Time* (New York: Harper Business, 2015), 37–38.

209 Pfeffer, *Leadership BS*, 39.

210 Burt, "Social Contagion and Innovation," 1289.

way" among your colleagues and superiors, which might be difficult to prove otherwise. The general acceptance of what is "best" is an efficient shortcut to the arduous process of consensus building.[211]

THE VALUE OF BEST PRACTICES

The spread and adoption of high-quality best practices can lift all boats when they are rigorously selected and adopted with vigilance.

RAISING THE BAR, ACROSS THE BOARD

Handwashing in hospitals is now a best practice due to the decades of research that demonstrated its effectiveness in reducing disease transmission and showed how hospitals could increase physician adoption of the practice. The adoption of this inarguable and simple practice required keen attention to detail and fine-tuning in every hospital.

Best practices in digital purchasing have improved from laborious processes to streamlined one-click transactions. Now, thanks in large part to industry leaders such as Amazon and the proliferation of affordable plug-and-play tools, many companies offer streamlined customer experiences. Now, digital experiences for small and large companies alike have converged on a standard and best practices.

Foundations, academics, governments, and consultancies are providing sustainability best practices that can help organizations

---

211 Joe Osburn, Guy Caruso, and Wolf Wolfensberger, "The Concept of 'Best Practice': A Brief Overview of Its Meanings, Scope, Uses, and Shortcomings," *International Journal of Disability, Development and Education* 58, no. 3 (September 2011): 216, https://doi.org/10.1080/1034912X.2011.598387.

improve their operations. Some of these efforts are explicit guidelines that are adapted to local contexts. Others are guiding principles that are supported by a menu of options that one can choose from.

All of this is for the good. In each instance, the best practice was thoroughly tested and adoption was guided by the principle that local adaptation may be necessary.

We run into trouble when ideas spread that are biased in their perspective—they may be good for the practitioner, but not for the practice itself—and adopted without ongoing vigilance.

THE DANGERS OF BEST PRACTICES

Our belief and confidence in following a best practice can lead to a continuation of a practice that is in reality outworn. It can also result in complacency and resistance to searching for and attempting something new.

BEST PRACTICES BLIND US TO POTENTIAL WEAKNESSES AND LIABILITIES

Our overconfidence and belief in best practices can dull critical thinking. They promise certainty and safety and tempt us to turn off our vigilance in understanding what's going on beneath the surface. If performance is lagging, we are not likely to look at the best practice as the cause. Rather we look to blame external factors or call it a fluke.

Often, we fail to ask the simple question, *Best for whom?* Is it better for the company or its customer? Is it better for the teacher or the student, the doctor or the patient? Is it better for the police or the citizenry? Unfortunately, the answer to the question—*best for whom?*—and the importance of the question itself is often clear only in hindsight.

POOR BEST PRACTICES CAN DAMAGE AN ENTIRE SECTOR

Once a sector converges around a best practice, there is often less effort spent in seeking a better approach. When this practice has critical flaws, many organizations and the people they serve suffer downside risks. The following case study on reading instruction shows how an entire generation of teachers adopted an inspiring but ineffective teaching method that led to a national decline in literacy. (See the case study at the end of the chapter.)

WHAT WAS ONCE BEST MAY BE NO LONGER

When the conditions that once made a best practice work, change, the impact can be unexpected and damaging. For example, just-in-time manufacturing (JIT) and inventory management were considered a best practice for decades. *Harvard Business Review* rhetorically asked, "What's your excuse for not using JIT?"[212] Eventually, the pandemic and economic tariffs disrupted global supply chains. Manufacturers who had become accustomed to reliable just-in-time inventories did not maintain an expensive stock of supplies. Across the board, manufacturers were unable to produce their goods in a timely manner. Now, this once holy grail of efficiency is being reconsidered due to the volatility of the political and economic environment.[213]

---

212 Richard C. Walleigh, "What's Your Excuse for Not Using JIT?," *Harvard Business Review* (March 1986), https://hbr.org/1986/03/whats-your-excuse-for-not-using-jit.

213 Jennifer Blackhurst and Andrew Balthrop, "It's Time to Move Beyond Just-in-Time and Just-in-Case," *Supply Chain Management Review*, January 3, 2023, https://www.scmr.com/article/its_time_to_move_beyond_just_in_time_and_just_in_case.

YOU STOP LOOKING FOR SOMETHING BETTER

Once you have found and adopted the best practice there is little, if any, incentive to look for something better. As we learned in the chapter on the status quo effect, the search and evaluation of viable alternatives is a significant time and cognitive commitment. The consequence is that you stop scanning your environment in search of alternatives or even inspiration. When you stop scanning, you stop learning, innovating, and growing.

WHAT YOU CAN DO

We should approach best practices with caution. There are inherent limits to what we can extrapolate and apply from the experience of others. First, we don't exactly know what makes something work in the first place. And, there can be many obvious and subtle differences between our situation and another's. In short, the limitations of best practices, lessons learned, or advice is that they are offered and accepted with confidence when, in truth, we may not understand what makes them work and or appreciate their vulnerabilities.

Below are several strategies that will help us avoid the pitfalls of best practices.

REPLACE THE TERM "BEST PRACTICES" WITH "BEST FOR US NOW"

This slight turn of phrase does a couple of important things: (1) it acknowledges that a practice must work for you, not someone else; and (2) it puts a potential expiration date on a practice. What works for others, may not work for us. What works now, may not a year from now. We are best served by a modicum of humility, skepticism, and vigilance.

BE CURIOUS AND SKEPTICAL OF
ADVICE—VERIFY THE EVIDENCE

We should look for high-quality lessons learned that inspire us to think about how we can improve our own practice. A high-quality lesson learned comes from multiple sources, not just one, and is often communicated in the form of a guiding principle or working hypotheses that can be adapted and applied to new situations.[214]

Our job is to evaluate whether a best practice is a high-quality lesson learned.

We are well advised to be skeptical of best practices and "great advice" that is presented as new bold thinking, a breakthrough innovation, or the brainchild of a guru. By nature, we align ourselves with successful others. There are many psychological and economic incentives that go into creating new fads that are, at the end of the day, in service of selling books, expanding personal influence, and generating revenue.[215]

Rather than assuming that a practice is "best," management thinkers Jeffery Pfeffer and Robert Sutton suggest that you ask some basic questions:[216]

- **Is the practice associated with past success?** Get specific. How many times and under what conditions has the practice worked?
- **What are its limitations and why would it fail?**
- **Does the practice apply to your situation?** Is your situation (i.e., the business, the technology, the customers, a business model, the competitive environment) similar enough to some-

---

214 Patton, "Evaluation, Knowledge Management, Best Practices, and High Quality Lessons Learned," 33.

215 Jeffrey Pfeffer and Robert I. Sutton, *Hard Facts, Dangerous Half-Truths, and Total Nonsense: Profiting from Evidence-Based Management* (Brighton, MA: Harvard Business Review Press, 2006), 41–52.

216 Pfeffer and Sutton, *Hard Facts, Dangerous Half-Truths, and Total Nonsense*, 22.

one else's past situation that their practice will apply to your setting?

- **What assumptions does the idea or practice make about your people and organization?** What would have to be true about people and organizations for the idea or practice to be effective?
- **Which of these assumptions seem reasonable and correct?** Which seems wrong or suspect?
- **Would this idea or practice still succeed if the assumptions turned out to be wrong?**
- **Why do you think the past practice has been effective?**

We are often afraid to ask these questions because we would rather believe what we are hearing. But, our over-optimism can leave us vulnerable to and unprepared for the realities of the world.

UNDERSTAND HOW THE PRACTICE WORKS—CLARIFY THE MODEL

Adopting a new practice can be a leap of faith, but there is comfort in knowing that others are doing it too. The problem is, "if you can't explain the underlying logic or theory of why something should enhance performance, you are more likely engaging in superstitious learning, and may be copying something that is irrelevant or even damaging."[217]

By understanding the logic that makes the practice work, you will be able to assess whether it is right for you and adapt it to your specific context.

To illustrate how you can dissect a best practice and evaluate its applicability and value to you, I will use Google's popular

---

217 Pfeffer and Sutton, *Hard Facts, Dangerous Half-Truths, and Total Nonsense*, 8.

Design Sprint methodology for solving big problems quickly. It is considered a best practice for many in the digital and product development space. In brief, the Design Sprint method is a detailed five-day process that begins on Monday with mapping out your problem and choosing where to focus. On Tuesday, you sketch out a variety of solutions to this problem. Wednesday is decision-making, when you pick the solution and convert it into a testable hypothesis. On Thursday and Friday, you develop a prototype and test it with real customers.[218]

Below is a basic framework for identifying "how a system works at all."[219]

Identify the Basic Mechanisms That Produce the Desired Results

In other words, define the elements of the practice that make it work. The underlying *mechanisms* that make design sprints work are:

- a compressed time frame that creates urgency for decisions that usually take months, if not years,
- quick feedback that surfaces problems early in the process, and
- customer engagement that prevents insular thinking and biases.

Identify the Features of the "Enabling Environment"

What needs to be true about your organization, customers, or competitive environment for the practice to work? In other words,

218   Jake Knapp, John Zeratsky, and Braden Kowitz, *Sprint: How to Solve Big Problems and Test New Ideas in Just Five Days* (New York: Simon and Schuster, 2016), 16.

219   Eugene Bardach, "Presidential Address—The Extrapolation Problem: How Can We Learn from the Experience of Others?," *Journal of Policy Analysis and Management* 23, no. 2 (March 2004): 209–211, https://doi.org/10.1002/pam.20000.

what does success of the practice depend upon? Success of the Design Sprint method depends upon:

- the willingness of decision-makers to deliberate quickly,
- the skill and ability to quickly create an adequate prototype that will generate useful customer feedback, and
- the ability to recruit representative customers to provide feedback.

If these conditions cannot be met, the viability and reliability of the Design Sprint method are compromised. Which brings us to...

Identify the Inherent Vulnerabilities of the Practice

The downsides of a practice could stem from the skills and resources required, organizational culture, or stakeholder buy-in. The vulnerabilities of the Design Sprint method include:

- The accelerated timeline may be inappropriate for complex, technical, or risky solutions.
- The possibility that decision-makers may not buy into the method and the results may not go anywhere.
- The level of skill needed to produce a good prototype is beyond your grasp and you cannot rely on customer feedback.

These vulnerabilities show how a method can be successful in one organization, and not another. They serve as a basis for you to evaluate the potential of a practice in your organization.

By sketching out how a practice works, you can test the veracity of its logic and most importantly understand how it does or doesn't apply to your specific context. You can reduce the inherent uncertainty of applying a new practice.

CHAPTER SUMMARY

- "Best practices" can become a dogma that keeps us from trying something new and critically evaluating the effectiveness of what we are doing or searching for something better.

- Best practices begin as local knowledge about what works in one place, which becomes a universal standard for what generally works the best.

- Best practices satisfy our need to feel and appear competent, increase the ease of our own decision-making, bolster our confidence, and allow us to learn from the experience of others, which is helpful in ambiguous situations.

- When best practices are thoroughly tested and adapted to the specifics of a situation, they can improve the practice of an entire sector.

- The dangers of best practices are the result of the confidence we place in them, which can blind us to their weaknesses and keep us from looking for better alternatives. When outworn practices are held by an entire sector (e.g., adherence to "balanced literacy" to teach reading), the whole sector suffers.

- The downsides of best practices can be mitigated by replacing the term "best practices" with "best for us now." This slight turn of phrase captures the idea that something that works for you may not work for another, and something that works now may not work later.

- Generally speaking, one should be skeptical and curious about the "great" advice of others. Ask about the evidence for and assumptions underlying the advice of others. Don't assume it will apply to the specifics of your situation. Rather, understand in detail how the practice works and the conditions needed for it to work.

CASE IN POINT: RESISTANCE OF LEADERSHIP DOGMA

HALF-TRUTHS AND FALLACIES OF
LEADERSHIP BEST PRACTICES

Leadership has become a central focus, and one could say fascination, of organizations and our culture more broadly. Since the 1970s, attention and respect shifted from the practice of *management* to *leadership*. The *leader* is considered "something of a swashbuckling hero" while the manager is a "bureaucratic bore." The leader is an "innovator" and an "original" who inspires trust, while the manager is an "administrator," just a "copy" who relies on systems of control.[220]

As our culture became more "leadership-centric," a $150 billion leadership industry was more than happy to develop current and potential leaders with professional development and training, coaching, and higher education. Despite this gigantic investment, several leadership researchers argue that the results of leadership have never been worse. "Humankind is suffering from a crisis of confidence in those who are charged with leading wisely and well."[221] In fact, by many accounts, the workplace is "dire with disengaged, disaffected, dissatisfied employees everywhere."[222] Heartbreaking and hilarious at the same time, one study showed that 35 percent of responding workers report they would forgo a substantial raise to see their boss fired.[223]

This clear-eyed and sharp-tongued group of leadership researchers is calling out the failures of this industry to produce quality leadership. They are calling out the misleading half-truths and fallacies that are commanding high prices while producing miserable results. They call our attention to popular leadership maxims that conceal dangerous vulnerabilities.

---

220 Barbara Kellerman, *The End of Leadership* (New York: Harper Business, 2012), 31.

221 Kellerman, *The End of Leadership*, 31.

222 Pfeffer, *Leadership BS*, 10.

223 Pfeffer, *Leadership BS*, 13.

Below are five misguided "best practices" of leadership that they debunk.

Fallacy #1: Leaders Are Responsible for Corporate Performance, and Charismatic Leaders Are Transformational

In our culture and organizations, we often think of the CEO as the most important person in a company. The leader is credited and blamed for an organization's performance even if the forces that determine success and failure are beyond their control. This strong bias toward attributing the cause of events to prominent people—rather than complex social or economic dynamics—is known as "the fundamental attribution error."[224] Studies show that most of an organization's performance is caused by larger forces such as industry effects and year-over-year economic changes. We don't recognize the real constraints on CEO action and appreciate the role followers play in supporting, informing, and shaping their organizations.

Leadership scholar, Rakesh Khurana, details the rise and continued popularity of the charismatic superstar CEO, such as Lee Iacocca and Steve Jobs. Different from the company men of yore who rose through the ranks, the charismatic CEO has a magical quality with the "power to perform miracles—to bring a dying company back to life...or to vanquish much larger more powerful foes." He is an outsider, "someone who could shake things up and put an end to business as usual." As one director said of the appointment of an outsider CEO, "He is not beholden to anyone... You turn to the outsider and then you can watch the blood spray. You don't see many examples of internal candidates getting to the top of the system and then laying waste to the existing culture." Khurana describes the common thread of the outsider CEO: destabilization and full surrender from all involved.[225] Though some organizations can destabilize and become more vibrant, doing so carries great risk for any organization that tries it—many fail.

---

224 Rakesh Khurana, "The Curse of the Superstar CEO," *Harvard Business Review* 80, no. 9 (September 2002): 62, https://hbr.org/2002/09/the-curse-of-the-superstar-ceo.

225 Khurana, "The Curse of the Superstar CEO," 62–66.

Fallacy #2: A Leader's Vision and Strategy Can Be Removed from Implementation and Operations

Management scholar Henry Mintzberg is an outspoken critic of some taken-for-granted leadership practices that he argues are damaging companies and their world around them. He argues that teaching leadership through case studies—many times removed from the realities they represent—reinforces the misguided notion that strategy can be distanced from operations and hands-on implementation. Mintzberg argues this approach diminishes the role and power of people doing the work in organizations who know how things can be done better, which is a springboard for strategy.[226] Moreover, he argues that this top-down leadership style amplifies the destructive disconnect between many leaders and their organizations, expressing itself through lavish executive compensation and business strategies that incentivize short-term profits over longer-term productivity.

Fallacy #3: Feel Good Leadership Is Effective Leadership

Management researcher Jeffery Pfeffer argues that the preponderance of feel-good content and advice generated by the leadership industry belies the reality of the working world. Charismatic leaders say things they don't do—even if they believe what they say—and offer their followers uplifting myths and fables that are often blatantly untrue. We like to believe these stories as they speak to the workplace that we want to see, yet rarely exists. As reality sets in, the inspiration conjured by the motivational speaker quickly dissipates into disappointment and cynicism. It certainly does not create real change. Rather it leaves its listeners unprepared for the political realities of their organization.[227]

One of the most dedicated and fiercest critics of the leadership industry is Barbara Kellerman, a scholar of leadership, who describes the leadership teachings as "ceaselessly, exhaustingly sunny." The leadership teachings are exclusively focused

---

226 Drew Hansen, "Why MBA Programs Don't Produce Leaders," *Forbes*, October 4, 2011, https://www.forbes.com/sites/drewhansen/2011/10/04/why-mba-business-school-not-leaders/?sh=35f768d2cf8d.

227 Pfeffer, *Leadership BS*.

on the individual leader—not their followers or their broader organization—but "these single individuals, these leaders or would-be leaders...free-floating agents fixated largely if not entirely on themselves: on enhancing their experience and expertise on developing their skill set and on expanding their self-awareness, self-development, self-improvement, and...self-importance." With simple and quickly taught lessons that focus solely on you—the most important person—the leadership industry has devolved into feel-good narcissism, where it will likely stay. People are willing to invest significant money in their potential as a leader, seeing themselves as a person who is "separate from and, and possibly even superior to, everyone else."[228] The problem is organizations work because many people work together to build and maintain a functioning system.

Fallacy #4: MBAs Are Good Leaders, Harvard MBAs Are Even Better

Henry Mintzberg analyzed the impact that having an MBA has on CEO performance. He analyzed nineteen Harvard CEOs who "had made it to the top" and showed that a majority, ten, "seemed clearly to have failed, meaning that their company went bankrupt, they were forced out of the CEO chair, a major merger backfired, and so on." He found the performance of another four to be questionable. Only five out of nineteen Harvard MBAs did an adequate job.

After Mintzberg published these findings in Forbes, he wrote a book on the subject and analyzed 444 CEOs. His research found that companies headed by MBAs declined more quickly; "the MBA degree is associated with expedients to achieve growth via acquisitions...[which showed] up in the form of reduced cash flows and inferior return on assets." Even as MBA-led companies underperformed, compensation of the MBA CEOs increased, indeed about 15 percent faster than the others. Apparently, they had learned how to play the "self-serving" game."[229]

---

228 Barbara Kellerman, *Professionalizing Leadership* (New York: Oxford University Press, 2018), 121–124.

229 Henry Mintzberg, "MBAs as CEOs: Some Troubling Evidence," *Henry Mintzberg* (blog), February 22, 2017, https://mintzberg.org/blog/mbas-as-ceos.

Fallacy #5: Change or Die

We often hear the urgent maxim "Change or Die." Jeffery Pfeffer warns would-be change agents of the real perils and sobering failure rates: 30–60 percent of new products fail to realize profits; downsizing among a large sample of S&P 500 firms showed that layoffs did not realize a return on assets and it could take eighteen months to realize any costs savings; total quality improvements can have a negative effect on innovation; Enterprise Resource Planning (ERP) projects can take twice as long, cost twice as much, and have a 30 percent cancel rate before completion.[230] And yet, transformational change remains the executive's siren song.

---

230 Pfeffer and Sutton, *Hard Facts*, 162–164.

CASE IN POINT: RESISTANCE OF EDUCATIONAL DOGMA

THE SPREAD OF A PHILOSOPHY AND
THE RISE OF ILLITERACY

Since the early 2000s, "balanced literacy" was considered the best way to teach children how to read. In contrast to phonics, which teaches students how to sound out letter sequences, balanced literacy "focuses more on stories, context, and illustrations. It's learning to read a word by considering the meaning of the story and what word might fit into the themes and the images on the page."[231]

The balanced literacy curriculum was created by Lucy Calkins, a famous and charismatic education professor at Columbia University. Beginning in the late 1970s, Professor Lucy Calkins championed the philosophy of "child-driven learning" and developed a pioneering curriculum for writing that emphasized writers finding their voice to spark an interest in writing, rather than the traditional focus on grammar, spelling, and penmanship. Calkins was also widely known and beloved for her respect and support for teachers.[232]

Calkins expanded her child-driven approach to reading. Calkins' balanced literacy curriculum was "based on a vision of children as natural readers" who did not require sounding out words to understand them.[233] For over twenty years, Calkins' balanced literacy was wildly popular and profitable as it became the prominent curriculum for teaching reading. Despite little research to support its effectiveness, more than 15,000 elementary schools—including New York

---

231 Michael Barbaro, "The Fight Over Phonics: Why American Schools Are Changing How Reading Is Taught," June 6, 2023, in *The Daily*, produced by Mooj Zadie, Will Reid, Rikki Novetsky, and Clare Toeniskoetter, podcast, https://www.nytimes.com/2023/06/06/podcasts/the-daily/reading-school-phonics.html.

232 Dana Goldstein, "Lucy Calkins Retreats on Phonics in Fight Over Reading Curriculum," *New York Times*, May 22, 2022, https://www.nytimes.com/2022/05/22/us/reading-teaching-curriculum-phonics.html.

233 Barbaro, "The Fight Over Phonics."

City and some of the nation's largest school systems—used a balanced literacy curriculum.[234]

Yet, as early as the 1990s, neuroscience was demonstrating, through the help of MRI machines, that reading is a "profoundly auditory" activity that happens through an auditory translation in the brain, which would be supported and instructed by phonics. Essentially, "the brain links three components together: awareness of how a word sounds when spoken, its meaning, and its spelling."[235] In short, the science showed that phonics would support how we naturally learn to read.

Though a wealth of scientific evidence supporting phonics existed for decades, it took years of parent advocacy, hard-hitting journalism, and dismal literacy performance across the nation for teachers and school districts to change reading curriculum and include phonics.

Some have described literacy as a national crisis. By 2020, only 49 percent of third graders across the country are proficient in reading. Eighty percent of Chicago school children do not read at grade level. Many have called for Lucy Calkins to apologize for having failed the nation's schoolchildren in their most foundational educational task.[236]

Now that the scientific and performance results are clear, many are struggling to make sense of how they and the "balanced literacy" approach could have gone so wrong. One reporter who covered this issue for years describes the reckoning of teachers:

---

234 Goldstein, "Lucy Calkins Retreats on Phonics."

235 Rick Harrison, "How Teaching Kids to Read Went So Wrong: Emily Hanford Visits ISPS to Discuss the Science and Politics of Reading Instruction," Yale University Institute for Social and Policy Studies, May 12, 2023, https://isps.yale.edu/news/blog/2023/05/how-teaching-kids-to-read-went-so-wrong-emily-hanford-visits-isps-to-discuss-the.

236 Barbaro, "The Fight Over Phonics."

They had really enjoyed going to those summer training programs with Lucy Calkins. They admired her. They loved reading her books. And for teachers who just had that feeling maybe that they weren't reaching all the kids that they wanted to reach, who tried their best for years—to find out that all this time, there was powerful, persuasive evidence that other methods are more effective—it was devastating emotionally, psychologically devastating for many educators.[237]

The story of Lucy Calkins, "balanced literacy" and "child-centered learning" is that of a "best practice" that led a nation of educators astray. It is a powerful example of how the desire to believe in something can override the nagging sense that something isn't working. It shows how what is good for the practitioner can come at the expense of the practiced upon. It shows how easy it is to "bask in the reflected glory" of charismatic individuals and look away from the evidence that the practice simply doesn't work.

237 Barbaro, "The Fight Over Phonics."

Groupthink

MUTUALLY ASSURED DELUSIONS

"The whole animal kingdom demonstrates the fundamental law that species whose members are incapable of facing the battle for self-preservation, gather new strength through herd life."

—ALFRED ADLER, 1927

You are likely to encounter groupthink when the decisions are tough, there is a lot at stake, and you are working with a tight-knit group. Perhaps you are selling your initiative to a group of complacent executives who brush off the urgency that you see. Perhaps you are trying to build buy-in with another department to adopt a new practice or technology, and they seem strangely dead set against you.

Here are a few examples of groupthink at play:

- A new marketing director advocates for a new product. At every turn, he is met with staunch resistance from the team responsible for the product development. They are not going to be told what to do, especially by an outsider. The ambitious newcomer eventually leaves the organization, saying that he "felt like an organ rejected by its host."

- "There is nothing wrong with our offerings" was a constant refrain from this museum. The executive team was unanimous in its belief that there was no need to change the exhibits or the customer experience or grow its customer base. All they needed to do was raise prices. They believed attendance declines were evitable. The result is fewer people attending, slimmer margins, no investments in the facility, and general stagnation.

- One-on-one, Jack was a completely collegial and collaborative soul. However, in the presence of his boss and the executive team, he literally became a different person. The pressure to conform to the group's adversarial management style resulted in Jack becoming sharply critical and uncollaborative with people outside his team. His transformation is like Jekyll and Hyde.

The social dynamics of a group strongly influence individual behaviors. The pressure to conform and support the majority impacts decision-making. Groupthink can create blinders that keep a group from recognizing the need to change. Groupthink makes it uncomfortable to be the lone advocate of an idea.

THE NATURE OF GROUPTHINK

Major change requires vigilant decision-making—thinking through the risks, opportunities, and alternatives. It can be cognitively difficult and emotionally wrenching. Change may require people to let go of something and someone they care deeply about. It may require leaving an outworn decision behind. If the decision is challenging and stressful, individuals and groups tend to wish the situation away, talk themselves out of urgency, and seek comfort in the solidarity of others.

THE DRIVE FOR UNANIMITY

Yale psychologist Irving Janis studied groups in all varieties of settings ranging from high-level policymakers and executives in organizations to groups trying to quit smoking. Janis observed a strong need for group members to concur with one another in amicable solidarity.

In the 1970s, Janis introduced the world to the phenomenon of groupthink. He defines it as *"a mode of thinking that people engage in when they are deeply involved in a cohesive in-group whose members, striving for unanimity, override their motivation to realistically evaluate alternative courses of action."*[238] The result can be poorly made and regretful decisions.

Janis identified eight symptoms of groupthink:[239]

- **Illusion of Invulnerability.** Members of the group ignore obvious danger, are overly optimistic, and are willing to take extraordinary risks.

- **Collective Rationalization.** Members of the group develop rationalizations to explain away any warning that is contrary to the group's thinking.

- **Illusion of Morality.** Members of the group believe their decisions are morally correct and ignore any ethical consequences of their decisions.

- **Excessive Stereotyping.** Members of the group construct negative stereotypes of rivals outside the group.

- **Pressure for Conformity.** Members of the group apply pressure to anyone in the group who expresses any doubt about the group's illusions, stereotypes, decisions, or rationales.

- **Self-Censorship.** Members of the group withhold dissenting

---

238   Irving L. Janis, *Victims of Groupthink: Psychological Studies of Foreign-Policy Decisions and Fiascoes* (Boston: Houghton Mifflin, 1972), 9.

239   Janis, *Victims of Groupthink*, 105–106.

views, keep silent about their misgivings, and minimize the importance of their doubts.

- **Illusion of Unanimity.** Members of the group falsely perceive that everyone agrees with the group's decision; silence is seen as consent.
- **Self-appointed Mindguards.** Some members of the group appoint themselves to the role of group protector from adverse information that might threaten group complacency.

Groupthink can manifest in a collective state of over-optimism or denial. Hopeful beliefs are held intact as challenging evidence and voices are either ignored, forgotten, or dismissed.

As a result of groupthink, the group quickly closes ranks around a decision. They can compromise with each other and move toward a central position or adopt the position of the majority or those in power.

THE BREEDING GROUNDS OF GROUPTHINK

Groupthink is most likely to occur when group cohesion is high, the group is insulated from outsiders, and it lacks a methodical approach to decisions. Under these conditions, there may be "strong pressures toward uniformity" that encourage group members "to avoid raising controversial issues, questioning weak arguments, or calling a halt to soft-headed thinking."[240] With a cohesive group, leadership can bend the group's thinking by expressing the slightest preference.

Research shows that some situations and features of our organizations create pressure to conform and trigger groupthink.

---

240 Irving L. Janis and Leon Mann, *Decision Making: A Psychological Analysis of Conflict, Choice, and Commitment* (New York: Free Press, 1977), 130.

Consensus-based group decision-making is more conducive to groupthink. When all members of the group must agree to a decision, like a jury, pressures to conform will be higher as unanimity is required for the group to complete the task of making a decision and achieve its goals.

Situations with high stress, high risk, high reward, and low hope can trigger groupthink. Groupthink can function as a coping mechanism for groups that have much to lose and much to gain. If there is little hope in the search for alternatives, group members assuage each other's fear with reassurance that they are doing the right thing. When a group with low confidence feels high stress, they will reassure one another to boost their esteem. New and complex technologies that have a profitable upside with a low likelihood—but potentially disastrous—downside are prone to groupthink.

Lastly, **when an uncertain leader is surrounded by ignorant advisors** who cannot provide clarifying information, the group will rely on the comfort of consensus.

In general, the dislike of anxiety and the need for hope creates a "universal unwillingness to listen" and a contagion of ignorance.[241]

CAUSES OF GROUPTHINK

The potential for groupthink to show up in our personal and professional lives is great, because generally speaking, we would rather concur than argue. The underlying causes of groupthink make us human; we need to belong.

---

241 Roland Bénabou, "Groupthink: Collective Delusions in Organizations and Markets," *The Review of Economic Studies* 80, no. 2 (April 2013): 447, 454, https://doi.org/10.1093/restud/rds030.

OUR NEED TO BELONG IS A FUNDAMENTAL HUMAN MOTIVATION

We rely on others to satisfy our deepest needs, and we have a strong desire to belong in groups. Psychologists demonstrate that the need to belong is a fundamental human motivation. This research shows that:

- **We form bonds with others very easily** and "form favorable views with whomever [we] spend time with."[242] We even form bonds with people we previously disliked. In short, we readily make friends and align with groups.

- **We are very reluctant to break bonds.** We labor to preserve our relationships and are deeply distressed when they end. Part of our anxiety about death is based on our fear of loneliness. Leaving others behind for new jobs and relocations is painful. Even temporary groups (e.g., training cohorts, therapy groups) try to maintain bonds as their experience ends.[243]

- **Belonging provides significant emotional rewards.** Generally speaking, "happiness in life is strongly correlated with having some close, personal relationships."[244] Research suggests that the type of relationship doesn't make much difference.

- **We automatically mimic people to gain acceptance.** Without awareness, we mimic the facial expressions, mannerisms, cadence of speech, accents, postures, and even the moods of others to build rapport.[245] The slightest perception of anoth-

---

242 Baumeister and Leary, "The Need to Belong," 501–502.

243 Baumeister and Leary, "The Need to Belong," 502, 520.

244 Baumeister and Leary, "The Need to Belong," 506.

245 Tanya L. Chartrand and Jessica L. Lakin, "The Antecedents and Consequences of Human Behavioral Mimicry," *Annual Review of Psychology* 64, no. 1 (September 2012): 300, https://doi.org/10.1146/annurev-psych-113011-143754.

er's behavior will influence our own.[246] Decades of research show that mimicry builds bonds, increases group cohesion, and acts as a "social glue."[247]

- **Exclusion and breaking bonds are incredibly painful.** The lack of relationships, the dissolution of bonds, and the feelings of exclusion are incredibly painful and distressing. In fact, social exclusion creates a feeling of "being isolated and hopeless in a potentially hostile world."[248]

BELONGING TO A GROUP IS HELPFUL

Humans have always sought the protection of groups. "When other people are in groups, it is vital to belong to a group oneself."[249]

For a group to forward a collective goal, the group needs to agree amongst itself. If everyone has a different opinion, a group will accomplish very little. Effective collaboration and collective action rely upon the concurrence of a group.[250]

Other people are important sources of knowledge and information. Disagreement produces tension that we need to resolve by convincing others of our position or moving toward theirs. Instinctively we know that "the average of the opinions of any two people is more likely to be correct than the opinion of either individual."[251]

---

246 Chartrand and Bargh, "The Chameleon Effect," 906.

247 Jessica Lakin et al., "The Chameleon Effect as Social Glue: Evidence for the Evolutionary Significance of Nonconscious Mimicry," *Journal of Nonverbal Behavior* 27, no. 3 (2003): 150, https://doi.org/10.1023/A:1025389814290.

248 Baumeister and Leary, "The Need to Belong," 506.

249 Baumeister and Leary, "The Need to Belong," 499.

250 Lee Ross and Richard E. Nisbett, *The Person and the Situation: Perspectives of Social Psychology* (London: Pinter & Martin, 2011), 45.

251 Ross and Nisbett, *The Person and the Situation*, 44–45.

WE ARE SOCIALIZED INTO GROUPS
AND ADOPT THEIR NORMS

When we enter an organization, get promoted, or assume a new job, we are socialized into our role and the culture that surrounds it. During these moments of transition, when we are most anxious, we adopt the norms of the group and learn the "long-standing 'rules of thumb'…matter-of-fact prejudices, models of social etiquette and demeanor, certain customs and rituals suggestive of how members are to relate to colleagues, subordinates superiors, and outsiders."[252]

A consequence of our socialization is that group members are likely to share a "conventional wisdom" that will guide and narrow their collective perspectives. Likewise, group members are not to challenge their common and foundational assumptions.

WE NEED OTHERS TO COPE WITH LIFE AND STRESS

Research shows that "having other people available for support and assistance can enhance coping and provide a buffer against stress." Simply belonging to a group can reduce stress. Major decisions often require choosing between competing or impossible demands. The agreement of a group provides "mutual support" that helps "all group members to cope with the stresses of decision-making" and "bolster the decision maker's self-esteem."[253]

252 John Eastin Van Maanen and Edgar Henry Schein, "Toward a Theory of Organizational Socialization" (working paper, Massachusetts Institute of Technology, 1979): 1, https://dspace.mit.edu/bitstream/handle/1721.1/1934/?sequence=1.

253 Janis, *Victims of Groupthink*, 202.

THE VALUE OF GROUPTHINK

In some respects, groupthink is, in its subtle forms, indistinguishable from a team that supports one another. Thus, groupthink has benefits for an organization that are akin to effective collective action.

TIGHT-KNIT AND UNIFIED GROUPS ARE FORMIDABLE

Tight-knit groups make each other feel confident that they are making the right decision. This kind of self-esteem can be powerful in organizations. It can lead to bold and coordinated action.

GROUPS THAT CONVERGE AROUND DECISIONS CAN MOVE FORWARD

A tight-knit group that agrees with each other has the advantage of getting things done. In contrast, groups plagued by bickering, infighting, and indecision are inefficient and often ineffective. Being of like mind allows a group to move forward efficiently.

SUPPORTIVE GROUPS CAN HELP EACH OTHER CHANGE

Being in a group that encourages each other can help individuals change.[254] The effectiveness of group therapy depends on "engendering a sense of belongingness" that provides group members with a sense of safety and acceptance that facilitates change.

---

254 Baumeister and Leary, "The Need to Belong," 520.

THE DANGERS OF GROUPTHINK

If your change effort requires adoption from a tight-knit group (especially one wary of "outsiders") with a vested interest in the status quo, the possibility of encountering ironclad and collective resistance is high.

Groupthink can wreak havoc on the decision-making processes and lead to potentially regrettable decisions.

GROUPTHINK RESULTS IN DECISIONS THAT LACK VIGILANCE

Highly cohesive and unanimous groups suffer from insular and biased processes and perspectives. They limit consideration of alternatives and do not re-examine their thinking or identify potential obstacles.

GROUPTHINK RESULTS IN MUTUALLY ASSURED DELUSIONS

Consensus provides a group with the reassurance that everyone is right. In order to maintain their confidence, the group may suppress and deny bad news through:

- *Over-optimism* that occurs when the group "maintains hopeful beliefs by discounting, ignoring, or forgetting...data."[255] Over-optimism nullifies bad news.
- *Information aversion* that occurs when the group avoids relevant information to avoid discovering a bad outcome.[256]

For instance, people avoid checkups and refuse to take medical tests because they are afraid of what they might learn. Mutual

---

255 Bénabou, "Groupthink," 430.

256 Bénabou, "Groupthink," 432.

fund managers seek more information about their portfolios when the market is up versus down. People will even pay money to avoid learning their exact IQ.[257]

Put simply, people like hope and dislike anxiety. When a group faces a hard truth, it generates a "universal unwillingness to listen." In organizations, the leader's delusions spread across the organization, resulting in "mutually assured delusions."[258]

WE AGREE WITH MAJORITIES AND
DO NOT CHALLENGE THEM

A wealth of research demonstrates that we feel strong pressure to join majorities. People who may not agree with the majority "start with the assumption that the majority is correct, even when it is not, and that they themselves are in error. By contrast, they assume that the differing minority is incorrect, and in fact, manifest outright derision toward them. They fear the disapproval that results from maintaining or joining a minority view. A study of 225 juries showed that the majority position on the initial ballot was the final verdict in 85 percent of cases.[259]

The flock to the majority creates convergent thought processes that seek to justify the majority opinion rather than challenge it with disconfirming evidence. As a majority solidifies its position, underlying assumptions are not challenged, and thinking is shallow and unexamined. Thinking becomes convergent. Conversely, when minority viewpoints are confidently and consistently voiced,

---

257   Bénabou, "Groupthink," 431–432.

258   Bénabou, "Groupthink," 430, 447.

259   Charlan Jeanne Nemeth, "Differential Contributions of Majority and Minority Influence," *Psychological Review* 93, no. 1 (1986): 23, 25, https://doi.org/10.1037/0033-295X.93.1.23.

they inspire deep examination of assumptions and creative exploration of ideas. Minority viewpoints spark divergent thinking.

GROUPTHINK CAN LEAD TO POOR IF NOT DISASTROUS DECISIONS

Irving Janis documented major fiascos resulting in insular thinking, the drive to concur, defensive avoidance of warnings, and an overall soft-headed approach to weighty matters. He detailed wishful thinking that prolonged the Vietnam War and the misjudgments that led up to Pearl Harbor.[260] In both cases, leaders and their advisors ignored warnings and failed to take appropriate action.

The impact of groupthink can have huge consequences. Groupthink can result in:

- **Avoidable errors** that can be caught with procedural rigor
- **Over-optimism** that results in poor risk-taking
- **Inaction** in the face of warnings that the group minimizes or ignores

Major change disrupts the status quo and those who have a vested interest in maintaining it. You will need to ensure that group deliberations are rigorous and do not revert to complacency.

WHAT YOU CAN DO

Humans are deeply inclined to seek solidarity, reassurance, and approval. We physically imitate our way into acceptance and hand over our independence of thought in order to align with others.

---

260 Janis and Mann, *Decision Making.*

Given this, we should not expect ourselves or our colleagues to be immune from groupthink.

How can we maintain group cohesion—like-mindedness, shared values, and mutual respect—and avoid concurrence-seeking? How can we maintain group momentum without pursuing the wrong course of action?

The solutions below can strengthen the norms and mindsets of groups so they can avoid clinging to outworn decisions and evaluate the possibilities of change.

LEVERAGE A GROUP TO SUPPORT CHANGE

You can form a new group or leverage an existing one to foster support for your change. An amicable group provides one another with coping mechanisms needed to weather disruptive change. They provide each other with confidence and reassurance. They help each other rebound from setbacks. You should tap into this power.

You can also use a group to sway others who may be riding the fence. Also, if the majority of the group favors the change effort, the odds are that the rest of the group will follow.

Your goal is to harness the benefits of comradery while fostering open-mindedness and critical thinking.

DISSENT WHEN YOU BELIEVE THE MAJORITY IS INCORRECT

Generally, we are reluctant to voice an opinion at odds with the majority for fear of rejection and ridicule. Consequently, many viewpoints are unexpressed and solutions unexplored.[261]

Research demonstrates that dissent improves the quality of

---

261 Nemeth, "Differential Contributions of Majority and Minority Influence," 29.

GROUPTHINK · 189

thinking and decision-making processes. **The presence of only one dissenter reduces the conformity of a group** as "any break in the unanimity of the majority, even by error, may signal the appropriateness of independent judgment," which can lead to original thinking.[262] While the convergent thinking of a majority "constrains and focuses attention," a divergent view of a minority can "stimulate reappraisal of the situation," which helps the group identify better solutions.[263]

Below are simple strategies for a dissenter to influence the majority opinion.

1. **Be consistent in your viewpoint.** Being consistent is more effective than being extreme.
2. **Be confident.** Little tricks like sitting at the head of the table can sway opinion.[264] How could someone so confident be wrong?
3. **Be authentic.** Authentic dissent provokes unbiased and independent thinking.[265] Note: the "devil's advocate" technique for challenging arguments is not an authentic form of dissent. Rather it's a role-playing technique that is not as persuasive as a genuine opinion. It can even backfire and cause the group to double down on their argument and falsely believe they are being diligent.

---

262 Charlan Jeanne Nemeth and Barry M. Staw, "The Tradeoffs of Social Control and Innovation in Groups and Organizations," in *Advances in Experimental Social Psychology* Vol. 22, edited by Leonard Berkowitz (Cambridge, MA: Academic Press, 1989), 193.

263 Nemeth and Staw, "The Tradeoffs of Social Control and Innovation," 200.

264 Nemeth and Staw, "The Tradeoffs of Social Control and Innovation," 187.

265 Charlan Jeanne Nemeth et al., "Improving Decision Making by Means of Dissent," *Journal of Applied Social Psychology* 31, no. 1 (July 2006): 43, https://doi.org/10.1111/j.1559-1816.2001.tb02481.x.

CREATE GROUP NORMS THAT FOSTER DISSENT

You can proactively encourage group members to challenge their assumptions.

Explicitly invite the challenge. I've seen this done simply and effectively when a leader asks, "What are we missing here?" or, "Where is the weakness in this argument?" The same leader will sometimes say, "I get a little worried when we are all in agreement." Over time and with consistency, these prompts become group norms.

Articulate underlying assumptions by asking, "What needs to be true for this to be a good option?"[266] This simple question shifts a group's deliberations away from their common beliefs toward objectively verifiable conditions that can be tested in reality.

GENERATE ALTERNATIVES AND EVALUATE THEIR CONSEQUENCES

When we face difficult decisions, we often use simplified decision-making methods that rely on "a few rock-bottom principles" that reduce the complexity of our problem so that we can make intuitive judgments, a "crude form of satisficing."[267] When the group converges around a preferred option, other potentially superior options are not explored or considered. This lack of vigilance can lead to regret.

For Irving Janis, the goal is to produce regret-proof decisions, which can only be achieved with rigorous consideration of alternatives from a variety of perspectives. To this end, you need a

---

266 A.G. Lafley and Roger L. Martin, *Playing to Win: How Strategy Really Works* (Brighton, MA: Harvard Business Press, 2013), 186.

267 Janis and Mann, *Decision Making*, 39.

decision-making process and framework to ensure that important decisions have fulsome options.

Janis developed a decision-making framework (slightly modified version below).

ADAPTION OF JANIS'S FRAMEWORK

The Problem/Solution:			The Decision:	
	Option A	Option B	Option C	Option D
Consequences to Self	+	+	+	+
	–	–	–	–
Consequences to most Impacted Person(s)	+	+	+	+
	–	–	–	–
Consequences to Others	+	+	+	+
	–	–	–	–
How would you feel if you made this choice?				
What would people important to me think if I made this choice?				
What needs to be true for this to be a good decision?				

The framework visually demonstrates the variety of alternatives for the decision as well as the depth of consideration. For each alternative, it is important to consider their consequences from (1) a tangible (more rational) and intangible (more emotional and moral) perspective; and (2) from the perspective of impacted parties, such as the decision maker(s), key stakeholders, or the organization itself.

Most importantly, the process should probe the consequences

deeply and emotionally to break through defensive rationalizations. Janis stressed that difficult and emotionally fraught decisions should not be rushed. **The process should allow decision-makers to emotionally process their decisions so they will be able to stand by them and accept the consequences without regret.**

Additional methods for generating more alternatives and improving group deliberations:

- **Splinter the group into multiple working groups to simultaneously explore alternatives.** This will ensure a greater variety of options are generated and prevent premature consensus. I often begin brainstorming sessions with an exercise known as "alone together." Before groups even form, each individual has to write down their ideas for alternatives to the problem.
- **Convene a session to develop the contingencies for the working decision.** This will help the group consider the preferred decision more deeply and possibly identify new information that would affect the decision before it's final.

CONFRONT RATIONALIZATIONS AND COMPLACENCY

Sometimes groups persist with "outworn decisions" because they put up a "defensive facade that makes [them] impervious to rational appeals." Familiar rationalizations subdue doubt and dull vigilance. You may need to confront such rationalizations with emotionally provocative tactics, such as:

- **Arousing fear and exaggerating risks.** Groups that feel invulnerable tend to minimize risks and ignore warnings. You can provoke deeper and more emotional thinking about the consequences of a decision. Ask each group to imagine the most dire consequences of their decision. Have them reflect on this alone and then share. Then, ask the group to note new thoughts about the decision and alternatives that come to mind.[268]

- **Engage group members in role-playing.** Complacent groups may not consider the perspective of others in their decision-making. There are a couple of approaches to consider. Ask group members to take the opposing perspective and prepare a brief speech arguing against your decision. Janis observed a prison administrator change his mind about installing TVs in the prison after he role-played a convict advocating for televisions. Another approach involves creating a headline that announces your decision. Ask group members to imagine how an impacted stakeholder would respond to reading the headline.

Note: When arousing emotions to make decisions, look for the "optimal level of fear arousal" that evokes emotions, without leading to overwhelm or defensiveness.

Role-playing and giving voice to someone else's perspective can be an intuitive and effective way of broadening one's perspective.[269]

AVOID INSULAR THINKING

An insular group is less likely to challenge itself, question its assumptions, or search for alternatives. To break through insular thinking:

- **Invite knowledgeable and respected outsiders** to meetings to challenge the thinking of core group members.[270] The out-

---

268 Janis, *Victims of Groupthink*, 361.

269 Janis, *Victims of Groupthink*, 362.

270 Janis, *Victims of Groupthink*, 214.

sider should be brought in before consensus is reached to avoid bolstering the decision. The role of the interloper is to listen carefully, grasp ideas quickly, and look for new alternatives, "hidden catches," unforeseen consequences, and sensitivities. The goal is not to resolve the guest's considerations. Rather, your goal is to stimulate and capture new inputs to the decision-making process.

- **Encourage group members to consult trusted advisors.** Ideally, this is done throughout the process at key junctures—when alternatives are identified, consequences are enumerated, and the preliminary decision made. By regularly checking in with outsiders, group members will hear additional perspectives that challenge rationalizations or present new alternatives.[271]

AVOID PREMATURE DECISIONS

A group might quickly close ranks and quickly converge around a decision. As a consequence, the preferred alternative may be seriously flawed, and a better choice is not even considered. To ward off premature closure:

- **Conduct a second-chance meeting.** After a preliminary decision is made, hold a *second-chance meeting*, in which group members express lingering doubts as vividly as possible. They can revisit any aspect of the decision. The *second-chance meeting* allows the group to make sure it understands the full implications of its decision.
- **Conduct a contingency meeting** that identifies the risks of the preliminary decision and develops contingency plans for them. The goal is to forecast the reactions of important stake-

---

271 Janis, *Victims of Groupthink*, 213.

holders or competitors and the consequences of potentially perilous decisions so that you can be prepared. Then, you develop preparations for major contingencies and identify warning signs that trigger each contingency. Contingencies help a group to articulate warnings in a way that cannot easily be dismissed and ignored.[272]

- **Make the decision, sober and drunk.** In 45 AD, Herodotus said of the Persians, "If an important decision is to be made, they [the Persians] discuss the question when they are drunk, and the following day…when they are sober. If they still approve it, it is adopted; if not, it is abandoned. Conversely, any decision they make when they are sober is reconsidered afterwards when they are drunk."[273] As the mind loosens with inebriation, lingering doubts or a different course of action may come to the surface.

CHAPTER SUMMARY

- Groupthink can create blinders that keep a group from recognizing the need to change. Moreover, the pressure to conform makes it uncomfortable to be the lone advocate of an idea.
- Groupthink occurs when the need to concur with one another and strive for solidarity is stronger than the need to realistically evaluate a situation or alternatives.
- There are eight symptoms of groupthink: (1) illusion of invulnerability, (2) collective rationalization, (3) illusion of morality, (4) excessive stereotyping, (5) pressure for conformity, (6) self-censorship, (7) illusion of unanimity, (8) self-appointed mindguards.

---

272 Janis, *Victims of Groupthink*, 217–218.

273 Herodotus, *The Histories* 1.133.

- Groupthink can result in over-optimism or denial. Hopeful beliefs are held intact as challenging evidence and voices are either ignored, forgotten, or dismissed.
- Groupthink is most likely to occur when group cohesion is high, the group is insulated from outsiders, and it lacks a methodical approach to decisions. It can also happen when decisions require consensus, stress and risks are high, and uncertain leaders are surrounded by ignorant advisors.
- Groupthink is caused by our need to belong to groups. Groups provide us with emotional satisfaction and help us cope. They provide us with information and are necessary to move forward with collective goals.
- The camaraderie and cohesion of groupthink have value. Tight-knit groups are confident, can make decisions readily, and can get things done. As group therapy shows, groups can help their members change.
- The dangers of groupthink are poor decision-making that lacks vigilance, an overly optimistic and deluded group that avoids challenging information, and a lack of dissension that can spark new thinking.
- You can harness the power of group cohesion—like-mindedness, shared values, and mutual respect—and avoid concurrence-seeking. Form a group or leverage an existing one to foster support for change. Remember, the group can help each other change. To avoid the pitfall, dissent and encourage dissent if the group is missing something or potentially wrong. You may need to explicitly invite a challenge: "What are we missing here?"
- Confront rationalizations that seem familiar and consult people outside the group.
- In decision-making, explore many alternatives and their implications from different perspectives. Avoid premature closure on decisions; fast decisions can lead to regret.

CASE IN POINT: RESISTANCE OF COLLECTIVE PRACTICES

GROUPTHINK AND THE NORMALIZATION OF CORPORATE CORRUPTION

The dynamics of groupthink that cause insular groups to be resistant to rational critique and make bad decisions also lead to corporate corruption. Specifically, the ability of a group to rationalize decisions, exert social pressures to conform, and quell dissent are the bedrocks of corporate corruption. These dynamics explain how people engaged in corruption fail to see their acts as unethical and actively perpetuate corruption.

We will briefly examine how corrupt actions spread and become norms within an organization that are passed on to generations of newcomers. We will explore how corruption is:

- Institutionalized through a slippery slope of decisions and actions
- Socialized through group norms and social cocoons
- Rationalized among members of a group

In closing, we will explore why corruption is resistant to change and why whistleblowing is such a brave action.

CASE IN POINT: CORRUPTION TAKES A VILLAGE

Corruption is institutionalized when an initial corrupt act creates a permissive environment that begets more corrupt acts. The slippery slope effect explains this moral loosening. *Slippery slope decision-making rationalizes current corrupt practices as defensible because they are similar to acceptable past practices.* The initial corrupt act becomes an organizational precedent. People simply assume that past decisions and actions were rational.[274] From here, small steps continue along a corrupt path. But, each step is so small that it does not appear entirely different from acceptable practices.[275] For example, what began as a one-time optimistic spin on an SEC filing became a pattern of intentional misrepresentations that covered up poor financial performance.[276]

Over time, repetition of unethical behavior numbs a person's moral sensitivity and one finds themselves "down a road that one would have not taken if the destination was clear at the outset."[277]

As the organization continues to realize the upsides of corrupt practices, they become embedded in the organization's structures, processes, budgets, and goals. Eventually, corruption becomes an automatic everyday practice that "takes more conscious effort to discontinue than to continue."[278]

---

274 Blake E. Ashforth and Vikas Anand, "The Normalization of Corruption in Organizations," in *Research in Organizational Behavior* Vol. 25, edited by Roderick M. Kramer and Barry M. Staw (Greenwich, CT: JAI Press, 2003), 8, https://doi.org/10.1016/S0191-3085(03)25001-2.

275 Ann E. Tenbrunsel and David M. Messick, "Ethical Fading: The Role of Self-Deception in Unethical Behavior," *Social Justice Research* 17, no. 2 (June 2004): 228, https://doi.org/10.1023/B:SORE.0000027411.35832.53.

276 Catherine M. Schrand and Sarah L. C. Zechman, "Executive Overconfidence and the Slippery Slope to Financial Misreporting," *Journal of Accounting and Economics* 53, nos. 1–2 (February–April 2012): 311, https://doi.org/10.1016/j.jacceco.2011.09.001.

277 Ashforth and Anand, "The Normalization of Corruption in Organizations," 29.

278 Ashforth and Anand, "The Normalization of Corruption in Organizations," 11.

Sometimes the organization comes to depend upon and even budget the yields of corruption. Examples abound. Wells Fargo established aggressive crossing-selling goals that resulted in the creation of 2 million accounts without customer authorization over a five-year period.[279] Three generations of comptrollers at Gulf Oil mindlessly carried out the practice of laundering corporate funds to politicians long after the instigating comptroller left.[280]

SOCIAL COCOONS FOSTER AND ENFORCE CORRUPTION

Research shows our perception of ethical behavior is influenced more by our peers than our own judgment. At the bottom, corporate criminals are "conformists" who are shaped by social influence.[281]

Corruption is incubated within social cocoons. Social cocoons are groups within a larger organization that have unique norms and solutions to the problems they face. Social cocoons are created as:

- Veteran employees model the expected and accepted behaviors for newcomers.
- Newcomers are encouraged to affiliate and bond with veterans.
- Corrupt acts are viewed and described in a positive light.
- Any misgivings that a newcomer has are attributed to their own naïveté or shortcomings.[282]

---

279 Brian Tayan, "The Wells Fargo Cross-Selling Scandal," Rock Center for Corporate Governance at Stanford University Closer Look Series: Topics Issues and Controversies in Corporate Governance No. CGRP-62 Version 2, Stanford University Graduate School of Business Research Paper No. 17-1, Stanford University, Stanford, CA, December 2016, revised January 2019, 4, https://papers.ssrn.com/sol3/papers.cfm?abstract_id=2879102.

280 Ashforth and Anand, "The Normalization of Corruption in Organizations," 8.

281 Ashforth and Anand, "The Normalization of Corruption in Organizations," 26.

282 Vikas Anand, Blake E. Ashfort, and Mahendra Joshi, "Business as Usual: The Acceptance and Perpetuation of Corruption in Organizations," *Academy of Management Perspectives* 18, no. 2 (May 2004): 45, https://doi.org/10.5465/ame.2004.13837437.

Group members compartmentalize life within the cocoon so that the cocoon's norms remain localized. When they re-enter life outside the cocoon, they are often ethical and law-abiding citizens.

Group members enforce compliance with corrupt group norms first through punishments, such as verbal harassment and sabotage, then through exclusion and rejection. This eventually leads the non-compliant to quit.[283]

Arthur Anderson created an insular social environment by offering newcomers exclusive opportunities to become partners. "'They all knew that their chances of making partner were slim... But there was that big fat brass ring at the end.' Thus...new recruits were unlikely to raise any sticky questions that could deprive them of their chance at the brass ring."[284]

CORRUPT GROUPS RATIONALIZE THEIR BEHAVIORS

Rationalizations help groups ethically bleach and normalize unacceptable behaviors.

Below are common strategies to rationalize corruption.

- **Euphemistic language** disguises unethical acts with abstract, neutral, and bureaucratic terms (e.g., illegal accounting practices are "aggressive" accounting practices).[285]
- **The denial of responsibility** allows people to believe that they had no other choice (e.g., "everybody does it" or "the boss made me do it").[286]

---

283 Ashforth and Anand, "The Normalization of Corruption in Organizations," 33.

284 Anand, Ashforth, and Joshi, "Business as Usual," 45.

285 Tenbrunsel and Messick, "Ethical Fading," 226–228.

286 Anand, Ashforth, and Joshi, "Business as Usual," 40.

- **The denial of an injury or a victim** allows people to believe that no one is harmed or transforms the victim into someone who deserves their fate (often cited when people steal from corporations or the IRS).[287]
- **Social weighting (e.g., "we are not so bad")** enables corrupt employees to "condemn the condemners" or compare themselves with others even worse.[288]
- **Appeal to higher loyalties** occurs when employees argue that unethical behavior is in service of a more important and higher goal (e.g., police officers perjure themselves out of loyalty to a colleague).[289]

Corrupt groups use rationalizations to assuage any concerns that what they are doing is wrong.

CORRUPT BEHAVIORS ARE RESISTANT TO CHANGE

All of the forces of groupthink are on display in corrupt organizations. Corporate corruption is created and maintained through groups who one small step at a time ethically stray and adopt norms that support corrupt behavior. They rationalize their behavior to each other, assuage any doubts, and bolster each other's confidence. They create their own insular world in which unethical behavior is acceptable, socialized, and enforced. Unethical behaviors become part of a daily routine that is divorced from moral decision-making.

Corruption is resistant to change, like any institutionalized practice that is adopted and enforced by a group with an incentive to justify itself. A brief examination of whistleblowing explains why. The threat or fear of retaliation "greatly reduce[s] the likelihood that an observer of wrongdoing will intend to blow the whistle."[290]

287 Anand, Ashforth, and Joshi, "Business as Usual," 41.

288 Anand, Ashforth, and Joshi, "Business as Usual," 42.

289 Anand, Ashforth, and Joshi, "Business as Usual," 42.

290 Jessica R. Mesmer-Magnus and Chockalingam Viswesvaran, "Whistleblowing in Organizations: An Examination of Correlates of Whistleblowing Intentions, Actions, and Retaliation." *Journal of Business Ethics* 62, no. 3 (December 2005): 290, https://doi.org/10.1007/s10551-005-0849-1.

In fact, retaliation is greatest when the wrong-doing is most frequent and severe. In these organizations, "it is more likely that a cultural norm actively operates to continue and support the transgressions" and the whistleblower is perceived as transgressing the group's norms. Thus, the corrupt group will activate its enforcers to silence the dissent of whistleblowers.

By actively enforcing corrupt norms on dissenters and newcomers and rationalizing and routinizing corrupt practices, the corrupt organization "becomes resistant not only to change, but to examination."[291]

---

291 Ashforth and Anand, "The Normalization of Corruption in Organizations," 15.

CASE IN POINT: RESISTANCE TO HARD DECISIONS

COMMON DECISION-MAKING MIND TRAPS

We put up defenses when confronted with hard choices. Unwittingly, we avoid disturbing information in an attempt to preserve our decision from challenge. Janis identifies several common tactics used to defensively bolster our positions.[292] When faced with hard choices, we often:

- *Defensively procrastinate* when there is no deadline and little hope. We may evade information and fail to respond in an urgent situation.

- *Misjudge and minimize warnings.* We may look for loopholes and exceptions that explain away warning signs.

- *Invent new arguments to support our decision* to feel comfortable in our decision. We cherry-pick data and arguments to enhance our case and stifle doubt.

- *Don't look ahead and consider ominous implications.* We will avoid thinking about the potentially disturbing consequences of our decision or explain them away with reassuring interpretations.

- *Forget details that would help us interpret challenging information accurately.* Our selective memories allow us to forget something that, if remembered, would challenge our thinking once we realize the full significance of our decision.

- *Shift responsibility and seek out expert "others" who will take over entirely.* We find a way to foist the decision onto someone else.

- *Bolster our argument by avoiding challenging information* or selectively exposing ourselves to supporting information.

- *Become hypervigilant and indiscriminately open ourselves to information* when there is high stress and little time. We become overwhelmed with information overload.

---

292 All information from this list comes from Janis and Mann, *Decision Making*, 125–129, 205.

Threat Rigidity

BATTEN DOWN THE HATCHES

"People often can't solve problems unless they think they aren't problems."

—KARL WEICK, 1984

Change can be threatening. When we feel threatened, a switch flips, we put our heads down, hole up, and shy away from the situation. Threats make us feel out of control and we respond by controlling what little we can, whether it's the right response or not. This instinctual reaction is known as threat rigidity, and it's common to executives, middle managers, and front-line staff. It can undo a change effort.

Below are a few examples of how major change can trigger significant resistance.

- A regional attraction invested more than $1M in new technology that would replace an ineffective system patched together by countless Band-Aids. The project experienced technical challenges and budget overruns. The implementation consultants flagged each technical and budget risk with urgency. On their side, the client began to think the project was not viable. As the alarm bells of risk kept ringing and a viable technical path had yet to be found, the client began to believe the consultants were acting in bad faith, the project would never work, and they would be left holding the bag. With only one month before launch, they decided to live with the system they knew and pulled the plug on the project.

- A flurry of news reports about excess spending in higher education has prompted the Governor to call for spending cuts within the state's public university. This prompts the Provosts to scrutinize spending by the Deans, who in turn begin to claw back funds from departments and programs. News spreads fast: "Watch your budgets, $200K just disappeared from the math department." Budget managers hide and hoard as much funding as possible. Program heads and faculty double down on the necessity of their course offerings. Calls to collaborate on interdisciplinary programs are met with fierce resistance.

- For many years, this company was the occasional target of animal activists, protests, and tough news stories about the ethics of their operations. The stance of the executive team was strident denial that anything was wrong and staunch resistance to change anything. Rather than reach out to activist groups to discuss the issues or find common ground, which could have nullified their opposition, they chose to circle their wagons. Most press and external relationships were assumed to be adversarial which only fueled the flames resulting in increasingly negative press and lawsuits.

THE NATURE OF THREAT RIGIDITY

Let's ground ourselves in a definition. *Threat rigidity is "the general tendency for individuals, groups and organizations to behave rigidly in threatening situations."*[293] Let's unpack a bit more. What is a

---

[293] Staw, Sandelands, and Dutton, "Threat Rigidity Effects in Organizational Behavior," 502.

"threatening situation"? Threatening situations are urgent situations in which we stand to lose something and feel out of control. On the other hand, opportunities are situations in which we stand to gain something and feel in control.[294] Our perception of personal control can determine how we react to urgent situations and how we assess gains and losses.

Below is a summary of the conditions that make us feel out of control versus in control.[295]

We are *in control* when we have	We are *out of control* when
autonomy in determining how to respond.	our activities will be constrained or determined by others.
freedom to choose whether or not to respond.	we lack the competence and capabilities needed to meet the demands of the situation.
access to the resources and means to resolve the issue.	the situation is beyond the limits of our endurance.
competence to deal with the issue.	
the ability to predict and know what is going to happen.	
coping strategies that will help us endure challenging times.	

RIGIDITY IN INDIVIDUALS, GROUPS, AND ORGANIZATIONS

Our rigid response to threatening and out-of-control situations plays itself out in individuals, groups, and organizations.

When *individuals* feel under threat, a physical response kicks in. We become physically alert, anxious, and on edge.

---

294 Jackson and Dutton, "Discerning Threats and Opportunities," 384.

295 All information in the following table comes from Jackson and Dutton, "Discerning Threats and Opportunities," 384; Thompson, "Will It Hurt Less if I Can Control It?," 95–98.

Our range of vision constricts, and we literally see less as we focus on the most important visual cues in front of us. Mentally, we become overwhelmed and revert to habitual and overlearned responses as recently acquired techniques and training are forgotten.[296] We become less flexible in problem-solving and less able to perceive the situation accurately. Essentially, we stereotype the situation as a threat.

When *groups* feel under threat from an outside force, they come together and strengthen their bond. The group centralizes control and supports the actions of its leader. They become more uniform and less tolerant of dissent as the group needs to move forward on its collective goals. Note: if the threat comes from within the group, it will splinter with blame and dissension.[297]

When *organizations* are in threatening situations, they centralize authority and restrict the number of decision-makers to the highest level of the organization.[298] Rather than improvise, they use formal and standard operating procedures to coordinate action. Like individuals, organizations fall back on "well-learned strategies" and rely heavily on past experiences and familiar sources of information.[299] Typically, organizations may also focus on efficiency and cost savings.

There is an interesting caveat to how organizations respond to threat. Sometimes threats can motivate new spending. That said, the operations that support the new investments don't change. If anything, the greater the investment, the tighter the controls

---

296 Staw, Sandelands, and Dutton, "Threat Rigidity Effects in Organizational Behavior," 504; Karl E. Weick, "The Collapse of Sensemaking in Organizations: The Mann Gulch Disaster," *Administrative Science Quarterly* 38, no. 4 (December 1993), https://doi.org/10.2307/2393339.

297 Staw, Sandelands, and Dutton, "Threat Rigidity Effects in Organizational Behavior," 508–510.

298 Staw, Sandelands, and Dutton, "Threat Rigidity Effects in Organizational Behavior," 514.

299 Prithviraj Chattopadhyay, William H. Glick, and George P. Huber, "Organizational Actions in Response to Threats and Opportunities," *The Academy of Management Journal* 44, no. 5 (October 2001): 950, https://www.jstor.org/stable/3069439.

and oversight. Even if you break through budget rigidity, you will likely encounter routine rigidity.[300]

In general, when an individual, group, or organization faces a threat, it will constrict information, control what it can, and conserve its resources.[301]

CAUSES OF THREAD RIGIDITY

For individuals and organizations, threat rigidity is caused by our need to control what we can when we feel out of control. It is also the byproduct of our tendency to see and be more responsive to bad information. For this reason, threats spread like contagions.

OUR NEED FOR CONTROL LIMITS PERCEPTION, ACTION, AND RISK-TAKING

We feel threatened when we believe we do not have the power, ability, or resilience to manage or control a situation.[302] When we feel threatened and out of control, we become overwhelmed and anxious. Our knee-jerk response is to (1) constrict our perceptions to our immediate surroundings and (2) limit our actions to familiar strategies. In short, we regress and act in short-sighted ways.[303]

Feelings of fear and anxiety "favor cautious risk-averse decision-making" that comes with low reward options.[304] We

---

300 Clark G. Gilbert, "Unbundling the Structure of Inertia: Resource versus Routine Rigidity," *Academy of Management Journal* 48, no. 5 (October 2005): 757–758, https://doi.org/10.5465/amj.2005.18803920.

301 Staw, Sandelands, and Dutton, "Threat Rigidity Effects in Organizational Behavior," 516.

302 Jackson and Dutton, "Discerning Threats and Opportunities," 384.

303 George Loewenstein, "Out of Control: Visceral Influences on Behavior," *Organizational Behavior and Human Decision Processes* 65, no. 3 (March 1996): 274, https://doi.org/10.1006/obhd.1996.0028.

304 G. F. Loewenstein et al., "Risk as Feelings." *Psychological Bulletin* 127, no. 2 (March 2001): 9, https://doi.org/10.1037/0033-2909.127.2.267.

try to control what we can when we feel threatened. **Our need to feel in control causes us to make our world smaller, manageable, and familiar.**

This explains why many organizations under direct threat are more likely to take inward-facing conservative actions that focus on things they can control (e.g., spending, decision-making, staff levels). Notably, if an organization faces an external threat to its core competency—its reason for being—it is more likely to take riskier externally directed actions to restore a sense of control and ultimately survive.[305] Both conservative inward-facing actions and riskier externally-directed actions are attempts to reclaim control.

BAD EVENTS GET MORE ATTENTION THAN GOOD

At any one time, too much is going on and we have to prioritize what we give our limited attention to. We are essentially "cognitive misers" who have to focus on what's important.[306] The research is clear—we give bad events more attention than good ones. A series of studies asked participants if they wanted to hear the bad or good news first, and 77–88 percent said they wanted the bad news first. Organizationally, managers are more likely to interpret strategic issues as threats, unless there is strong evidence to do otherwise.[307] It appears that negative events are simply easier for us to recognize.[308]

---

305   Chattopadhyay, Glick, and Huber, "Organizational Actions in Response to Threats and Opportunities," 949–951.

306   Roy F. Baumeister et al., "Bad Is Stronger than Good," *Review of General Psychology* 5, no. 4 (December 2001): 340, https://doi.org/10.1037/1089-2680.5.4.323.

307   Jackson and Dutton, "Discerning Threats and Opportunities," 385.

308   Paul Rozin and Edward B. Royzman, "Negativity Bias, Negativity Dominance, and Contagion," *Personality and Social Psychology Review* 5, no. 4 (November 2001): 301, https://doi.org/10.1207/S15327957PSPR0504_2.

Our ability to adapt and survive could depend on this negative bias. One bad day can undo years of good ones. It may be that "humans and animals show heightened awareness of and responded more quickly to negative information because it signals the need for change."[309] **Change prompted by a threat allows us to adapt to our environment.** Ultimately, our ability to respond to threats and adapt helps us improve, thrive, and achieve the stability that comes with our ability to meet life's challenges.

THE SENSE OF THREAT SPREADS LIKE A CONTAGION

Groups are more likely to converge on negative emotions, especially noticeable emotions like anxiety. We are far less likely to notice someone sitting in quiet contemplation compared to a nervous person in distress. When we are in groups, we naturally adapt our moods to match the mood of the group. If the group is upset by a setback, we will be more somber. Not only do we mimic emotion in our mannerisms, but we feel the emotion itself. The sense of threats and anxiety can become self-perpetuating as the negativity escalates between group members.[310] Most importantly, we won't recognize the influence of contagion.

THE VALUE OF THREAT RIGIDITY

Threat rigidity is almost an instinctual response designed to keep the individual, group, or organization functioning in extremely challenging situations. It conserves and focuses our energies on the most necessary functions. Threat rigidity keeps us alert and

---

309 Baumeister et al., "Bad Is Stronger than Good," 358.

310 Sigal G. Barsade, "The Ripple Effect: Emotional Contagion and its Influence on Group Behavior," *Administrative Science Quarterly* 47, no. 4 (December 2002): 647–648, https://doi.org/10.2307/3094912.

highly responsive to danger and bolsters internal controls to ensure we act in a coordinated fashion.

OUR SENSITIVITY TO THREATS KEEPS US VIGILANT AND RESPONSIVE

As individuals and organizations, we are on the lookout for bad news and events that can harm us. We dedicate more time and attention to surveilling for threats than opportunities, and we deliberate more about bad events. In contrast, continued good news can make us complacent.

There is one very important caveat to this potential virtue—if we are overwhelmed and in denial that a threat exists, we become less responsive and overly cautious.

WE REDUCE ERRORS BY STRENGTHENING INTERNAL CONTROLS

When faced with a control-reducing threat, organizations are more likely to take "conservative internally directed actions" and rely on "increased formalization and standardization of procedures [that] ensure coordination of organizational action" and compliance of lower-level staff with organizational directives.[311] When faced with a threat, coordination and control are heightened concerns because the risk and cost of errors are more consequential. Control is an attempt to reduce the possibility of error.

---

311 Staw, Sandelands, and Dutton, "Threat Rigidity Effects in Organizational Behavior," 514.

WE CAN ACT IN CONCERT BY CENTRALIZING AUTHORITY

Dissension could prove disastrous under threat. The natural inclination to come together, support leadership, and centralize authority allows organizations to more quickly take coordinated action. This, in turn, allows the organization to be more decisive and responsive to the threat.[312]

THE DANGERS OF THREAT RIGIDITY

Even though our sensitivity to bad events makes us more vigilant and responsive, we can easily become overwhelmed with anxiety. Individually, overwhelm can cause us to cognitively shut down, try to escape, or deny the problem. Within our organizations, anxiety is contagious and can result in excessive control and caution that limits the generation and consideration of creative solutions.

The dangers of behaving rigidly under threat are critical when the pace of change exceeds an organization's ability to respond.

INTERNAL CONTROLS MAKE US LESS CREATIVE AND NIMBLE

When faced with a control-reducing threat, organizations focus internally on what they can control. This can result in a restriction of information as communication channels become standardized, hierarchical, and centralized. As the organization leans on standardization and formalized processes, it becomes less adaptive at a time when it needs to be highly adaptive.

When faced with a vital threat (e.g., loss of core customer segments), an organization might respond and invest in new resources. Nonetheless, research shows that even with new invest-

---

312 Staw, Sandelands, and Dutton, "Threat Rigidity Effects in Organizational Behavior," 514.

ments, organizations are likely to rely on their standard routines. If anything, the oversight of the new investment increases the rigidity of their actions.[313]

CENTRALIZATION LIMITS THE GENERATION OF SOLUTIONS

As authority is centralized and hierarchical and greater emphasis is placed on control, fewer people within the organization are engaged in decision-making, problem-solving, and experimentation. This dramatically decreases the number and variety of solutions the organization can mount against its threat. This means that the organization is more likely to rely on its well-learned strategies that may or may not be up to the task.

ANXIETY CREATES RISK-ADVERSE DECISIONS

Anxiety can spread like contagion across an organization and affect perception and decision-making. When we feel anxious, we are more likely to imagine the negative consequences of a decision. When we experience anxiety early on, as we collect and process information, it has a significant impact on subsequent analysis and decision-making.[314] Many studies show that fear and anxiety lead to cautious risk-averse decision-making and a focus on maintaining internal controls.[315] When the organization experiences a significant or novel threat, a cautious approach may not be adequate.

---

313   Gilbert, "Unbundling the Structure of Inertia," 749.

314   Sigal G. Barsade, Constantinos G.V. Coutifaris, and Julianna Pillemer, "Emotional Contagion in Organizational Life," *Research in Organizational Behavior* 38 (January 2018): 144, https://doi.org/10.1016/j. riob.2018.11.005.

315   Loewenstein et al., "Risk as Feelings," 266.

SCAPEGOATING HELPS US FEEL MORE IN CONTROL

When we are confronted with a threatening and inexplicable situation, we bolster our sense of control by creating a scapegoat. Scapegoating can function like a self-protective mechanism designed to reduce a sense of threat.[316] Rather than imagine large forces or chaos being the cause of malady, scapegoats provide us with a clear and easy-to-understand explanation of why something bad is happening. Scapegoating helps us "maintain the perception that the external world is orderly, predictable, and stable (rather than chaotic and dangerous)."[317] Scapegoats also provide a satisfying means to solve the problem—punish the scapegoat. This strategy is often seen when CEOs are threatened by poor corporate performance.[318]

WHAT YOU CAN DO

A threat is defined as a situation in which we perceive an urgent and high-stakes situation that we cannot control or potentially endure. Under threat, we experience stress and anxiety which constrict our thinking and result in greater centralization and control in organizations. Constriction and control can override the creative thinking and adaptation necessary to meet the demands of the situation. This constriction can inhibit our ability to change as we batten down the hatches. There are many strategies you can employ individually and organizationally.

---

316 Blake E. Ashforth and Raymond T. Lee, "Defensive Behavior in Organizations: A Preliminary Model," *Human Relations* 43, no. 7 (July 1990): 628, https://doi.org/10.1177/001872679004300702.

317 Zachary K. Rothschild et al., "A Dual-Motive Model of Scapegoating: Displacing Blame to Reduce Guilt or Increase Control," *Journal of Personality and Social Psychology* 102, no. 6 (2012): 1149, https://doi.org/10.1037/a0027413.

318 Warren Boeker, "Power and Managerial Dismissal: Scapegoating at the Top," *Administrative Science Quarterly* 37, no. 3 (September 1992), https://doi.org/10.2307/2393450.

DECREASE THE SENSE OF THREAT

A heightened sense of threat creates anxiety, and too much of this does not bring out the best in us. When we consider a situation a serious "threat," we trigger an instinctual fearful response that makes us more controlling and risk-averse and shuts down our more creative impulses that can help navigate and manage uncertain situations.

Ironically, we are most able to deal with a problem when we do not believe one exists.

If your change effort has the potential to threaten someone's competence, control, or status, you are well served to reduce the sense of threat.

There are a couple of things you can do to reduce the sense of threat:

1. **Identify and reinforce any opportunities.** Help people re-appraise a potentially threatening situation into one that can provide very clear and concrete opportunities. Don't forget that we easily perceive threats, but opportunities will need to be spelled out in unmistakable terms and repeatedly communicated for this to sink in.

2. **Present the change effort in a nuanced way with an optimistic tone.** The perceptions of threats are the result of knee-jerk understandings. By mentally labeling a situation as a "threat," we reduce its complexity and, in all likelihood, close off the exploration of opportunities. In essence, we pre-determine our relationship with it. A genuinely positive tone and approach can help set the emotional stage for an open-minded assessment.

FOSTER A SENSE OF CONTROL

We consider something a threat when it makes us feel out of control. By fostering the belief, if not the reality, of control, you can neutralize the sense of threat, mitigate its impact, and possibly transform it into an opportunity.

Several strategies can enhance our sense of control over a situation.

Create predictability. Provide information that helps people understand and predict what will happen. Clear timelines help us prepare for what's coming and allow us to relax during interim periods. Predictability "lessens cognitive overload. A person who can predict when the event will occur does not have to keep searching the environment for signs" that something is about to happen.[319] Avoid the element of surprise as it will keep people on edge, waiting for the next shoe to drop.

Create opportunities to participate in decision-making. When you include staff in a decision-making process and allow them to weigh in on alternatives, they will have a greater sense of control over their futures. Note: It's more important that you solicit input than accept it. Often, we can accept decisions that we don't agree with, if we believe we were genuinely heard. Be authentic in your listening.

Give people discretion on how change is implemented. You can provide the high-level direction and outcomes that need to be achieved. Then, let go a little and give others latitude to interpret the change for themselves and determine the best way to make the change a reality in their world.

---

319 Thompson, "Will It Hurt Less if I Can Control It?," 96.

MAKE THE CHANGE MEANINGFUL

We have a greater ability to endure hardship when it is attached to something that is important to us. You can help people navigate difficult change by giving it meaning and connecting it to something they care about. Research shows that soldiers reported less severe pain than civilians after surgery because their injuries had meaning for them.[320]

Another way to make change meaningful is to encourage people to see it as part of their plan. We can tolerate adversity when it is "seen as a part of a plan rather than a random event. Individuals seem to have a need to see the events in their lives as part of an orderly, meaningful world, such as part of the plans of God, or flowing from their own plans and goals."[321] For instance, the loss of a job is less stressful if it is believed to flow from one's trajectory in life or values.

FOSTER CONFIDENCE AND HOPE

Threats arouse our belief, more than the reality, that we are not up to the task.

The fear of threat is reduced when we believe that we have the resources and ability to handle a situation. You enhance the confidence of your staff by providing the time, tools, and support needed to develop the skills they will need to succeed.

Foster a sense of hope that your team can deal with challenges. Hope in our abilities helps us imagine a potential threat as an opportunity; we must believe that we can be successful.

One of the most important factors in our ability to handle

---

320 Thompson, "Will It Hurt Less if I Can Control It?," 98.

321 Thompson, "Will It Hurt Less if I Can Control It?," 99.

stress during organizational challenges is our belief, more than the reality, in our ability to control a given situation.[322]

DEAL WITH UNCERTAINTY BY MAKING A DECISION

When you are in an ambiguous or chaotic situation and under stress, you can "put your world in order" by running it through a decision-making process.[323] The process of identifying goals and priorities, collecting information, and evaluating options provides leaders with a sense of control and confidence they need to manage threats.

Research conducted on companies dealing with extreme uncertainty, hostile competitors, and fast-paced environments shows how decision-making can be an essential process for navigating change.

Below are lessons learned from the companies that successfully used quick decision-making to survive, as well as the ill-fated paths taken by their failing counterparts.

- **Have a clear and explicit goal to anchor your actions** (e.g., "To be the best machine on the market"). When you can tap into proactive organizational goals, agreement can be achieved more quickly. In contrast, a failed firm was guided only by its Chairman's opportunistic reaction.[324]
- **Be on top of your data and operations.** The management teams from successful firms were tuned in to the real-time details of their operations. They had developed an intuition

322 Susan Ashford, "Individual Strategies for Coping with Stress during Organizational Transitions," *The Journal of Applied Behavioral Science* 24, no. 1 (February 1988): 21, https://doi.org/10.1177/0021886388241005.

323 L. J. Bourgeois and Kathleen M. Eisenhardt, "Strategic Decision Processes in High Velocity Environments: Four Cases in the Microcomputer Industry," *Management Science* 34, no. 7 (July 1988): 826, https://doi.org/10.1287/mnsc.34.7.816.

324 Bourgeois and Eisenhardt, "Strategic Decision Processes in High Velocity Environments," 828.

that allowed them to develop options, deliberate, and decide quickly, together. In contrast, failed firms had visionary and disconnected CEOs and management that occasionally evaluated their high-level data.

- **Conduct a short and intense decision-making process.** This keeps the team focused on the decision and makes the process a priority. Speed can be critical in launching an effective response. Companies that successfully navigated threats acted quickly, approximately three months for major decisions. Failing firms took up to twenty months for a major decision.
- **Identify and evaluate many alternatives to solve the problem.** The decision-making process should emphasize breadth over depth. By evaluating many alternatives, decision-makers look at the strengths and weaknesses of each, to identify the most viable. This process increases their confidence.
- **Get input from the management team and lower-level staff.** Input from different perspectives tests the viability of options, avoids surprises, and prevents the escalation of commitment that can come with having only one option (the fallbacks are known).[325]
- **Make the decision.** The successful companies used "qualified consensus" to make decisions. It goes like this. The management team attempts to reach a consensus. If it occurs, the decision is made. If it doesn't, the CEO will make the choice, often in consultation with trusted advisors.[326] Input from the management team, staff, and advisors keeps the CEO from being isolated, anxious, and restricted from information. Input also keeps the politics at bay that can come from people

---

325 Kathleen M. Eisenhardt, "Making Fast Strategic Decisions in High-Velocity Environments," *The Academy of Management Journal* 32, no. 3 (September 1989): 555, https://www.jstor.org/stable/256434.

326 Eisenhardt, "Making Fast Strategic Decisions in High-Velocity Environments," 562.

feeling excluded. Even though the CEO acts in an autocratic manner, executives have a sense of relief and focus that comes from a decision being made.[327] Essentially, successful firms have a "let's get on with it" attitude, while failed firms lack a decisive and bold CEO.

- **Integrate the decision with existing tactical plans and functional areas.** The decision is considered through the lens of existing tactical plans, budgets, and operations. Bringing the decision down to earth turns a highly ambiguous situation into a tangible one that can be evaluated. This gives decision-makers a better understanding of the decision. Additionally, successful firms empower subsequent functional leaders with functional decisions.

In sum, the firms that dealt with their uncertain and threatening environments by forcing them through a compressed and intense decision-making process were successful. They needed to make uncertainty more clear and actionable; a decision-making process accomplishes this. In a difficult situation, decision-making increased their competence and control, which improved their ability to manage a threat.[328]

EXPECT THE UNEXPECTED

Resilient organizations can manage threats because they do not expect things to go as planned, they're aware of problems, and have the mindset and resources necessary to deal with them.[329] In contrast, brittle organizations take the absence of failure to mean that

---

327 Bourgeois and Eisenhardt, "Strategic Decision Processes in High Velocity Environments," 830.

328 Eisenhardt, "Making Fast Strategic Decisions in High-Velocity Environments," 566.

329 Weick and Sutcliffe, *Managing the Unexpected*, 97.

there are no troubles on the horizon. Brittle organizations are easily overwhelmed by discrete shocks and deviations from the norm.[330]

Below are strategies to develop organizational resilience.

Develop awareness of your situation. Resilient organizations are on the lookout for anomalies and try to "make sense of weak signals."[331] When we dial into the details of our situation, we are more likely to see nuance that can help us devise a better response. As we communicate our individual perspectives, we can develop a shared understanding of the situation, and the organization can take collective action.

Just as firefighters "size up" a fire scene and continually build a mental picture of the burning house and surrounding community, organizations need the capacity to represent and understand a threatening situation.[332] Disasters occur when you "lose the capacity to represent the event and account for what is happening."[333]

Doubt your conventional wisdom. Resilient organizations continually doubt the relevance of their past experience and question their assumptions and received wisdoms. Doubt makes organizations "receptive to alternative perspectives, which result in the ability to anticipate the unexpected."[334] Doubt creates an unease and sense that things may be unusual. It forces us to reconsider our understanding, think more flexibly, and defer to the expertise of others. Doubt is a good antidote to the mental numbing that can come from familiarity or repetition.

---

330 Timothy J. Vogus and Kathleen M. Sutcliffe, "Organizational Resilience: Towards a Theory and Research Agenda." In *Proceedings of the IEEE Internal Conference on Systems Man and Cybernetics* (Montréal, Canada, 2007), 3419, https://doi.org/ 10.1109/ICSMC.2007.4414160.

331 Vogus and Sutcliffe, "Organizational Resilience," 3420.

332 Gregory A. Bigley and Karlene H. Roberts, "The Incident Command System: High-Reliability Organizing for Complex and Volatile Task Environments," *Academy of Management Journal* 44, no. 6 (December 2001): 1291.

333 Weick and Sutcliffe, *Managing the Unexpected*, 105.

334 Timothy Vogus et al., "The Affective Foundations of High-Reliability Organizing," *Journal of Organizational Behavior* 35, no. 4 (February 2014): 594, https://doi.org/10.1002/job.1922.

ENGAGE IN NONSTOP TALK

Communication is critical to developing a shared understanding of an anomaly or changes in your environment that could become a threat. No one person has a complete picture of what's going on, inside or outside of an organization. **Through a patchwork of perspectives and the collective project of trying to make sense of it all, a collective understanding and plan for concerted action will emerge.** You should encourage people to speak up about their observations and concerns. Resilient organizations recognize "speaking up as valuable even when the result is that production is stopped unnecessarily."[335] Executives in organizations that succeed in fast-paced and threatening environments are in constant communication with each other about real-time observations. Nonstop talk facilitates a more accurate understanding of what is going on and what you should do about it.

CHAPTER SUMMARY

- Change can be threatening. It can trigger an instinctual response that pulls back and becomes rigidly controlling.
- Threat rigidity is the tendency for individuals, groups, and organizations to behave rigidly in threatening situations.
- We consider something a threat when we stand to lose something and feel out of control. We consider something an opportunity when we stand to gain something and feel in control.
- Under threat, we become anxious, our vision constricts to our immediate surroundings, and we revert to overlearned habitual responses. Our problem solving diminishes, and we become less flexible.

---

335 Vogus and Sutcliffe, "Organizational Resilience," 3419.

- Under threat, groups come together, consolidate control, support their leader, and become less tolerant of dissent.
- Under threat, organizations centralize authority and lean into hierarchy and standard operating procedures. They rely heavily on past experience.
- Threat rigidity is caused by feeling overwhelmed and anxious. This in turn causes us to constrict information, control what we can, and conserve our resources. The sense of threat can spread like contagion; bad events get more of our attention than good.
- Threat rigidity provides value. Organizations reduce the possibility of errors by increasing internal controls. They can also act in concert by centralizing authority.
- Conversely, internal controls can make us less creative and nimble in a situation that demands flexibility. Centralization limits the exchange of ideas and generation of solutions. Anxiety can make us risk-averse.
- You can mitigate the impact of threatening and ambiguous situations by running them through a decision-making process, which provides a sense of control and confidence needed to manage threats.
- Expect the unexpected and don't assume things will go as planned. By being on the lookout and doubting your assumptions, you can develop a resilience for dealing with problems.
- Do everything you can to reduce the sense of threat, and identify and reinforce opportunities. You can foster a sense of control by creating predictability, opportunities for decision-making, and discretion for how change is implemented.
- Foster a sense of confidence and hope that helps people believe that they have the resources and ability to handle a situation. Connect the change to something they care about—make it meaningful.

CASE IN POINT: RESISTANCE TO
MANDATES AND SANCTIONS

THREAT RIGIDITY AND THE RESPONSE
TO NO CHILD LEFT BEHIND

Passed in 2002, No Child Left Behind (NCLB) was a bipartisan law that aimed to close the achievement gap between poor and minority students and those more advantaged by requiring every child to be proficient in reading and math by 2014.[336]

Schools that failed to meet NCLB standards faced a series of progressive sanctions and "cascading punishments—beginning with mandated tutoring and going all the way to school takeover."[337] Education Secretary Arne Duncan later reflected on NCLB, saying it "'created dozens of ways for schools to fail and very few ways to help them succeed or to reward success.'"[338] In essence, the policy created a threat for struggling schools.

The University of California conducted two case studies to determine if the NCLB's threat of sanctions created a rigid response in struggling California schools. In both cases, researchers found the "increased accountability, high-stakes standardized testing, and *teacher-proof* instruction" had the effect of constricting teacher's autonomy, flexibility, and motivation.[339] The studies confirmed responses consistent with threat rigidity: "unilateral decision-making,

336 Alyson Klein, "No Child Left Behind: An Overview," *Education Week*, April 10, 2015, https://www.edweek.org/policy-politics/no-child-left-behind-an-overview/2015/04; Motoko Rich and Tamar Lewin, "No Child Left Behind Law Faces Its Own Reckoning," *New York Times*, March 22, 2015, https://www.nytimes.com/2015/03/22/us/politics/schools-wait-to-see-what-becomes-of-no-child-left-behind-law.html.

337 Alan J. Daly, "Rigid Response in an Age of Accountability: The Potential of Leadership and Trust," *Educational Administration Quarterly* 45, no. 2 (April 2009): 169, https://doi.org/10.1177/0013161X0833049.

338 Rich and Lewin, "No Child Left Behind Law Faces Its Own Reckoning."

339 Brad Olsen and Dena Sexton, "Threat Rigidity, School Reform, and How Teachers View Their Work Inside Current Education Policy Contexts," *American Educational Research Journal* 46, no. 1 (March 2009): 16, https://doi.org/10.3102/0002831208320573.

use of prescriptive programs and approaches, top-down directives, diminished agency, and a pervasive sense of fear for attempting new practices."[340]

In one case study of an underperforming California high school, the implementation of NCLB was especially fraught. Here, teachers experienced the tightening up of school procedures, increased pressure to standardize their practice, and very limited communications from the administration. One teacher talked about how "prescriptive textbooks ignore her professional training, her teaching experience, and her knowledge of the students in her classroom." Another complained, "We were told at various times over the course of the year: this is your bible, and I [as assistant principal] want to be able to walk into any English 1 class on a given Wednesday and see you all on the same page and on the same chapter." All teachers in one focus group felt uninformed: "It seems that the principal is listening to a very small cheerleading section and ignoring everybody else."[341]

Teachers were not encouraged to think differently about their teaching or learning or about the school's improvement.

> Instead, the whole of the reforms, the school climate, and the various actions by the administration appeared to encourage a lockstep emphasis on conformity which silenced opportunities for creative thinking. School conditions did not encourage innovative ideas; instead they emphasized managing resources efficiently, controlling teaching and bracing for attack.[342]

The school became a "besieged work environment" that "created teacher hostility and a disenfranchisement."[343] Things reached a boiling point, and eventually, twenty teachers spearheaded a successful effort to oust the principal.

---

340 Daly, "Rigid Response in an Age of Accountability," 205.

341 Olsen and Sexton, "Threat Rigidity, School Reform, and How Teachers View Their Work," 27.

342 Olsen and Sexton, "Threat Rigidity, School Reform, and How Teachers View Their Work," 30.

343 Olsen and Sexton, "Threat Rigidity, School Reform, and How Teachers View Their Work," 15, 37.

Both case studies suggest that NCLB's sanctions created a threatening environment for school administrators that cascaded down to educators. For struggling schools, these punishments "prevent exploration of the instructional approaches needed to reach diverse student populations."[344] This research suggests that the rigidity of response might explain why 75 percent of the struggling schools in California assigned to NCLB's "program improvement" status were unable to exit.

344 Daly, "Rigid Response in an Age of Accountability," 205.

CASE IN POINT: RESISTANCE TO BUSINESS MODEL THREATS

THE RIGID RESPONSE OF PRINT NEWSPAPERS TO DIGITAL PUBLISHING

A multi-year study detailed the perception and responses of eight newspaper organizations to the emergence and threat of digital publishing.[345] Online publishing would demand major adjustments within news organizations, including features that differ from print (i.e., breaking news, live weather and traffic, searchable job databases, and items for sale) and a different business model with distinct costs and revenue streams.

The case study shows an industry that was slow to recognize what digital could mean for their business and slow to invest resources to build their own digital capabilities. When they finally invested money in digital, almost all of them centralized authority to the CEO, reduced experimentation in digital offerings, and focused on print resources rather than developing new digital capabilities. They reacted rigidly. There was one notable exception that broke the rigidity mold and responded with innovation and flexibility.

I will highlight the main phases of this story.

Phase 1 (Early 1990s)
Digital Is a Novelty, Just Getting Started. No Threat. No Action.

All eight organizations failed to perceive or respond to the threat of online publishing. Online was often considered a novelty, and organizations had trouble selling online to print advertisers. There was very little overlap between the large print customer base and digital users. Print would be the primary business for the foreseeable future. In all eight companies, early proposals to explore online stalled for two-plus years.

---

345 All information from this case study can be found in Gilbert, "Unbundling the Structure of Inertia."

Phase 2 (Mid-90s). Digital Is Coming and There Is Risk in Relying on Print. Wait and See.

Many organizations understood the risks of relying so heavily on traditional print customers. Yet, they did not respond with financial investments for online ventures. Rather, they reinvested in print and almost all conducted major studies estimating the effects of online cannibalization of their print business. Even though they knew that news consumption was moving toward a screen, they opted for a wait-and-see approach.

Phase 3 ('97–'98). Digital Is Growing and It's a Threat. Spend Money.

Most managers in the organizations studied were concerned about online publishing; they saw it as a threat: "We thought we could lose half of our circulation." Others worried about their cash cow—the classifieds—that represented as much as 60 percent of newspaper profits.

The growing worry resulted in significant financial investments in digital; budgets and staff grew as much as 400 percent. Notably, investments were not inspired by growing markets or new revenue streams. Rather, they were triggered by the fear of losing 20–30 percent of classified ad revenue.

The perception of threat mobilized resources and financial investments. But, the infusion of cash was accompanied by a controlling and rigid management style and quashed the innovation needed to launch a successful digital venture.

Put another way, the threat of digital overcame resource rigidity, but it created routine rigidity.

In almost every organization studied (minus the notable exception), rigidity was clear:

- **The CEO and Managing Director centralized authority** and assumed control over the strategy.

- **Business plan templates were imposed**, and sometimes the CEO approved new hires.
- **Experimentation was constricted** by the sheer pace of rapid growth. There was simply no time to reconsider and adjust course.
- **Online features were oriented toward the existing print business** rather than creating distinct products and revenue streams. For instance, the print classified business was in charge of online classifieds out of fear of cannibalization.

In short, the online business was seen and managed through the lens of print. Almost all, with one exception, created an online product that was merely an extension of print newspapers.

Researchers observed one notable exception. In this organization, the CEO was advised by a friendly outsider from Silicon Valley. This external perspective might have been instrumental in charting a distinct strategy for the organization. This organization did several things differently from the rest of the pack:

- **They created a separate online venture** with autonomy from the newspaper. The online team had its own management, salesforce, and brand.
- **The digital team was located in a different building** more than a mile away from the print newspaper.
- **Half of the digital content came from sources other than the newspaper**, its lead stories differed, and it included a searchable database and interactive forums.
- **Digital had its own business model.**

Essentially the organization ran two distinct ventures (print and digital) that were structurally separated.

This differentiated structure allowed the newspaper to maintain its defensive position and more traditional operating model while the online venture could assume a more innovative posture that could capitalize on new opportunities and new technologies. The CEO would switch hats and adopt the mindset of each group. This structural differentiation of online from print also decoupled the organization's threats from opportunities. It managed the print business understanding the threat of digital while it launched a new digital venture that could take advantage of opportunities. It allowed each team to keep their motivations simple and focus on their respective businesses.

Change Cynicism

KNOWING GLANCES, ROLLING EYES

"People who invariably believe in another's integrity are likely to be taken advantage of by those who lack it."

—JAMES DEAN JR., 1997

Cynicism takes a variety of forms. Here are a few examples:

- A newly hired consultant inherited the deep suspicions from staff who were burnt by consultants who promised the world and left them holding the bag. At every turn, she had to justify her recommendations. The smallest bump in the road was met with, "Here we go again."
- An organization struggled to reverse declining revenues with a combination of budget cuts and unrealistic revenue goals. The CEO preferred expensive trips around the globe to the embittered office. A small group of staff started a grass-roots insurgency on social media exposing the excesses of the C-suite. Within weeks, the CEO was ousted.
- An enthusiastic executive launched yet another change effort, the latest in a string of efforts started before others were completed. Launched with fanfare and great promise, the effort fell flat on the staff who had seen this before. No one was

committed this time around. From the sidelines, the staff watched the program falter and become what it was destined to be—yet another failure.

- A vocal group of staff called on the CEO to take stronger stances on political and social issues. The CEO was reluctant to wade into territory unrelated to the organization's mission. The staff were frustrated by the CEO's inaction; they started to doubt that the CEO actually cared. Distrust toward the CEO grew as it eroded once-strong relationships. Unable to lead, the CEO eventually left.

Cynicism can be painful for everyone involved. The cynical employee works for an organization they don't trust. The object of cynicism, often leadership, can feel bewildered and alone. Cynicism can run deep and as a result, be deeply intractable. It can destroy a change effort before it even starts.

THE NATURE OF CYNICISM

At the heart of cynicism is the doubt or disbelief about another's motives for their decisions or actions. Different from skepticism, which is the doubt about the *viability* of a course of action, cynicism involves doubt about *viability* and *motives*.[346]

---

346 David J. Stanley, John P. Meyer, and Laryssa Topolnytsky, "Employee Cynicism and Resistance to Organizational Change," *Journal of Business and Psychology* 19, no. 4 (June 2005): 436, https://doi.org/10.1007/s10869-005-4518-2.

CYNICISM IS BASED IN REALITY

Cynicism involves "a real loss of faith" in the leaders of change efforts or in the organization itself.[347] *Cynicism is an employee's "response to a history"—an actual experience that went badly.* Eventually, enough evidence accumulates that leads the employee to conclude that the organization or its leaders lack integrity.

Note: this chapter examines situational cynicism and is not an attempt to understand dispositional cynicism, a personality type.

There are two varieties of cynicism in workplaces. Employees can be cynical about their *organization* or about *specific change efforts.*

Organizational cynicism *is the belief that one's organization lacks integrity.* Organizational cynics believe that "the practices of their organizations betray lack of such principles as fairness, honesty, and sincerity." These folks may believe such principles are "sacrificed to expediency, and that unscrupulous behavior is the norm."[348] Those cynical of the whole organization believe self-interest permeates decision-making and leadership is unreliable.

Cynicism toward one's organization is more likely to form when there are:

- Excessive executive compensations and perks
- A history of harsh organizational layoffs or budget reductions that result in heavier workloads[349]
- A disconnect between executives and the real operations of an organization
- A belief that leaders are motivated by self-interest

---

347 Arnon E. Reichers, John P. Wanous, and James T. Austin, "Understanding and Managing Cynicism about Organizational Change," *Academy of Management Perspectives* 11, no. 1 (February 1997): 48, https://doi.org/10.5465/ame.1997.9707100659.

348 James W. Dean, Pamela Brandes, and Ravi Dharwadkar, "Organizational Cynicism," *The Academy of Management Review* 23, no. 2 (April 1998): 346, https://doi.org/10.2307/259378.

349 Dean, Brandes, and Dharwadkar, "Organizational Cynicism," 344.

- A belief that decisions are motivated by short-term or narrow interests[350]

Organizational cynicism likely requires system-wide reform of practice and process. This could include rehabilitation of how communications are structured, decisions are made, employees are treated, and executives are compensated.

Change cynicism is a more narrowly focused doubt about the motives and abilities of "those responsible" for the change effort.[351] Change cynicism can occur "when a succession of change efforts fail [and] employees feel initially disappointed and betrayed."[352]

Cynicism toward a change effort is likely to form when there are:

- a history of repeated failed change efforts,
- a belief that their leaders are lazy, incompetent, or lack integrity, and
- previous change efforts were launched with lofty announcements and followed by haphazard implementation and failure.[353]

Cynicism of the whole organization and/or specific change efforts can result in a collective, "Why bother?" Cynicism will decrease people's willingness to expend extra effort and commit to change—key ingredients for transformational change.

---

350 Quy Nguyen Huy, Kevin G. Corley, and Matthew S. Kraatz, "From Support to Mutiny: Shifting Legitimacy Judgments and Emotional Reactions Impacting the Implementation of Radical Change," *Academy of Management Journal* 57, no. 6 (March 2014): 1670, https://doi.org/10.5465/amj.2012.0074.

351 John P. Wanous, Arnon E. Reichers, and James T. Austin, "Cynicism about Organizational Change: Measurement, Antecedents, and Correlates," *Group & Organization Management* 25, no. 2 (June 2000): 135, https://doi.org/10.1177/1059601100252003.

352 Rebecca Abraham, "Organizational Cynicism: Bases and Consequences," *Genetic, Social, and General Psychology Monographs* 126, no. 3 (September 2000): 272, https://pubmed.ncbi.nlm.nih.gov/10950198.

353 Abraham, "Organizational Cynicism," 272.

THE CAUSES OF CYNICISM

Organizations roll out change efforts with the promise that the organization will realize greater profits, efficiency, competitive advantage, or happier customers. Employees are asked to take on additional responsibilities, absorb the stress of change, and trust that their sacrifice will be rewarded. As requests are made of employees, they naturally form expectations that their organization is obligated to repay. They develop implicit *psychological contracts* with their organization.[354] **Psychological contracts form when we believe our contributions obligate our organization to reciprocate our extra effort in the form of recognition, growth advancement, or job security.**

BROKEN TRUST CAUSES CYNICISM

Initially, we are willing to go above and beyond and make sacrifices—in other words, take a risk and be vulnerable—because we *trust* our organization will honor its part of this implicit contract.[355] The greater our trust, the greater our willingness to take risks.

We form trusting relationships with organizations and leaders that demonstrate *ability, integrity, and good will* toward their employees. When an organization or leader fails to demonstrate this, they will struggle to engender the trust and commitment necessary for managing difficult change.[356] They have also laid the groundwork for resistance.

Where trust is damaged and the psychological contract is violated, cynicism is born.

---

354 Rousseau, "Psychological and Implied Contracts," 124–126.

355 Mayer, David, and Schoorman, "An Integrative Model of Organizational Trust," 712.

356 Mayer, David, and Schoorman, "An Integrative Model of Organizational Trust," 715.

THE VALUE OF CYNICISM

Cynicism performs a vital role for individuals and organizations. It can be the voice of conscience for an organization, a form of self-protection to people, and offer information that should not be ignored.

CYNICISM HOLDS LEADERSHIP ACCOUNTABLE

On the organizational level, "cynics may provide a necessary check on the temptation to place expediency over principle or the temptation to assume that self-interested or underhanded behavior will go undetected. In their particular manner, cynics may act as a voice of conscience for the organization."[357]

FOR INDIVIDUALS, CYNICISM KEEPS US FROM BEING TAKEN ADVANTAGE OF

Cynicism prevents us from trusting and being vulnerable to people who will likely betray us. It is a logical response that protects us and prevents us from taking poor risks.

FOR THE ORGANIZATION, CYNICISM IS A SOURCE OF VALUABLE INFORMATION

Cynicism is born in reality. It is the symptom of deeper problems (e.g., disconnect between leadership and operations, unfair treatment of employees, poor management) that need to be addressed.

---

357 Dean, Brandes, and Dharwadkar, "Organizational Cynicism," 347.

THE DANGERS OF CYNICISM

The consequences of cynicism on organizations, employees, and change efforts can be profound, damning, and long-lasting.

CYNICAL EMPLOYEES SUFFER EMOTIONALLY

Our emotional responses to violations of justice, fairness, and trust run deep and linger; they are "hot feelings" that include betrayal, bitterness, and contempt.[358]

RELATIONSHIPS WITH THE ORGANIZATION MAY NOT RECOVER

Even though our emotions may fade over time, they may not return to "normal." When our sense of fairness and mutual obligation is broken, the entire relationship is called into question, and it may never become trustworthy.[359]

CYNICAL EMPLOYEES ARE MORE LIKELY TO RESIST CHANGE AND WITHHOLD VITAL COMMITMENT AND SUPPORT

They are less motivated and willing to go above and beyond for change efforts.[360] Essentially, change initiatives are "reduced to mere acts of compliance with organizational directives rather than selfless acts stimulated by an intent to help the organization."[361]

---

358 Rousseau, "Psychological and Implied Contracts," 129.

359 Mayer, David, and Schoorman, "An Integrative Model of Organizational Trust," 349.

360 Reichers, Wanous, and Austin, "Understanding and Managing Cynicism about Organizational Change," 51.

361 Abraham, "Organizational Cynicism," 278.

CYNICISM CONTRIBUTES TO CHANGE FATIGUE

Too much change at once creates stress, strain, and exhaustion; we are past our ability to cope. Change fatigue results as we withdraw in an "attempt to conserve energy."[362]

CYNICISM FEEDS ITSELF

Cynicism is not easily combatted. "Once employees become distrustful of management's motives, it will likely be difficult to convince them their concerns are not justified—the words and deeds required to convey this information will themselves be questioned," which creates an "escalating cycle of cynicism."[363]

Cynicism forms in the absence of effective communication. When employees fail to see or hear about progress, cynicism fills the void.

Cynicism can become a "self-fulfilling prophecy" as cynics withhold the support necessary for a change effort to succeed. Cynical beliefs about the organization's ability to change are reinforced as a project falters or fails.

Managers are more likely to become cynical about employees if their attempts to overcome cynicism fail. They may withhold information, focus on compliance, and not include employees in decision-making. In turn, employee cynicism will deepen.[364]

---

362 Jeremy B. Bernerth, H. Jack Walker, and Stanley G. Harris, "Change Fatigue: Development and Initial Validation of a New Measure," *Work & Stress* 25, no. 4 (December 2011): 333, https://doi.org/10.1080/026783 73.2011.634280.

363 Stanley, Meyer, and Topolnytsky, "Employee Cynicism and Resistance to Organizational Change," 457.

364 Stanley, Meyer, and Topolnytsky, "Employee Cynicism and Resistance to Organizational Change," 457.

WHAT YOU CAN DO

Intense cynicism toward the organization is a sign of deep organizational problems that require systemic reform, which may be beyond your control.

As in all things, the details of the situation matter, and there is hope in many situations with a mindful and forthright approach.

UNDERSTAND AND DEAL WITH THE PAST

Deal with past failures head-on; don't ignore them. Cynicism is based in reality, and you should know this reality. By identifying underlying issues and problems, you can uncover information relevant to your change effort. It is important to understand if the cynicism is specific (e.g., to a past change effort or leader) or if it applies to the organization itself. If people are cynical of change, due to past failures, you can explain why this time is different in specific and believable ways.

Note: not acknowledging past failures can be interpreted as attempts to hide mistakes, which can easily be interpreted as a lack of integrity, which can be insurmountable.

BUILD AND LEVERAGE YOUR PERSONAL CREDIBILITY

Credibility "can take years to be earned, but it can be lost in an instant. Credibility grows minute by minute, day by day...but it can be lost with one thoughtless remark or inconsistent act or one broken agreement."[365]

When people are cynical of past change efforts or the organization, your personal credibility may be critical in repairing trust and building support for change.

---

365 Kouzes and Posner, "The Credibility Factor," 32.

Research on credibility shows several ways for leaders to build personal credibility:

- **Demonstrate honesty and integrity.** Research shows that honesty is the most important quality of leaders. It's simple; good leaders "do what they say they are going to do."[366]
- **Demonstrate trust and "ante up first."** We form trusting relationships when we take a risk and assume another will eventually reciprocate. Good leaders "ante up first."[367]
- **Stand up for your beliefs.** Confusion over what a leader stands for leads to misunderstanding, stress, and conflict.
- **Know the people that you serve.** Know what your staff and stakeholders aspire to care about and value. Listen to them deeply. Listening and understanding why staff may be cynical about the change effort or organization will help you understand what needs to be fixed in order to build back trust and commitment.
- **Be enthusiastic, energetic, and positive about the future.** Speak with passion and communicate what excites you as a person. Enthusiasm can be contagious; it begins with you. Be positive; "the essence of leadership is to energetically reflect back to the institution how it best thinks of itself."[368]

FILL THE VOID, COMMUNICATE

- **Communicate successes, no matter how small.** Change happens one step at a time. People can easily miss the progress around them as it happens day by day. Remember that in the absence of communication cynicism fills the void.[369]

---

366 Kouzes and Posner, "The Credibility Factor," 30.

367 Kouzes and Posner, "The Credibility Factor," 30.

368 Kouzes and Posner, "The Credibility Factor," 32.

369 Wanous, Reichers, and Austin, "Cynicism about Organizational Change," 149.

- **Explain why there may be a lack of progress or why it is slow.** Help people understand the situational factors and the complexities involved so they are less likely to blame individuals.[370]
- **Explain the management perspective and rationale for decisions.** The more people understand the reasoning behind decisions, the more likely they are to accept them. Understanding *why* a decision is made is as important as *what* the decision is.[371]
- **Do everything you can to avoid surprises.**[372] The stress caused by change is due as much to the uncertainty of what's going to happen as to the material facts of the change itself.[373]

KEEP PEOPLE INVOLVED

By engaging people directly in the process, you give them control and a sense of ownership over something that could be disempowering or threatening. You honor their knowledge and competence. You also create two-way communications and allow for personal commitment.

Involve people in the decisions that affect them. People who have a voice in a decision are more likely to consider it to be fair.[374]

Specifically, involve people in implementation planning. This will give people a sense of control over their jobs. By involving staff in planning, especially in the implementation phase, they

---

370 Wanous, Reichers, and Austin, "Cynicism about Organizational Change," 149.

371 Wanous, Reichers, and Austin, "Cynicism about Organizational Change," 150.

372 Wanous, Reichers, and Austin, "Cynicism about Organizational Change," 150.

373 Jeremy B. Bernerth et al., "Justice, Cynicism, and Commitment: A Study of Important Organizational Change Variables," *The Journal of Applied Behavioral Science* 43, no. 3 (September 2007): 321, https://doi.org/10.1177/0021886306296602.

374 Bernerth et al., "Justice, Cynicism, and Commitment," 307.

have the opportunity to discover how the change can help them personally and professionally.[375]

DEMONSTRATE (OR PROVE) THE INTEGRITY OF YOUR ORGANIZATION

When an organization fails to treat people respectfully, manage processes in good faith, and distribute rewards and sacrifices equitably, it breaks implicit contracts, damages trust, and ultimately causes cynicism toward the whole organization.

To combat *organizational cynicism*, you will need to:

1. **Treat employees fairly and with respect.** We expect to be treated with politeness, dignity, and respect by people in positions of power. We also expect information to be candid, thorough, reasonable, timely, and relevant to us as individuals.[376]

2. **Administer processes fairly.** Major changes should be guided by fair procedures that:

   A. apply consistently across individuals,

   B. apply consistently over time,

   C. are free of bias,

   D. use accurate and relevant information when making decisions,

   E. allow participants to take corrective action if they disagree,

   F. conform to ethical standards, and

   G. consider the opinions of those affected by the outcome.[377]

3. **Distribute resources, rewards, and sacrifices fairly.** We expect the benefits of the organization's success to be shared

---

375 Abraham, "Organizational Cynicism," 285.

376 Bernerth et al., "Justice, Cynicism, and Commitment," 305.

377 Bernerth et al., "Justice, Cynicism, and Commitment," 305.

with the employees who made it possible. Likewise, if organizational change requires sacrifice, it too should be shared. Executive perks, inequitable pay scales, and downsizing focused on lower-level employees exacerbate and create organizational cynicism. Overcoming this will require a commitment to systemic reforms.

4. **Communicate the fairness of the process.** It is just not enough to act fairly. You must tell people that you followed fair procedures. When people suspect something to be unfair, they look at the process that was followed. In cases of downsizing, you must demonstrate that workforce reductions were fairly and humanely administered with generous benefits and support such as outplacement services. Be transparent and clear that you were unbiased, objective, and that you rigorously evaluated alternatives.[378]

REPAIR BROKEN TRUST

People doubt the motives of their leaders as a result of real experiences that damaged trust. To build support for your change effort, you may need to repair trust.

First, you must understand *how* trust was broken. Was it the result of a *lapse of competence* (e.g., we didn't have the right skill set to implement the project correctly) or a *failure of integrity* (e.g., someone deliberately hid mistakes or did not tell the truth)?

If trust was damaged due to a *lapse of competence*, research indicates the following can be effective:

- **Apologize and accept responsibility and blame for past failures.** In accepting blame for the past, you signal your intention to accept responsibility for the future. While the

---

378 Bernerth et al., "Justice, Cynicism, and Commitment," 311.

admission of guilt can diminish trust, people are willing to forgive isolated failures of generally competent people.[379]

- **Be sincere and express genuine remorse.** Research shows that remorse has the largest single effect in generating forgiveness.[380] Apologies are effective in repairing trust if they are sincere and express remorse and guilt. Sincere remorse indicates that the transgressor is repairable.

- **Promise that you will do better.** Promises can quickly restore trust in the short term. But promises must be followed by observable trustworthy actions.[381]

- **Above all, perform trustworthy deeds.** Alone, trustworthy actions can restore trust in the long term.[382] Any path to restoring trust requires consistent trustworthy deeds that demonstrate your integrity.

If trust was broken due to a *violation of integrity*, deception, or underhandedness, the path of repair is much harder. Research shows that apologies for violations of integrity only confirm that one is a dishonest person.[383] This is not to say that one should not accept responsibility for lapses of integrity; rather, you should do everything to avoid violations of integrity.

Violations of trust can be *ambiguous* and interpreted as a lack

---

379 Peter H. Kim et al., "When More Blame Is Better than Less: The Implications of Internal vs. External Attributions for the Repair of Trust after a Competence- vs. Integrity-Based Trust Violation," *Organizational Behavior and Human Decision Processes* 99, no. 1 (January 2006): 51, https://doi.org/10.1016/j.obhdp.2005.07.002.

380 Kinshuk F. Sharma, David Schoorman, and Gary A. Ballinger, "How Can It Be Made Right Again? A Review of Trust Repair Research," *Journal of Management* 49, no. 1 (April 2022): 379, https://doi.org/10.1177/01492063221089897.

381 Maurice E. Schweitzer, John C. Hershey, and Eric T. Bradlow, "Promises and Lies: Restoring Violated Trust," *Organizational Behavior and Human Decision Processes* 101, no. 1 (September 2006): https://doi.org/10.1016/j.obhdp.2006.05.005.

382 Schweitzer, Hershey, and Bradlow, "Promises and Lies," 21.

383 Kim et al., "When More Blame Is Better than Less," 51.

of competence or integrity (e.g., incorrectly filing your tax return to pay less tax). In this case, trust is more effectively repaired by framing the violation as a lapse in competence.

CHAPTER SUMMARY

- Cynicism and a lack of trust can run deep within an organization and can destroy a change effort from the outset.
- Cynicism is the doubt or disbelief about another's motives for their decisions or actions. It is based on a history of real experiences that make an employee conclude their organization and its leader lack integrity.
- Employees can be cynical of an unscrupulous organization that lacks fairness, honesty, and sincerity. They can be cynical of change efforts led by leaders that lack credibility or efforts that are the latest in long string of failures.
- Cynicism is caused by damaged trust and violation of implicit expectations we have of our organization.
- Cynicism has a value. It can be a voice of conscience for the organization and hold leaders accountable. Cynicism keeps us from being taken advantage of. It is also a sign of deeper problems within the organization.
- The harms of cynicism to the employee include emotional distress and suffering. Relationships with the organization may never rebound, and cynical employees will withhold their support for the organization and its change effort.
- Cynicism can become a self-fulfilling phenomenon. It fills the void of communications and project setbacks. Cynical employees beget cynical managers.
- Cynicism can be a sign of significant organizational problems and can be hard to manage. That said, you should understand and deal with the past, head-on.

- Always communicate; cynicism fills the void. Communicate about small successes, no matter how small. Explain the lack of progress or problems. Give people enough information to understand your perspective and rationale. Avoid surprises.
- Keep people involved in decisions that impact them. Show you respect them.
- Demonstrate and communicate the integrity and fairness of processes and the distribution of resources (and sacrifices). Treat employees fairly and with respect. Communicate and listen in an authentic manner.
- You may need to repair broken trust. Do so carefully. The obvious rules apply if trust was broken as a result of incompetence: apologize, be sincere, promise to do better, and perform trustworthy deeds. Generally speaking, people forgive incompetence—you can improve. If trust was broken as a result of a lack of integrity or deception, then you are in trouble; it takes only one dishonest act to confirm you are a dishonest person. Avoid this.

CASE IN POINT: RESISTANCE TO LEADERSHIP DISCONNECTS

"CYNICISM WILL NOT BE TOLERATED": FROM SUPPORT TO CYNICISM TO MUTINY

An in-depth and long-term study of a large technology company's attempt at radical transformation shows how support can turn into cynicism and then mutiny.[384]

The 50,000-person company was fast losing its market share; profits declined approximately 70 percent from the previous year. Investors and the board were demanding a change.

The company brought in a new CEO with extensive high-tech experience who broke up the "monolithic bureaucratic structure" into separate business units and installed a new management team to reduce costs by 25 percent.

The company budgeted $1.2 billion for restructuring to achieve its cash flow targets within three years. To define how the company could improve its financial performance, the top management team engaged 40 "veteran" senior middle managers who in turn enlisted 500 other middle managers. This group suggested a total of 250 projects, of which 150 received funding.

Early on, middle managers were supportive of transformation efforts. Rank-and-file employees supported the new CEO who promised to reduce workloads before downsizing staff, or as he put it "remove the work before we remove the job." He committed to high-quality customer service—a point of competitive advantage—and manageable workloads.

---

384 All information can be found at Huy, Corley, and Kraatz, "From Support to Mutiny," 1656–1670.

Moreover, they appreciated that they were a part of the change: "I like very much that the top managers have given me the opportunity to show what I am capable of." Another said, "I think many of us were selected for our ability, our interest in making changes in achieving a challenge."

Employees even understood that the downsizing was necessary and believed the company was "a very good citizen" by offering generous severance packages.

As the transformation transitioned from formulation to implementation, challenges emerged that led middle managers to rethink their initial optimism and positive judgments of the top management team. Within one year, only 38 percent of employees believed that the company "had a sincere interest in their well-being" and more than 60 percent rated their morale as "fair to very poor."

Many projects were delayed and underperforming. Middle managers complained that the top management team was not providing sufficient support. Middle managers felt the pressure of the three-year time frame bearing down on them. "Failure is not an option" was often repeated, and projects that should have been reconsidered or canned went nowhere.

While the CEO was focused externally, the top management team was overwhelmed. More people than expected took generous severance packages, which left many middle managers stretched thin, overworked, and fatigued.

Middle managers started to believe that the CEO's promise not to remove people before work had not been kept.

Disappointment was especially felt in the customer service department where "middle managers were under intense pressure to deliver good customer service, while managing the collective anxiety and resentment of their line employees who were learning new competencies, while at the same time subject to downsizing...and geographical consolidation." The IT that was promised to improve productivity went vastly over budget and required years of additional development. Without new technology, workloads increased.

Resentment was evident in customer service. One middle manager put it this way: "They say that the greatest priorities are customer service. Yet all the actions demonstrate that the highest priority is short-term, financial results... People are not naïve."

Finally, widespread bitterness prompted the issuance of a memo to middle managers stating, "Cynicism will not be tolerated; we are in a position of leadership, and must project hope and confidence in difficult times."

The CEO and the top management team lost all legitimacy as their middle managers regarded them as "mercenaries of change" motivated by "short-term mandates to make a lot of money" instead of the long-term health of the organization.

Employees believed that the CEO and top management team were disconnected from the realities of their customers and their operations. The pressure to deliver on the financial goals became increasingly intense and exacerbated their fatigue.

At this point, middle managers delayed implementation of any directives they didn't agree with.

After three years, it was clear that the program would not succeed. In a quick attempt to reach financial targets, the top management team cut 3,000 customer service employees.

This was the last straw for middle management. They saw the downsizing as a panicked decision that showed once more how little top management knew or cared. One HR manager said, "This action will kill customer service, and this company is going to live or die on service."

Middle managers openly defied the downsizing order.

Shortly after the revolt, the CEO quit. A new CEO was hired, and the top management team was dissolved. The transformation effort was a failure.

In sum, this large-scale radical effort built substantial early support from middle management by leveraging their *competence* and giving them *control* to define the details of the transformation effort. However, leadership became disconnected from middle management and operations, and the promises of leadership became disconnected from their actions. Their *integrity* was compromised, and cynicism resulted in a mutiny.

Reflections

I started this journey with a fire in my belly to help brave leaders who put their reputations on the line to attempt big and difficult things in their organization. My motivation was to help them understand and overcome resistance to organizational change.

After two years of research on the nature of resistance, I have landed in a place far from where I started. I have found myself in a place of deep empathy for people who struggle with change and a new understanding of the value of resistance.

Even though we are not stuck in the past, we are tethered there. Day in and day out as we go to work, we find ways to build competence and community. We create meaning in our jobs to make peace with our workplaces. We make investments that build over time. Change can disrupt this peace and render our sacrifices irrelevant. In this context, resistance is one way we try to restore the balance we struck and the truce we made.

I would like to conclude this book with some personal reflections that were born out of how this journey has changed me.

I have changed my mind in some key respects. I would like to share with you these revelations of hindsight. These represent moments that I wish I could do over and mindsets I wish I could have adjusted. It is my hope these insights will be helpful to you.

REFLECTION #1: LEADERSHIP AND VISION
DO NOT HAVE THE RIGHT OF WAY

Before this book, I believed that leaders of change were responsible for making big things happen and visions of the future moved organizations forward. I loved giving myself over to an idea, developing plans, and convincing others that my path forward was the best one for the organization. I would wake up at 4:00 a.m. to do my "big picture" work. Though I managed operations well, in my heart of hearts, I believed that my "big picture" for the future was superior to the practice of the current day. My ego was gratified by the idea that I could engineer an organization with my mind.

Now, I have a more profound appreciation for operational details and the people who hold the knowledge of how to get things done in an organization. Compared to "the big picture," the details are easily considered small things. But these small things are potentially the most critical. In changing a small thing, you can potentially pull on a thread that undoes a larger tapestry. Many executives are disconnected from on-the-ground realities, and it is often people at lower levels of an organization who know the most about how it works. This working knowledge is a potential source of rightful resistance when the "big picture" puts something in jeopardy.

REFLECTION #2: LEADING CHANGE IS NOT
MUSCLING YOUR WAY TO THE FINISH
LINE—IT'S EARNING SUPPORT

I have led change efforts that took two years to secure funding and another two to implement. By the time I've hatched an idea, developed a bullet-proof plan, and sold the issue across the organization, I was all in. I was highly confident in my vision and believed it was worth investment and sacrifice. I was intensely focused on the end goal and thought of the organization as a lethargic force. All of its demands for stakeholder engagement, budgetary approvals, and risk calculations were obstacles that I would need to muscle my way through to succeed. In this world, I needed to win. My focus on the finish line was singular and intense—my commitment escalated. In general, I believe the organizational demands and process of leading transformational change often result in the leader's over-commitment and potential rigidity.

I still believe that leading major complex change efforts requires strength and perseverance. Now, I more fully appreciate the risks inherent in disruptive change and the value that perspectives other than mine can bring to the table. Now, I would not assume to know exactly what the finish line should even be. I would assume that my vision has flaws, and I would orchestrate a process to identify and shore up the weaknesses. I would try harder to listen to my harshest critic. I would do as much as I can to make the change good for the people that it impacts the most. I would bring them into the process early and consult them often. I would be willing to change the change.

REFLECTION #3: STABILITY MAKES CHANGE MEANINGFUL

I had a saying, a truism, I coined to describe the herculean challenge of changing well-established organizations: The status quo is the most powerful force on earth, second only to water. My attitude toward the status quo—the way things have always been—was instinctively adversarial. Its sheer staying power blocked progress, and I was itching to shake things up. I did not consider constancy and security as something of value that I needed in my work life.

Now I see the status quo as a source of stability—something we all rely on—and a precondition for change. I now see stability as a key feature, not a bug, of organizations. Stability is what makes an organization and its people reliable. I have come to understand that stability makes change meaningful. It is against a stable backdrop that we can see something move. I have come to understand that stability makes change sustainable. You cannot change everything at once. Without stability, change would be chaos.

REFLECTION #4: CHANGE MEANS LETTING GO OF THE PERSON THAT WE WERE

The research shows that it doesn't matter how much better something else might be; we don't want to let go of what we've got.

We hold on tightly to what we have, to the way we work, and to the people we work with. We can grow oddly fond of systems and processes and may have a hard time explaining why. We take comfort in knowing what we are doing.

I can't help but think that we are reluctant to let go because we doubt that we may ever have it that good again, no matter how much we may complain about our current condition. We build up skills, knowledge, and relationships that allow us to feel accomplished. Change can take us back to the starting line.

Deep down, we may know that what we have now has been hard-won, and the next time we may not win. Perhaps we believe that our competence, success, and comfort are completely contextual. Change the context and we risk having nothing.

Our attachment to the status quo is not just about holding on to a system, process, or structure. It's about holding onto the person that we believe we were. We were the person who knew what to expect and could handle almost any situation. We were the person that others could rely on to get a job done. We were the person who felt good about themselves and what they could accomplish. We were the person "in the know." We had confidence.

Change means letting go of the person that we were with no guarantee that we can become that person again.

REFLECTION #5: LEADING CHANGE IS EXERCISING POWER WITH EMPATHY AND RESPONSIBILITY

You can think of managing change as a simple dynamic. On one hand, someone is initiating and leading change—the change-maker. On the other hand, there are people who must respond, accommodate or implement the change—the change-takers. Change-makers are permitted to disrupt things, and they have power over those who are impacted by the change. They can redesign processes and systems, reconstitute teams and reporting structures, and they can hire and fire. The change-maker is sanctioned to disrupt, which can cause anxiety as people have to relearn something they once knew well and likely take pride in. The change-maker has the power to introduce uncertainty about someone's future. The change-maker can create a sense of overwhelm, alienation, and loss of purpose.

I hope you will exercise your power with empathy and responsibility.

Empathy comes from understanding that all of us are impacted by change on a deeper level and at some point we all resist change. Disruptive change threatens our basic needs for ease, purpose, integrity, control, competence, belonging, and stability. I hope to forever supplant the self-serving stereotype of a small-minded and misguided resistor with a portrait of a complex human motivated by fundamental needs that can, yes, resist change, but also accomplish great things made possible by working together.

Responsibility comes from understanding that you build support for change by managing the needs of people impacted by it. You can also mismanage and ignore these needs, which will as predictably result in resistance. You, the change-maker, have the power, information, and influence to create the conditions that drive major change and make this change good for the people it impacts.

And so the question is, What will you do with your sense of *empathy and responsibility?*

One day we lead, the next day we follow. We all walk in the shoes of resistance at different points in our lives. The time will come when you too will suffer the uncertainty of not knowing your place in a new world or how to navigate it. Today, you have the opportunity to model leadership that you could—when the time comes—gratefully follow.

Acknowledgments

It's a funny thing, writing a book. It's physically and socially isolating. And yet, as I take stock of all the people who have helped me along the way, I feel such a deep sense of human connection and gratitude. This journey has been a rocky road with some highs and many lows. Were it not for the people acknowledged on these few pages who sustained me intellectually and emotionally, this book would not exist.

You will see a long list of accomplished thinkers who have contributed to my understanding of resistance in the bibliography. I would recommend that you read any work cited there. There are a handful who have made a deep and lasting impact on how I understand change, organizations, and management. In the long and quiet hours of reading and writing, I had many conversations in my head with these folks and developed a fondness for them. At this point, they feel like friends.

To the Fords (Jeffery and Laurie), you paved my way to truly understand resistance and have the courage to stand up for it. To John Bargh, your research—profound and disquieting—introduced me to a subterranean version of myself that I don't even know what to make of. To Roy Baumeister, you go so deep into what it means to be human; you also convinced me to stay near people. To Martha Feldman, thank you for reclaiming the notion of "routine" as something dynamic and vital and in so doing elevating the people who keep them going. To Jane Dutton, for your many insights along the way and for showing us how alive organizations are below the top rungs. To Charlan Nemeth, for demonstrating how the lone voice can move many and planting the seeds of personal courage. Barry Staw, with decades of service to your field, you bring clarity and humanity to how we act and react in organizations and helped me see a few not-so-flattering tendencies in myself. To Michael Tuschman, your frameworks of organizational identity and design helped resolve seeming contradictions. To Dennis Gioia, for showing how "who we are" is so bound up with how we understand and navigate change. To Jeffery Pfeffer and Barbara Kellerman, for shaking me by the collar and helping me to recognize outworn and self-serving notions of leadership and most importantly to move on. To Gerry Salancik, within two pages you catapulted to the top of my list of people I would most want to have a beer with. I wish you had lived longer. Finally, to Karl Weick, I have very few regrets, but one is not having studied you sooner. I have no doubt that life would have been different and I would have been wiser.

I am truly grateful for the folks who took the time to provide feedback when my ideas were in their early, insecure, and not-so-pretty stages. Some of you were a firehouse while others delivered the bad news surgically. All were incredibly helpful and generous. Thanks to Pari Sabety, Emily Eakin, Watt Hamlett, Sandra Rowe, Brian Williams, Terrence Metz, Dave Acup, Kiva LaTouche, Michael Ward, Misty McLaughlin, Jessica Langelaan, Frank Popp, Matthew Worwood, and Doug Harrison. Many thanks to Jonathan Palmer who was for so many years a generous, wise and compassionate partner in making change. I would also like to thank Shannyn Lee for setting things in motion. For keeping them going, I owe a huge hug to Karyn Ruth White, who picked me up when I was down and kept me real.

To my wonderful publishing team. Thanks to Mark Chait for seeing my mission so clearly and enthusiastically. You gave me a big boost when I needed it most. To Maggie Rains, Emmy Koziak, and Caroline Hough for being such genuine and supportive partners.

The impetus for this book was to help people like my clients who are trying to steer complex ships in the right direction. They invited me into their hard problems, and I am truly grateful to have had the opportunity to help them engineer change in their organizations. My thanks to Amanda Krause, Paula Hunker, Aalok Kanani, Melanie Tonlan, Amy Middleton, Laura DuBuys, and Jeff Sailer. To Sara Hobel and Liza Ehrlich, I can't thank you enough for being my closest partners in so many respects while this book was written.

Oh friends, I could not have weathered these storms were it not for you. Thank you for your endless patience and support to keep going. I've always said that my life would boil down to a handful, and here you are. All my love to Amity Worrel, Paxton Barnes, Nader Sadre and Lauren Muir, Colleen McCann, Kathi Schaeffer, Judy Frimer, Alison Power, and Marie Keen.

To Mom and Dad, I thank you for living a life that gives me the confidence and courage to go against the grain. To my wombmate Jill who, from moment zero, has been a partner through thick and thin. Dennis and Gloria, thank you for all the love and support.

No one has literally stood by my side more over the past two years in writing this book than my elderly dogs, Joan and Bill. These constant companions have taught me so much about resistance to change. In their demand that each day be like the one before, I can see routine at work along with their need for ease. In their unyielding pecking order (Joan #1), I see their need for stability within our group. In their insistence that the family always stay together on our walks, I see their need for belonging. In their refusal to walk another five feet without a treat, I see their need for control. In their constant vigilance for anything that could rupture the sanctity of our home, I see purpose. I thank them for tethering me to the lighter side of life.

Lastly, to Steven. I had no idea what I was signing myself up for in writing a book. Whatever it was, I signed you up too—but forgot to ask. We close out this chapter in the story of our thirty wonderful years together. Now, with nothing but a blank page before us, we lift our pen.

About the Author

JAN KADERLY is the founder of Brave Bird Consulting (www. gobravebird.com), which helps purpose-driven organizations develop strategies that stake a claim, galvanize people, and leave a mark on the world.

For twenty-five years, Jan has led major change in large and complex organizations. Whether it's leading an award-winning global campaign that led to a US ivory ban, overhauling digital infrastructure and citizen engagement programs, or redefining the identity of an organization, Jan's work has been transformational.

Organizations emerge prepared to lead millions of people to action, use systems to develop better relationships, and understand themselves in new ways that inspire pride and growth.

This type of disruptive change has never been a victory march. It has always encountered resistance. Now, Jan is taking her knack for rigorous methodology and commitment to learning from the very best thinkers to help organizations understand and embrace resistance.

Jan regularly speaks at conferences and lectures at universities, including New York University, Columbia, and the University of Connecticut.

Jan was raised on farms—soybean in Ohio and cotton and sheep in the Texas panhandle. She was a lucky beneficiary of affordable higher education, earning a bachelor's degree from the University of Texas and a master's degree from the University of Pennsylvania (thanks to a fellowship). Jan's life passions are understanding what makes collectives succeed and fail, elderly dogs, cooking dumplings, and singing wildly out of key.

Bibliography

Abraham, Rebecca. "Organizational Cynicism: Bases and Consequences." *Genetic, Social, and General Psychology Monographs* 126, no. 3 (September 2000): 269–292. https://pubmed.ncbi.nlm.nih.gov/10950198.

Albert, Stuart, and David A. Whetten. "Organizational Identity." In *Research in Organizational Behavior* Vol. 7, edited by Barry M. Staw and Larry L. Cummings, 263–295. Greenwich, CT: JAI Press, 1985.

Anand, Vikas, Blake E. Ashfort, and Mahendra Joshi. "Business as Usual: The Acceptance and Perpetuation of Corruption in Organizations." *Academy of Management Perspectives* 18, no. 2 (May 2004): 39–53. https://doi.org/10.5465/ame.2004.13837437.

Argote, Linda, and Jerry M. Guo. "Routines and Transactive Memory Systems: Creating, Coordinating, Retaining, and Transferring Knowledge in Organizations." *Research in Organizational Behavior* 36 (2016): 65–84. https://doi.org/10.1016/j.riob.2016.10.002.

Ashford, Susan J. "Individual Strategies for Coping with Stress during Organizational Transitions." *The Journal of Applied Behavioral Science* 24, no. 1 (February 1988): 19–36. https://doi.org/10.1177/0021886388241005.

Ashforth, Blake E., and Vikas Anand. "The Normalization of Corruption in Organizations." In *Research in Organizational Behavior* Vol. 25, edited by Roderick M. Kramer and Barry M. Staw, 1–52. Greenwich, CT: JAI Press, 2003. https://doi.org/10.1016/S0191-3085(03)25001-2.

Ashforth, Blake E., and Yitzhak Fried. "The Mindlessness of Organizational Behaviors." *Human Relations* 41, no. 4 (April 1988): 305–329. https://doi.org/10.1177/001872678804100403.

Ashforth, Blake E., and Raymond T. Lee. "Defensive Behavior in Organizations: A Preliminary Model." *Human Relations* 43, no. 7 (July 1990): 621–648. https://doi.org/10.1177/001872679004300702.

Ataee, Ramezan Ali, Mohammad Hosein Ataee, Ali Mehrabi Tavana, and Mahmud Salesi. "Bacteriological Aspects of Hand Washing: A Key for Health Promotion and Infections Control." *International Journal of Preventative Medicine* 8 (March 2017): 16. https://doi.org/10.4103/2008-7802.201923.

Bandura, Albert. "Self-Efficacy Mechanism in Human Agency." *American Psychologist* 37, no. 2 (1982): 122–147. https://doi.org/10.1037/0003-066X.37.2.122.

Bardach, Eugene. "Presidential Address—The Extrapolation Problem: How Can We Learn from the Experience of Others?" *Journal of Policy Analysis and Management* 23, no. 2 (March 2004): 205–220. https://doi.org/10.1002/pam.20000.

Bargh, John A. "The Cognitive Unconscious in Everyday Life." In *The Cognitive Unconscious: The First Half Century*, edited by Arthur S. Reber and Rhianon Allen, 89–114. New York: Oxford University Press, 2022.

———. "It Was Social Consistency that Mattered All Along." *Psychological Inquiry* 29, no. 2 (October 2018): 60–62. https://doi.org/10.1080/1047840X.2018.1480586.

Bargh, John A., and Tanya L. Chartrand. "The Unbearable Automaticity of Being." *American Psychologist* 54, no. 7 (1999): 462–479. https://doi.org/10.1037/0003-066X.54.7.462.

Barsade, Sigal G. "The Ripple Effect: Emotional Contagion and its Influence on Group Behavior." *Administrative Science Quarterly* 47, no. 4 (December 2002): 644–675. https://doi.org/10.2307/3094912.

Barsade, Sigal G., Constantinos G.V. Coutifaris, and Julianna Pillemer. "Emotional Contagion in Organizational Life." *Research in Organizational Behavior* 38 (January 2018): 137–151. https://doi.org/10.1016/j.riob.2018.11.005.

Baumeister, Roy F., Ellen Bratslavsky, Catrin Finkenauer, and Kathleen D. Vohs. "Bad Is Stronger than Good." *Review of General Psychology* 5, no. 4 (December 2001): 323–370. https://doi.org/10.1037/1089-2680.5.4.323.

Baumeister, Roy F., Ellen Bratslavsky, Mark Muraven, and Dianne M. Tice. "Ego Depletion: Is the Active Self a Limited Resource?" *Journal of Personality and Social Psychology* 74, no. 5 (May 1998): 1252–1265. https://doi.org/10.1037//0022-3514.74.5.1252.

Baumeister, Roy F., and Mark R. Leary. "The Need to Belong: Desire for Interpersonal Attachments as a Fundamental Human Motivation." *Psychological Bulletin* 117, no. 3 (1995): 497–529. https://doi.org/10.1037/0033-2909.117.3.497.

Baumeister, Roy F., Kathleen D. Vohs, Jennifer L. Aaker, and Emily N. Garbinsky. "Some Key Differences between a Happy Life and a Meaningful Life." *Journal of Positive Psychology* 8, no. 6 (August 2013): 505–526. https://doi.org/10.1080/17439760.2013.830764.

Baumeister, Roy F., and Kathleen D. Vohs. "The Pursuit of Meaningfulness in Life." In *Handbook of Positive Psychology*, edited by C. R. Snyder and Shane J. Lopez, 608–618. New York: Oxford University Press, 2002.

Becker, Markus C. "Organizational Routines: A Review of the Literature." *Industrial and Corporate Change* 13, no. 4 (August 2004): 643–678. https://doi.org/10.1093/icc/dth026.

Bénabou, Roland. "Groupthink: Collective Delusions in Organizations and Markets." *The Review of Economic Studies* 80, no. 2 (April 2013): 429–462. https://doi.org/10.1093/restud/rds030.

Berger, Jonah. "Word of Mouth and Interpersonal Communication: A Review and Directions for Future Research." *Journal of Consumer Psychology* 24, no. 4 (May 2014): 586–607. https://doi.org/10.1016/j.jcps.2014.05.002.

Bernerth, Jeremy B., Achilles A. Armenakis, Hubert S. Field, and H. Jack Walker. "Justice, Cynicism, and Commitment: A Study of Important Organizational Change Variables." *The Journal of Applied Behavioral Science* 43, no. 3 (September 2007): 303–326. https://doi.org/10.1177/0021886306296602.

Bernerth, Jeremy B., H. Jack Walker, and Stanley G. Harris. "Change Fatigue: Development and Initial Validation of a New Measure." *Work & Stress* 25, no. 4 (December 2011): 321–337. https://doi.org/10.1080/02678373.2011.634280.

Bigley, Gregory A., and Karlene H. Roberts. "The Incident Command System: High-Reliability Organizing for Complex and Volatile Task Environments." *Academy of Management Journal* 44, no. 6 (December 2001): 1281–1299.

Boeker, Warren. "Power and Managerial Dismissal: Scapegoating at the Top." *Administrative Science Quarterly* 37, no. 3 (September 1992): 400–421. https://doi.org/10.2307/2393450.

Bourgeois, L. J., and Kathleen M. Eisenhardt. "Strategic Decision Processes in High Velocity Environments: Four Cases in the Microcomputer Industry." *Management Science* 34, no. 7 (July 1988): 816–835. https://doi.org/10.1287/mnsc.34.7.816.

Brewer, Marilynn B. "The Social Self: On Being the Same and Different at the Same Time." *Personality and Social Psychology Bulletin* 17, no. 5 (October 1991): 475–482. https://doi.org/10.1177/0146167291175001.

Brockner, Joel, Tom R. Tyler, and Rochelle Cooper-Schneider. "The Influence of Prior Commitment to an Institution on Reactions to Perceived Unfairness: The Higher They Are, The Harder They Fall." In "Process and Outcome: Perspectives on the Distribution of Rewards in Organizations." Special issue, *Administrative Science Quarterly* 37, no. 2 (June 1992): 241–261. https://doi.org/10.2307/2393223.

Brown, Andrew D., and Ken Starkey. "Organizational Identity and Learning: A Psychodynamic Perspective." *The Academy of Management Review* 25, no. 1 (January 2000): 102–120. https://doi.org/10.2307/259265.

Burt, Ronald S. "Social Contagion and Innovation: Cohesion versus Structural Equivalence." *American Journal of Sociology* 92, no. 6 (May 1987): 1287–1335. https://doi.org/10.1086/228667.

Chartrand, Tanya L., and John A. Bargh. "The Chameleon Effect: The Perception-Behavior Link and Social Interaction." *Journal of Personality and Social Psychology* 76, no. 6 (June 1999): 893–910. https://doi.org/10.1037/0022-3514.76.6.893.

Chartrand, Tanya L., and Jessica L. Lakin. "The Antecedents and Consequences of Human Behavioral Mimicry." *Annual Review of Psychology* 64, no. 1 (September 2012): 285–307. https://doi.org/10.1146/annurev-psych-113011-143754.

Chattopadhyay, Prithviraj, William H. Glick, and George P. Huber. "Organizational Actions in Response to Threats and Opportunities." *The Academy of Management Journal* 44, no. 5 (October 2001): 937–955. https://www.jstor.org/stable/3069439.

Chawla, Anuradha, and E. Kevin Kelloway. "Predicting Openness and Commitment to Change." *Leadership & Organizational Development Journal* 25, no. 6 (September 2004): 485–498. https://doi.org/10.1108/01437730410556734.

Cialdini, Robert B. *Influence, New and Expanded: The Psychology of Persuasion.* New York: Harper Collins, 2021.

Cialdini, Robert B., Richard J. Borden, Avril Throne, Marcus Randall Walker, Stephen Freeman, and Lloyd Reynolds Sloan. "Basking in Reflected Glory: Three (Football) Field Studies." *Journal of Personality and Social Psychology* 34, no. 3 (1976): 366–375. https://doi.org/10.1037/0022-3514.34.3.366.

Cialdini, Robert B., and Noah J. Goldstein. "Social Influence: Compliance and Conformity." *Annual Review of Psychology* 55, no. 1 (February 2004): 591–621. https://doi.org/ 10.1146/annurev.psych.55.090902.142015.

Daly, Alan J. "Rigid Response in an Age of Accountability: The Potential of Leadership and Trust." *Educational Administration Quarterly* 45, no. 2 (April 2009): 168–216. https://doi.org/10.1177/0013161X0833049.

David, Paul A. "Clio and the Economics of QWERTY." *The American Economic Review* 75, no. 2 (May 1985): 323–337. https://www.jstor.org/stable/1805621.

———. "Why Are Institutions the 'Carriers of History'?: Path Dependence and the Evolution of Conventions, Organizations and Institutions." *Structural Change and Economic Dynamics*5, no. 2 (December 1994): 205–220. https://doi.org/10.1016/0954-349X(94)90002-7.

Dean, James W., Pamela Brandes, and Ravi Dharwadkar. "Organizational Cynicism." *The Academy of Management Review* 23, no. 2 (April 1998): 341–352. https://doi.org/10.2307/259378.

Dittrich, Katharina, Stéphane Guérard, and David Seidl. "Talking about Routines: The Role of Reflective Talk in Routine Change." *Organizational Science* 27, no. 3 (January 2016): 678–697. https://doi.org/10.1287/orsc.2015.1024.

Djelic, Marie-Laure, and Sigrid Quack. "Overcoming Path Dependency: Path Generation in Open Systems." *Theory and Society* 36, no. 2 (March 2007): 161–186. https://doi.org/10.1007/s11186-007-9026-0.

Dutton, Jane E., Susan J. Ashford, Regina M. O'Neill, and Katherine A. Lawrence. "Moves that Matter: Issue Selling and Organizational Change." *Academy of Management Journal* 44, no. 4 (August 2001): 716–736.

Dutton, Jane E., Janet M. Dukerich, and Celia V. Harquail. "Organizational Images and Member Identification." *Administrative Science Quarterly* 39, no. 2 (June 1994): 239–263. https://doi.org/10.2307/2393235.

Eisenhardt, Kathleen M. "Making Fast Strategic Decisions in High-Velocity Environments." *The Academy of Management Journal* 32, no. 3 (September 1989): 543–576. https://www.jstor.org/stable/256434.

Elia, Fabrizio, Fabrizio Calzavarini, Paola Bianco, Renata Gabriella Vecchietti, Antonio Franco Macor, Alessia D'Orazio, Antonella Dragonetti, et al. "A Nudge Intervention to Improve Hand Hygiene Compliance in the Hospital." *Internal and Emergency Medicine* 17, no. 7 (October 2022): 1899–1905. https://doi.org/10.1007/s11739-022-03024-7.

Erasmus, Vicki, Thea J. Daha, Hans Brug, Jan Hendrik Richardus, Myra D. Behrendt, Margreet C. Vos, and Ed F. van Beeck. "Systematic Review of Studies on Compliance with Hand Hygiene Guidelines in Hospital Care." *Infection Control and Hospital Epidemiology* 31, no. 3 (March 2010): 283–294. https://doi.org/10.1086/650451.

Feldman, Martha S., and Brian T. Pentland. "Reconceptualizing Organizational Routines as a Source of Flexibility and Change." *Administrative Science Quarterly* 48, no. 1 (March 2003). https://doi.org/10.2307/3556620.

Fiol, C. Marlene. "Capitalizing on Paradox: The Role of Language in Transforming Organizational Identities." *Organizational Science* 13, no. 6 (December 2002): 653–666. https://doi.org/10.1287/orsc.13.6.653.502.

Fiol, Marlena, and Edward O'Connor. "Unlearning Established Organizational Routines – Part I." *The Learning Organization* 24, no. 1 (January 2017): 13–29. https://doi.org/10.1108/TLO-09-2016-0056.

Ford, Jeffrey D., and Laurie W. Ford. "Stop Blaming Resistance to Change and Start Using It." *Organizational Dynamics* 39, no. 1 (January–March 2010): 24–36. https://doi.org/10.1016/j.orgdyn.2009.10.002.

Ford, Jeffrey D., Laurie W. Ford, and Angelo D'Amelio. "Resistance to Change: The Rest of the Story." *Academy of Management Review* 33, no. 2 (April 2008): 362–377. https://doi.org/10.5465/amr.2008.31193235.

Freedman, Jonathan L., and Scott C. Fraser. "Compliance without Pressure: The Foot-in-the-Door Technique." *Journal of Personality and Social Psychology* 4, no. 2 (1966): 195–202. https://doi.org/10.1037/h0023552.

Gilbert, Clark G. "Unbundling the Structure of Inertia: Resource versus Routine Rigidity." *Academy of Management Journal* 48, no. 5 (October 2005): 741–763. https://doi.org/10.5465/amj.2005.18803920.

Gioia, Dennis A., and Kumar Chittipeddi. "Sensemaking and Sensegiving in Strategic Change Initiation." *Strategic Management Journal* 12, no. 6 (September 1991): 433–447. https://www.jstor.org/stable/2486479.

Gioia, Dennis A., Rajiv Nag, and Kevin G. Corley. "Visionary Ambiguity and Strategic Change: The Virtue of Vagueness in Launching Major Organizational Change." *Journal of Management Inquiry* 21, no. 4 (May 2012): 364–375. https://doi.org/10.1177/1056492612244722.

Gioia, Dennis A., Shubha D. Patvardhan, Aimee L. Hamilton, and Kevin G. Corley. "Organizational Identity Formation and Change." *Academy of Management Annals* 7, no. 1 (June 2013): 123–193. https://doi.org/10.5465/19416520.2013.762225.

Gioia, Dennis A., Majken Schultz, and Kevin G. Corley. "Organizational Identity, Image, and Adaptive Instability." *Academy of Management Review* 25, no. 1 (January 2000): 63–81. https://doi.org/10.2307/259263.

Grant, Adam M. "Relational Job Design and the Motivation to Make a Prosocial Difference." *Academy of Management Review* 32, no. 2 (April 2007): 393–417. https://doi.org/10.5465/amr.2007.24351328.

Hall, Stephen, Dan Lovallo, and Reinier Musters. "How to Put Your Money Where Your Strategy Is." *McKinsey Quarterly*, March 1, 2012. https://www.mckinsey.com/capabilities/strategy-and-corporate-finance/our-insights/how-to-put-your-money-where-your-strategy-is.

Hannan, Michael T., and John Freeman. "Structural Inertia and Organizational Change." *American Sociological Review* 49, no. 2 (April 1984): 149–164. https://doi.org/10.2307/2095567.

Huy, Quy Nguyen, Kevin G. Corley, and Matthew S. Kraatz. "From Support to Mutiny: Shifting Legitimacy Judgments and Emotional Reactions Impacting the Implementation of Radical Change." *Academy of Management Journal* 57, no. 6 (March 2014): 1650–1680. https://doi.org/10.5465/amj.2012.0074.

Jackson, Susan E., and Jane E. Dutton. "Discerning Threats and Opportunities." *Administrative Science Quarterly* 33, no. 3 (September 1988): 370–387. https://doi.org/10.2307/2392714.

Janis, Irving L. *Victims of Groupthink: Psychological Studies of Foreign-Policy Decisions and Fiascoes*. Boston: Houghton Mifflin, 1972.

Janie, Irving L., and Leon Mann. *Decision Making: A Psychological Analysis of Conflict, Choice, and Commitment.* New York: Free Press, 1977.

Kahneman, Daniel, Jack L. Knetsch, and Richard H. Thaler. "Anomalies: The Endowment Effect, Loss Aversion, and Status Quo Bias." *Journal of Economic Perspectives* 5, no. 1 (Winter 1991): 193–206. https://doi.org/10.1257/jep.5.1.193.

Kellerman, Barbara. *The End of Leadership.* New York: Harper Business, 2012.

———. *Professionalizing Leadership.* New York: Oxford University Press, 2018.

Khurana, Rakesh. "The Curse of the Superstar CEO." *Harvard Business Review* 80, no. 9 (September 2002): 60–66. https://hbr.org/2002/09/the-curse-of-the-superstar-ceo.

Kim, Peter H., Kurt T. Dirks, Cecily D. Cooper, and Donald L. Ferrin. "When More Blame Is Better than Less: The Implications of Internal vs. External Attributions for the Repair of Trust after a Competence- vs. Integrity-Based Trust Violation." *Organizational Behavior and Human Decision Processes* 99, no. 1 (January 2006): 49–65. https://doi.org/10.1016/j.obhdp.2005.07.002.

Knapp, Jake, John Zeratsky, and Braden Kowitz. *Sprint: How to Solve Big Problems and Test New Ideas in Just Five Days.* New York: Simon and Schuster, 2016.

Kouzes, James M., and Barry Z. Posner. "The Credibility Factor: What Followers Expect from Their Leaders." *Management Review* 79, no. 1 (January 1990): 29.

Krulee, Gilbert K. "The Scanlon Plan: Co-Operation Through Participation." *The Journal of Business* 28, no. 2 (April 1955): 100–113. https://www.jstor.org/stable/2350903.

Lafley, A. G., and Roger L. Martin. *Playing to Win: How Strategy Really Works.* Brighton, MA: Harvard Business Press, 2013.

Lakin, Jessica L., Valerie E. Jefferis, Clara Michelle Cheng, and Tanya L. Chartrand. "The Chameleon Effect as Social Glue: Evidence for the Evolutionary Significance of Nonconscious Mimicry." *Journal of Nonverbal Behavior* 27, no. 3 (2003): 145–162. https://doi.org/10.1023/A:1025389814290.

Lawler, Edward E., and Susan A. Mohrman. "Quality Circles After the Fad." *Harvard Business Review* 63, no. 1 (January 1985): 65–71. https://hbr.org/1985/01/quality-circles-after-the-fad.

Lesier, Fred G., and Elbridge S. Puckett. "The Scanlon Plan Has Proved Itself." *Harvard Business Review* 47, no. 5 (1969): 109–118.

Loewenstein, George. "Out of Control: Visceral Influences on Behavior." *Organizational Behavior and Human Decision Processes* 65, no. 3 (March 1996): 272–292. https://doi.org/10.1006/obhd.1996.0028.

Loewenstein, G. F., E. U. Weber, C. K. Hsee, and N. Welch. "Risk as Feelings." *Psychological Bulletin* 127, no. 2 (March 2001): 267–286. https://doi.org/10.1037/0033-2909.127.2.267.

Louis, Meryl Reis, and Robert I. Sutton. "Switching Cognitive Gears: From Habits of Mind to Active Thinking." *Human Relations* 44, no. 1 (January 1991): 55–76. https://doi.org/10.1177/001872679104400104.

Maddux, James E. "Self-Efficacy." In *Interpersonal and Intrapersonal Expectancies*, edited by Sławomir Trusz and Przemysław Babel, 41–46. New York: Routledge, 2016.

Martela, Frank, and Anne B. Pessi. "Significant Work Is about Self-Realization and Broader Purpose: Defining the Key Dimensions of Meaningful Work." *Frontiers in Psychology* 9 (March 2018): 363. https://doi.org/10.3389/fpsyg.2018.00363.

Martin de Holan, Pablo, Nelson Phillips, and Thomas B. Lawrence. "Managing Organizational Forgetting." *MIT Sloan Management Review* 45, no. 2 (Winter 2004): 45–51. https://sloanreview.mit.edu/article/managing-organizational-forgetting.

Massoud, Jacob A., Bonnie F. Daily, and James W. Bishop. "Reward for Environmental Performance: Using the Scanlon Plan as Catalyst to Green Organisations." *International Journal of Environment, Workplace and Employment* 4, no. 1 (January 2008): 15–31. https://doi.org/10.1504/IJEWE.2008.022255.

Mayer, Roger C., James H. Davis, and F. David Schoorman. "An Integrative Model of Organizational Trust." *Academy of Management Review* 20, no. 3 (July 1995): 703–734. https://doi.org/10.2307/258792.

McKnight, Patrick E., and Todd B. Kashdan. "Purpose in Life as a System that Creates and Sustains Health and Well-Being: An Integrative, Testable Theory." *Review of General Psychology* 13, no. 3 (September 2009): 242–251. https://doi.org/10.1037/a0017152.

Mesmer-Magnus, Jessica R., and Chockalingam Viswesvaran. "Whistleblowing in Organizations: An Examination of Correlates of Whistleblowing Intentions, Actions, and Retaliation." *Journal of Business Ethics* 62, no. 3 (December 2005): 277–297. https://doi.org/10.1007/s10551-005-0849-1.

Meyer, John P., and Lynne Herscovitch. "Commitment in the Workplace: Toward a General Model." *Human Resource Management Review* 11, no. 3 (Autumn 2001): 299–326. https://doi.org/10.1016/S1053-4822(00)00053-X.

Mowday, Richard T. "Reflections on the Study and Relevance of Organizational Commitment." *Human Resource Management Review* 8, no. 6 (Winter 1998): 387–401. https://doi.org/10.1016/S1053-4822(99)00006-6.

Murphy, Kevin R. "Performance Evaluation Will Not Die, But It Should." *Human Resource Management Journal* 30, no. 1 (October 2019): 13–31. https://doi.org/10.1111/1748-8583.12259.

Nag, Rajiv, Kevin G. Corley, and Dennis A. Gioia. "The Intersection of Organizational Identity, Knowledge, and Practice: Attempting Strategic Change Via Knowledge Grafting." *Academy of Management Journal* 50, no. 4 (August 2007): 821–847. https://doi.org/10.5465/amj.2007.26279173.

Nemeth, Charlan Jeanne. "Differential Contributions of Majority and Minority Influence." *Psychological Review* 93, no. 1 (1986): 23–32. https://doi.org/10.1037/0033-295X.93.1.23.

Nemeth, Charlan Jeanne, Joanie B. Connell, John D. Rogers, and Keith S. Brown. "Improving Decision Making by Means of Dissent." *Journal of Applied Social Psychology* 31, no. 1 (July 2006): 48–58. https://doi.org/10.1111/j.1559-1816.2001.tb02481.x.

Nemeth, Charlan Jeanne, and Barry M. Staw. "The Tradeoffs of Social Control and Innovation in Groups and Organizations." In *Advances in Experimental Social Psychology* Vol. 22, edited by Leonard Berkowitz, 175–210. Cambridge, MA: Academic Press, 1989.

Ocasio, William. "Towards an Attention-Based View of the Firm." *Strategic Management Journal* 18, no. S1 (December 1998): 187–206. https://doi.org/10.1002/(SICI)1097-0266(199707)18:1+<187::AID-SMJ936>3.0.CO;2-K.

Olsen, Brad, and Dena Sexton. "Threat Rigidity, School Reform, and How Teachers View Their Work Inside Current Education Policy Contexts." *American Educational Research Journal* 46, no. 1 (March 2009): 9–44. https://doi.org/10.3102/0002831208320573.

O'Reilly, Charles. "Corporations, Culture, and Commitment: Motivation and Social Control in Organizations." *California Management Review* 31, no. 4 (Summer 1989): 9–25. https://doi.org/10.2307/41166580.

O'Reilly, Charles A., and Jennifer A. Chatman. "Culture as Social Control: Corporations, Cults, and Commitment." In *Research in Organizational Behavior* Vol. 18, edited by Barry M. Staw and Larry L. Cummings, 157–200. Greenwich, CT: JAI Press, 1996.

———. "Organizational Commitment and Psychological Attachment: The Effects of Compliance, Identification, and Internalization on Prosocial Behavior." *Journal of Applied Psychology* 71, no. 3 (1986): 492–499. https://doi.org/10.1037/0021-9010.71.3.492.

Osburn, Joe, Guy Caruso, and Wolf Wolfensberger. "The Concept of 'Best Practice': A Brief Overview of Its Meanings, Scope, Uses, and Shortcomings." *International Journal of Disability, Development and Education* 58, no. 3 (September 2011): 213–222. https://doi.org/10.1080/1034912X.2011.598387.

Patton, Michael Quinn. "Evaluation, Knowledge Management, Best Practices, and High Quality Lessons Learned." *American Journal of Evaluation* 22, no. 3 (September 2001): 329–336. https://doi.org/10.1177/109821400102200307.

Pfeffer, Jeffrey. *Leadership BS: Fixing Workplaces and Careers One Truth at a Time.* New York: Harper Business, 2015.

Pfeffer, Jeffrey, and Robert I. Sutton. *Hard Facts, Dangerous Half-Truths, and Total Nonsense: Profiting from Evidence-Based Management.* Brighton, MA: Harvard Business Review Press, 2006.

Polites, Greta L., and Elena Karahanna. "Shackled to the Status Quo: The Inhibiting Effects of Incumbent System Habit, Switching Costs, and Inertia on New System Acceptance." *MIS Quarterly* 36, no. 1 (March 2012): 21–42. https://doi.org/10.2307/41410404.

Raffaelli, Ryan, Mary Ann Glynn, and Michael Tushman. "Frame Flexibility: The Role of Cognitive and Emotional Framing in Innovation Adoption by Incumbent Firms." *Strategic Management Journal* 40, no. 7 (February 2019): 1013–1039. https://doi.org/10.1002/smj.3011.

Ravasi, Davide, and Majken Schultz. "Responding to Organizational Identity Threats: Exploring the Role of Organizational Culture." *Academy of Management Journal* 49, no. 5 (June 2006): 433–458. https://doi.org/10.5465/AMJ.2006.21794663.

Reichers, Arnon E., John P. Wanous, and James T. Austin. "Understanding and Managing Cynicism about Organizational Change." *Academy of Management Perspectives* 11, no. 1 (February 1997): 48–59. https://doi.org/10.5465/ame.1997.9707100659.

Ross, Jerry, and Barry M. Staw. "Organizational Escalation and Exit: Lessons from the Shoreham Nuclear Power Plant." *Academy of Management Journal* 36, no. 4 (August 1993): 701–732. https://www.jstor.org/stable/256756.

Ross, Lee, and Richard E. Nisbett. *The Person and the Situation: Perspectives of Social Psychology*. London: Pinter & Martin, 2011. First published 1991 by McGraw-Hill (New York).

Rosso, Brent D., Kathryn H. Dekas, and Amy Wrzesniewski. "On the Meaning of Work: A Theoretical Integration and Review." *Research in Organizational Behavior* 30 (January 2010): 91–127. https://doi.org/10.1016/j.riob.2010.09.001.

Rothschild, Zachary K., Mark J. Landau, Daniel Sullivan, and Lucas A. Keefer. "A Dual-Motive Model of Scapegoating: Displacing Blame to Reduce Guilt or Increase Control." *Journal of Personality and Social Psychology* 102, no. 6 (2012): 1148–1163. https://doi.org/10.1037/a0027413.

Rousseau, Denise M. "Psychological and Implied Contracts in Organizations." *Employee Responsibilities and Rights Journal* 2, no. 2 (1989): 121–139. https://doi.org/10.1007/BF01384942.

Rozin, Paul, and Edward B. Royzman. "Negativity Bias, Negativity Dominance, and Contagion." *Personality and Social Psychology Review* 5, no. 4 (November 2001): 296–320. https://doi.org/10.1207/S15327957PSPR0504_2.

Rumelt, Richard P. "Precis of Inertia and Transformation." 2003. https://www.studocu.com/row/document/national-university-of-sciences-and-technology/electrical-engneering/berkeley-precis/64596594. Revised and abridged version of Richard P. Rumelt, "Inertia and Transformation," in *Resources in an Evolutionary Perspective: Towards as Synthesis of Evolutionary and Resource-Based Approaches to Strategy*, edited by Cynthia A. Montgomery, Norwell, MA: Kluwer Academic Publishers, 1995: 101–132.

Ryan, Richard M., and Edward L. Deci. "Self-Determination Theory and the Facilitation of Intrinsic Motivation, Social Development, and Well-Being." *American Psychologist* 55, no. 1 (January 2000): 68–78. https://doi.org/10.1037/0003-066X.55.1.68.

Salancik, Gerald R. "Commitment Is Too Easy!" *Organizational Dynamics* 6, no. 1 (Summer 1977): 62–80. https://doi.org/10.1016/0090-2616(77)90035-3.

Samuelson, William, and Richard Zeckhauser. "Status Quo Bias in Decision Making." *Journal of Risk and Uncertainty* 1, no. 1 (March 1988): 7–59. https://doi.org/10.1007/BF00055564.

Schrand, Catherine M., and Sarah L. C. Zechman. "Executive Overconfidence and the Slippery Slope to Financial Misreporting." *Journal of Accounting and Economics* 53, nos. 1–2 (February–April 2012): 311–329. https://doi.org/10.1016/j.jacceco.2011.09.001.

Schweitzer, Maurice E., John C. Hershey, and Eric T. Bradlow. "Promises and Lies: Restoring Violated Trust." *Organizational Behavior and Human Decision Processes* 101, no. 1 (September 2006): 1–19. https://doi.org/10.1016/j.obhdp.2006.05.005.

Sharma, Kinshuk, F. David Schoorman, and Gary A. Ballinger. "How Can It Be Made Right Again? A Review of Trust Repair Research." *Journal of Management* 49, no. 1 (April 2022): 363–399. https://doi.org/10.1177/01492063221089897.

Simonson, Itamar, and Barry M. Staw. "Deescalation Strategies: A Comparison of Techniques for Reducing Commitment to Losing Courses of Action." *Journal of Applied Psychology* 77, no. 4 (1992): 419–426. https://doi.org/10.1037/0021-9010.77.4.419.

Stanley, David J., John P. Meyer, and Laryssa Topolnytsky. "Employee Cynicism and Resistance to Organizational Change." *Journal of Business and Psychology* 19, no. 4 (June 2005): 429–459. https://doi.org/10.1007/s10869-005-4518-2.

Starbuck, William H. "Unlearning Ineffective or Obsolete Technologies." IOMS: Information Systems Working Papers, NYU Working Paper no. 2451/14188, New York University, New York, 1996. https://papers.ssrn.com/sol3/papers.cfm?abstract_id=1284804.

Staw, Barry M. "The Escalation of Commitment to a Course of Action." *Academy of Management Review* 6, no. 4 (October 1981): 577–587. https://doi.org/10.2307/257636.

———. "Knee-Deep in the Big Muddy: A Study of Escalating Commitment to a Chosen Course of Action." *Organizational Behavior and Human Performance* 16, no. 1 (June 1976): 27–44. https://doi.org/10.1016/0030-5073(76)90005-2.

Staw, Barry M., and Gerald R. Salancik, eds. *New Directions in Organizational Behavior.* Chicago: St. Clair Press, 1977.

Staw, Barry M., Lance E. Sandelands, and Jane E. Dutton. "Threat Rigidity Effects in Organizational Behavior: A Multilevel Analysis." *Administrative Science Quarterly* 26, no. 4 (December 1981): 501–524. https://doi.org/10.2307/2392337.

Szulanski, Gabriel, and Sidney Winter. "Getting It Right the Second Time." *Harvard Business Review* 80, no. 1 (January 2002): 62–69. https://hbr.org/2002/01/getting-it-right-the-second-time.

Tayan, Brian. "The Wells Fargo Cross-Selling Scandal." Rock Center for Corporate Governance at Stanford University Closer Look Series: Topics Issues and Controversies in Corporate Governance No. CGRP-62 Version 2, Stanford University Graduate School of Business Research Paper No. 17-1, Stanford University, Stanford, CA, December 2016, revised January 2019. https://papers.ssrn.com/sol3/papers.cfm?abstract_id=2879102.

Tenbrunsel, Ann E., and David M. Messick. "Ethical Fading: The Role of Self-Deception in Unethical Behavior." *Social Justice Research* 17, no. 2 (June 2004): 223–236. https://doi.org/10.1023/B:SORE.0000027411.35832.53.

Thera, Nyanaponika. *The Power of Mindfulness.* The Buddhist Society, 1968.

Thompson, Suzanne C. "Will It Hurt Less If I Can Control It? A Complex Answer to a Simple Question." *Psychological Bulletin* 90, no. 1 (1981): 89–101. https://doi.org/10.1037/0033-2909.90.1.89.

Tripsas, Mary, and Giovanni Gavetti. "Capabilities, Cognition, and Inertia: Evidence from Digital Imaging." Special issue, "The Evolution of Firm Capabilities." *Strategic Management Journal* 21, no. 10/11 (October–November 2000): 1147–1161, https://www.jstor.org/stable/3094431.

Tushman, Michael L., and Charles A. O'Reilly. "Ambidextrous Organizations: Managing Evolutionary and Revolutionary Change." *California Management Review* 38, no. 3 (July 1996): 8–29. https://doi.org/10.2307/41165852.

Tushman, Michael, Wendy K. Smith, Robert Chapman Wood, George Westerman, and Charles O'Reilly. "Organizational Designs and Innovation Streams." *Industrial and Corporate Change* 19, no. 5 (October 2010): 1331–1366. https://doi.org/10.1093/icc/dtq040.

Van Maanen, John Eastin, and Edgar Henry Schein. "Toward a Theory of Organizational Socialization." Working Paper, Massachusetts Institute of Technology, 1979. https://dspace.mit.edu/bitstream/handle/1721.1/1934/?sequence=1.

Verplanken, Bas, and Wendy Wood. "Interventions to Break and Create Consumer Habits." *Journal of Public Policy & Marketing* 25, no. 1 (April 2006): 90–103. https://doi.org/10.1509/jppm.25.1.90.

Vogus, Timothy J., Naomi B. Rothman, Kathleen M. Sutcliffe, and Karl E. Weick. "The Affective Foundations of High-Reliability Organizing." *Journal of Organizational Behavior* 35, no. 4 (February 2014): 592–596. https://doi.org/10.1002/job.1922.

Vogus, Timothy J., and Kathleen M. Sutcliffe. "Organizational Resilience: Towards a Theory and Research Agenda." In *Proceedings of the IEEE Internal Conference on Systems Man and Cybernetics*, 3418–3422. Montréal, Canada, 2007. https://doi.org/ 10.1109/ICSMC.2007.4414160.

Wanous, John P., Arnon E. Reichers, and James T. Austin. "Cynicism about Organizational Change: Measurement, Antecedents, and Correlates." *Group & Organization Management* 25, no. 2 (June 2000): 132–153. https://doi.org/10.1177/1059601100252003.

Weick, Karl E. "The Collapse of Sensemaking in Organizations: The Mann Gulch Disaster." *Administrative Science Quarterly* 38, no. 4 (December 1993): 628–652. https://doi.org/10.2307/2393339.

———. "Small Wins: Redefining the Scale of Social Problems." *American Psychologist* 39, no. 1 (1984): 40–49. https://doi. org/10.1037/0003-066X.39.1.40.

Weick, Karl E., and Kathleen M. Sutcliffe. *Managing the Unexpected: Sustained Performance in a Complex World.* 3rd ed. Hoboken, NJ: John Wiley & Sons, 2015.

———. "Mindfulness and the Quality of Organizational Attention." *Organization Science* 17, no. 4 (August 2006): 514–524. https://doi. org/10.1287/orsc.1060.0196.

Weick, Karl E., and Robert E. Quinn. "Organizational Change and Development." *Annual Review of Psychology* 50 (February 1999): 361–386. https://doi.org/10.1146/annurev.psych.50.1.361.

Whetten, David A. "Albert and Whetten Revisited: Strengthening the Concept of Organizational Identity." *Journal of Management Inquiry* 15, no. 3 (September 2006): 219–234. https://doi.org/10.1177/1056492606291200.

Whetten, David A., and Alison Mackey. "A Social Actor Conception of Organizational Identity and Its Implications for the Study of Organizational Reputation." *Business & Society* 41, no. 4 (December 2002): 393–414. https:// doi.org/10.1177/0007650302238775.

White, Robert W. "Motivation Reconsidered: The Concept of Competence." *Psychological Review* 66, no. 5 (September 1959): 297–333. https://doi. org/10.1037/h0040934.

Wood, Wendy. *Good Habits, Bad Habits: The Science of Making Positive Changes That Stick.* New York: Farrar, Straus and Giroux, 2019.

Wood, Wendy, and Dennis Rünger. "Psychology of Habit." *Annual Review of Psychology* 67 (January 2016): 289–314. https://doi.org/10.1146/ annurev-psych-122414-033417.

Yoong, Sze Lin, Alix Hall, Fiona Stacey, Alice Grady, Rachel Sutherland, Rebecca Wyse, Amy Anderson, Nicole Nathan, and Luke Wolfenden. "Nudge Strategies to Improve Healthcare Providers' Implementation of Evidence-Based Guidelines, Policies and Practices: A Systematic Review of Trials Included within Cochrane Systematic Review." *Implementation Science* 15, no. 1 (July 2020): 50. https://doi.org/10.1186/s13012-020-01011-0.

www.ingramcontent.com/pod-product-compliance
Lightning Source LLC
Chambersburg PA
CBHW071548210326
41597CB00019B/3159